HOLY ROLLERS
Murder and Madness in Oregon's Love Cult

HOLY ROLLERS

Murder and Madness in Oregon's Love Cult

T. McCracken
and
Robert B. Blodgett

CAXTON PRESS
Caldwell, Idaho
2002

Library of Congress Cataloging-in-Publication Data

McCracken, Theresa.
    Holy rollers: Murder and madness in Oregon's love cult /
Theresa McCracken and Robert B. Blodgett
        p. cm.
    Includes bibliographical references.
    ISBN 0-87004-424-9 (alk. paper)
    1. Creffield, Edmund, 1867?-1906. 2. Church of the Bride of Christ. I. Blodgett, Robert B. II. Title.

    BP605.C546M33 2002
    979.5'33--dc21

                                        2001058232

Lithographed and bound in the United States of America
CAXTON PRESS
Caldwell, Idaho
166980

DEDICATION

To my mom and dad
who, like O. V. Hurt,
unconditionally love their
sometimes wayward children.

T-

To Steve McLaughlin and
Don and Susan Unger for their
continued interest in the Creffield story

Robert

TABLE OF CONTENTS

ILLUSTRATIONS

ACKNOWLEDGMENTS

The sources for much of this story were hundreds of newspaper articles from the turn of the last century about Edmund Creffield and his followers.

For help finding copies of these newspapers, thanks go to Doris Tilles, Heidi Weisel, and Thelma Evans at the Oregon State University Library; to Rod Richards and Doris Flowers at the Multnomah County Library; to Martha Hawkes at the Newport Public Library; to the staff at the Newspaper Microfilm Collection at the University of Oregon Library.

Other sources for this story were records from the Oregon State Archives, the Washington State Archives, Superior Court of the State of Washington, King County; the Circuit Court of the State of Oregon for Multnomah County, the Circuit Court of the State of Oregon for Benton County, the Circuit Court of the State of Oregon for Lincoln County, the County Court of the State of Oregon for Linn County, the County Court of the State of Oregon for Benton County, the Oregon State Penitentiary, the Oregon State Insane Asylum, the Boys' and Girls' Aid Society of Oregon, the Salvation Army, the Federal Census of Oregon and Washington, the University of Washington Special Collections; Benton County, Oregon; Lincoln County, Oregon; Linn County, Oregon; Multnomah; County, Oregon; and King County, Washington.

Thanks go to these agencies and to the people in them who unearthed records and certificates for us. We don't know your names—or even the exact departments you work in—but be assured that your work is very much appreciated.

Thanks go to various societies and archives for the use of their photos and, for finding them, to their staff, including Jody Weeber, Steve Wyatt, and Loretta Harrison at the Oregon Coast

History Center; Mary Gallagher, Judy Juntunen, and Bill Lewis at the Benton County Historical Society and Museum; Colleen Neekerson and Judy Gibbs at the Alsi Historical and Genealogical Society; Terence S. Badger at the Washington State Archives; the Oregon State Archives; Sandy Macomber at the *Oregonian*; and the City of Seattle Municipal Archives.

For advice on the law and on court procedures, thanks go to William Morris (no relation to the Will H. Morris in the story).

Thanks go to Shirley—who like Cher has no last name—for sharing her personal knowledge about Edmund Creffield and his followers, for her enthusiasm about this project, and most of all for her attempts to keep us on track by calling frequently to ask: "Is the book done yet?"

Thanks go to others who also talked about their personal knowledge of the story. They are Elizabeth Bahn, William Baker, Robert Homer, Pauline Beach, Virginia Stevens, and Marilyn MacDonald.

Thanks go to Katherine and Charles McCracken, who read all dozen versions of this manuscript. Thanks go to others who made editorial suggestions: Wayne Cornell, our editor at Caxton Press; and fellow writers Toni Johnson, Paul Joannides, and Linda Crew.

Thanks go to Cindi Laws for putting us up (and putting up with us) when we were doing research in Seattle.

Robert B. Blodgett would like to give special thanks to Steve McLaughlin, and Don and Susan Unger, all of Corvallis, for their continued interest in the Creffield story and the research efforts that accompanied it.

T. McCracken would like to give special—and very belated—thanks to Carl White and Beth Lawrence, English teachers at East Lansing High School who said that—despite her having almost indecipherable handwriting, awful spelling, and her own rules of grammar—she should become a writer.

PROLOGUE

This is a story that has everything a good book should have: sex, mass insanity, the downfall of prominent families, murder, and sensational court trials.

And it's all true.

When Edmund Creffield and his followers made headlines in Oregon in 1903, it was page-one news—and not just in the Pacific Northwest, but around the country. Yet few today know who Creffield was, not even many folks in Waldport, where the final chapter of his story takes place.

Waldport is a small town—fewer than 2,000 today—the sort of place where everybody knows everything about everyone else. They even know everything about everyone else's parents and grandparents. The old-timers make sure of that. Go crabbing at the dock with one and he'll tell you about fishing in the old days "when you could walk across the Alsea Bay on the backs of salmon—which was a good thing because there wasn't a bridge in those days." He'll gladly tell you all about the Indians, the homesteaders, the loggers, and the lumber barons. He'll even tell you about the scoundrels and the madams. If you want to hear about something really outrageous, he'll tell you about Bo and Peep, a music professor and a nurse who not long ago convinced some in town that if they followed them, leaving behind everything—even their children—they would find salvation in a spaceship.

But asking an old-timer about Edmund Creffield is an offense. "We were always told to not talk about him," the old-timer will murmur, eyes cast down, "and I'm not going to. Why dredge up the dead? It'll only hurt the living. It was a one-time thing. Nothing like that could happen again. Or, anyhow, it couldn't ever happen again to *normal* people. Sane people. People like you and me."

What little most folks in town know was gleaned from a magazine article a student at Waldport High happened upon in the

1950s. The girl had never before heard of Edmund Creffield, but she knew almost everyone else mentioned in the piece. "Do you know who these people are?" she asked after reading the article aloud on the school bus. "Whose *mothers* these are? Whose *fathers* these are?" Everyone on the bus knew who they were because everyone in town knew who they were. They were some of the town's earliest settlers, some of the town's best-respected citizens.

That—not murder—may be the most unsettling part of this story. Unsettling because these were normal people. Sane people. People like you and me. If such things could happen to them, things like these might happen to anyone.

When the Waldport High students asked their parents for more information about the doings of Creffield and his followers, all were shushed up and told to never bring up the subject again. A group of men went up and down the coast buying and destroying every copy of the offending magazine they could find.

The young people obeyed their parents and never did bring up Creffield again.

And neither did anybody else in town.

Until now.

T. McCracken
Waldport, Oregon
September 2001

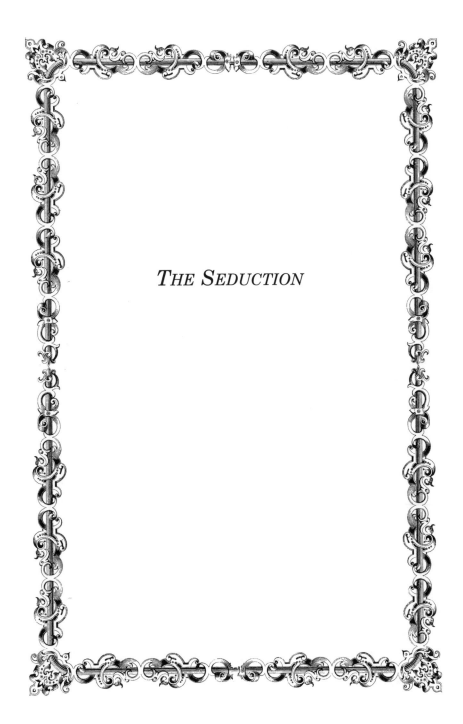

THE SEDUCTION

CHAPTER ONE

"TRUST ME,
BROTHERS AND SISTERS"

*In the beginning God created the heaven and
the earth.*—Genesis 1:1

"Trust me, brothers and sisters, I am God's exclusive messenger and He wants you to obey me implicitly. He wants you to join me in a life of deprivation, degradation—*and orgies.* In so doing, you will drive your families mad and they will have *you* committed to the insane asylum—the *loony* bin. Come, let us roll on the ground and pray."

Had Edmund Creffield said this during his first street corner sermon in Oregon in 1899 he would have had few if any followers. "Some sort of lunatic," people would have whispered to their children, grasping their hands as they sped away from him. Alas, Creffield didn't sound like a lunatic at first.

The secret to Creffield's charisma? Not his physical stature. Creffield was five-foot-six, 135 pounds, with light hair and pale blue eyes, "a very homely man"—or so said Burgess Starr. "But he attracted women wonderfully." And not just any women, but women who were the wives and daughters of respected men, women of high character and standing, God-fearing, decent women.

"His power over his followers, who were nearly all women,

was something wonderful," O. V. Hurt, Burgess Starr's brother-in-law, said. "They did whatever he said. They were dead to all human sympathies. They let their children, their husbands and their parents go uncared for and without a kind thought or word."

"Creffield was a hypnotist," Burgess said.

Louis Sandell, another of O. V.'s in-laws, said that Creffield had a "look that seemed to cast a spell over a person," and that he personally "felt more secure the farther away from him."

"During his schooling he made a particular study of mental telepathy and, it is claimed, became something of an expert in the science of thought transference," someone else said. Correspondence courses in hypnotism *were* popular at the time, courses that promised to "make women bend to your will."

A look that cast a spell? Mental telepathy? The science of thought transference? And these are statements made by people in this story who weren't eventually committed to the insane asylum.

As ludicrous as these all sounded, they were easier to accept than the idea that Edmund Creffield was God's exclusive messenger. But this is jumping ahead, for Creffield hadn't always held such power over people. In 1899 he was a soldier in the Salvation Army in Portland, Oregon, preaching with mixed success to anyone who would listen to him. When the Salvation Army had "opened fire" there twelve years earlier, they hadn't exactly been held in the highest esteem either. Thought of as a group of religious crackpots, members were routinely spat upon, pelted with rotten eggs, vegetables, and rocks, all the while thanking their tormenters, saying the attacks strengthened their determination. It was enough to drive the less righteous crazy.

By the time Creffield joined the organization, the Salvation Army had gained a certain amount of respectability. Initially it was thought he might make a promising officer and he was sent to Officer-Training School. His halo soon tarnished, though, as he began quibbling with his fellow soldiers—often about money, because wherever he was posted—The Dalles, eighty-five miles east of Portland; Oregon City, thirteen miles south of Portland; McMinnville, forty miles south-west of Portland; and Heppner, in eastern Oregon—donations plummeted. Donations were everything to the Salvation Army, or so Creffield claimed.

The Holy Ghost apparently didn't approve of this policy because in 1901 the Holy Ghost, Creffield said, directed him "not to solicit for money," and to leave the Salvation Army because "its people are not entirely of God."

"Creffield does not like to be controlled by others," said a fellow soldier, "but wants everything his own way, and that is why he left the Salvation Army."

No matter. Creffield resigned his position and went to, as he said, "tarry" with Martin L. Ryan at his Pentecostal Mission and Training School in Salem. Ryan's group was part of a Holiness Movement that taught the Bible in

Evening Telegram
Edmund Creffield in his Salvation Army uniform

its entirety, from the first word of Genesis to the last word of Revelation—"And if any man shall take away from the words of the book of this prophecy, God shall take away his part out of the book of life."—Revelation 22:19.

To Ryan, churches in America were honeycombed with sin and apathy. Just look at the what had happened to the Methodists. Many Methodists were practically infidels, leading lives filled with carnal and selfish desires. Go to the home of one and you might be invited to partake of worldly amusements and sinful pleasures such as card-playing, smoking, drinking, and dancing or, most objectionable, a discussion on Darwin's theory of evolution. Such things had no place in the lives of members of Ryan's group. Even if they had wanted to partake of these amusements, they had no time, for they went to evangelistic meetings nightly—not being content to attend services only on Sundays. These days Methodists pooh-poohed such meetings.

During his time with Ryan, a new doctrine was "revealed" to Creffield—he was God's Elect. He went to preach this new doctrine in Corvallis. Corvallis was in the heart of the Willamette Valley, the "Eden" at the end of the Oregon Trail. Thousands had came to the Oregon Territory for many reasons, but most came because there was the promise of land—free land that was productive beyond belief—preachers not being the only ones making astonishing claims. Peter Burnett, later governor of California, said: "Gentlemen, they do say, that out in Oregon the pigs are running about under the great acorn trees, round and fat, and already cooked, with knives and forks sticking in them so that you can cut off a slice whenever you are hungry."

When Creffield arrived in Corvallis, it was a small farming community and home to Oregon Agricultural College, a land-grant institution. People there led fairly orderly lives—ordinances had even recently been passed that prohibited livestock from roaming the streets at night.

Everybody knew everything about everyone else in town—the two papers, the Corvallis *Times* and the Corvallis *Gazette,* made sure of that. Everything was reported. Everything!

Go out of town—it was reported.

> *A swift journey on a bicycle was made Saturday by Frank Hurt. He went from Corvallis to Oregon City in six hours. It is not likely that the trip was ever made by wheel in so short a time.*
>
> The *Times*, October 26, 1901

Come back to town—it was reported.

> *Clarence Starr returned home Tuesday from Seaside, Oregon where he had been employed for several months in a sawmill. He relates an amusing story at the expense of the little pumpkin vine railroad that runs from Warrenton to Seaside. While en route home, traveling over this line, the train slowed down, that is, it went slower than usual and the whistle was repeatedly blown in vain efforts to "shoo" a cow off the track. It seemed impossible to make her give the right of way and a wearied passenger finally agreed to give her a start,*

which he did. She seemed quite alarmed at the demonstrations of the passenger and, throwing her tail to the breeze, continued her way on down the track at her liveliest gait. The passenger climbed back onto the "whole train" and the engine was turned loose to make up for the time lost. After about half an hour's run the train again slowed down and the shrill whistle resounded along the coast. The passenger inquired what was the matter now. He was answered by the conductor who stated that they had caught up with the cow.

The *Gazette,* November 1, 1901

Have a good day at work—it was reported.

Frank Hurt is reported to be doing exceedingly well in his position as shipping clerk at Ainsworth dock. A few days ago he checked a China steamer in and out. This is quite an undertaking and requires considerable knowledge and great accuracy. He is well spoken of by his employers.

The *Gazette,* December 3, 1901

Have a bad day at work—it was reported.

It was not a cyclone or a cattle stampede, though not many of the symptoms were lacking. It happened in Kline's store Saturday evening. The employees were boxing eggs for shipment. Victor Hurt stooped over an egg case and rummaged in the bottom, when a big rat ran up his arm on his shoulder, brandishing his tail in his face. Hurt, convinced that it was the panther reported at large west of town, fell over himself in terror and set up a commotion that brought all employees to the scene. Armed with brooms, pocket shears and bars of soap the boys began a chase that finally ended with the death of the rat just outside the front door. The only hurt sustained in the incident was by Hurt, whose nerves were so hurt that he still sees rats in every old box about the store.

The *Times,* May 29, 1901

Sometimes the most exciting items in the paper could be found in the church notes:

> *Unearthed! Exposed! Made public! Terrible tragedy! Full details! Names given! A blood stained bag! Ghastly contents to be exposed Saturday night 8 o'clock at the Salvation Army Hall, January 6th. Full particulars of greatest crime ever made public. All are welcome.*
>
> The *Gazette*, January 5, 1900

The crime that Creffield was about to commit in Corvallis was thought to be one of the greatest—if not *the greatest*—crimes ever made public in the city's history. At the time the papers dutifully followed and printed the details of this crime. Secrets were unearthed. Private lives were exposed. All of it was made public. Names were named. Reputations were stained. It was a terrible tragedy.

And every time people thought it couldn't get any worse, it did.

❦

Blessed are ye, when men *shall revile you, and persecute* you, *and shall say all manner of evil against you falsely, for my sake.*—Matthew 5:11

CHAPTER TWO

"GOD, SAVE US FROM
COMPROMISING PREACHERS"

Pow'r to heal the leper, Pow'r to raise the dead,
Pow'r to fill the empty pots with oil;
Is waiting for the worker who in Jesus' steps will tread,
And leave his life of ease for one of toil.

From the Reverend Knapp's
Bible Songs of Salvation and Victory

Alll churches, mainstream or fringe, begin pretty much the same way. It doesn't matter whether its founder is sincere in his faith or not—and there is no evidence to suggest that Creffield wasn't sincere in his. Step one in starting a church: Convince someone God exists. Easier, capture the attention of someone who already believes God exists. Better yet, capture the attention of a whole lot of people who already believe God exists. That's what Creffield did.

"Many members of the army here went over to the Comeouters, or Holy Rollers as they are sometimes designated," a dejected Salvation Army Lieutenant Manness said. "The work of the army has been very difficult because that organization seems to make a greater effort to win members of other churches than it does to win sinners."

When Creffield first preached his new doctrine to soldiers he knew from his Salvation Army days, he didn't say anything out-

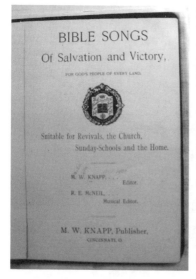

BIBLE SONGS
Of Salvation and Victory,
FOR GOD'S PEOPLE OF EVERY LAND.

Suitable for Revivals, the Church,
Sunday-Schools and the Home.

M. W. KNAPP,
Editor.
R. E. McNEIL,
Musical Editor.

M. W. KNAPP, Publisher,
CINCINNATI, O.

rageous. Mostly he preached about things they already believed in—the beauty of the "full Gospel," and how it taught peace and love. Nothing to object to there.

"If we ever expect to gain Heaven, and see the King in His beauty, we must live holy lives here on earth," Creffield preached. "The Word of God tells us to 'Follow peace with all men, and holiness, without which no man shall see the Lord.' In the Bible God speaks to men, and we must search the Scriptures to know the will of God concerning us, and after we have found out His will, the next thing is to do it."

And what spiritual gathering would be complete without singing? The hymnbook of choice for Creffield was the Reverend Martin Wells Knapp's recently published *Bible Songs of Salvation and Victory*, "for God's people of every land: suitable for revivals, the Church, Sunday-schools and the home."

Little by little, after gaining people's confidence, Creffield changed what he preached. He began to be critical of other churches and denominations.

> *When you get Him* [the Holy Ghost], *you'll bring consternation wherever you go. Peace ceases when you make your appearance. The so-called Christians of the modern Churches of to-day rise up in arms against you, and call you a "disturber of the peace," charging you with the crime of "breaking up their Churches."* . . .
>
> *The modern holiness folks (minus the fire) will call you a fanatic for preaching the baptism with the Holy Ghost and fire.*
>
> *You will be too hot for them; and when God gives you a message that cuts deep and strikes some of their idols, they cry, "Charity."* . . .
>
> [When you get the Holy Ghost] *you won't be anxious*

*about counting numbers and making a glowing report;
but you'll see people through on Pentecostal lines.*

*There are evangelists who were once all aglow, a
flame of fire. To-day they are a back number. What's the
cause? Compromise, human sympathy, shrinking from
persecutions, lowering God's standard a little, letting
down the bars and giving carnality a chance to creep in,
keeping silent when they should rebuke sin, grieving the
Spirit, and getting so at last that they can not detect the
devil creeping in.*

God, save us from compromising preachers!

Step two in starting a new church: Get people to believe one
has some sort of "direct connection" with God, that one is a special messenger from God—if not His *exclusive* messenger—sent
from Heaven to reveal the "divine truth." That's what Creffield
did.

After a time Creffield claimed he personally had reached
such a state of spiritual perfection that: "God revealed himself
to me. He came in the form of messages. He spoke to me. I heard
his voice."

At such a statement, no one fell to the ground prostrate in
front of him and asked for his divine guidance. They needed
more to go on than his simply saying God spoke to him. After
all, the town drunks—there were a few even in as idyllic a place
as Corvallis—routinely said God spoke to them. So Creffield
was asked to elaborate on how God revealed Himself to him—
did He come in spirit, or in person? Or maybe He used the tele-
phone as Corvallis had recently been wired.

"That cannot be explained or described," Creffield answered.
"It can only be experienced." Anyone, he said, could experience
the "power of receiving messages from God," anyone. Soldiers in
the Salvation Army. His doubters. Even Methodists.

As an added bonus, Creffield said that when people became
worthy of this sort of personal communion with God—were
receiving their own messages from the Almighty—their names
would be inscribed on a Holy Roll in Heaven. But they had to
act fast for there were a limited number of spaces on the Holy
Roll.

"God, have mercy," Creffield said in a thunderous tone.

Some in the gathering sat there rolling their eyes at one another, summing up their opinions of Creffield, God's Elect, by tapping a finger on their foreheads.

But at least one woman knelt with her eyes closed and whispered: "God have mercy."

"God will have victory tonight," Creffield said.

"God will have victory tonight," she whispered.

Some left the gathering—but not all.

Those who stayed knelt in prayer

"God, have mercy," Creffield said.

"God have mercy," the gathering whispered.

"God will have victory tonight," Creffield said.

"God will have victory tonight," the gathering whispered.

They all prayed for an hour, and, at Creffield's direction, the gathering began asking for forgiveness for their sins.

They all prayed for yet another hour, and without their realizing it, three hours had elapsed, and then four.

Creffield passed his hands back and forth over a woman, saying that "all forms of mental and bodily suffering could be cured by the laying on of hands."

When was the last time someone had said something like that at a Methodist service?

Not only could all forms of mental and bodily suffering be cured by the laying on of hands, but he, Creffield, God's Elect, a man with a direct connection to God, had special powers along these lines—or so he claimed.

"He seemed to be praying that the Lord would take her up bodily to heaven," one of the gathered said.

"God have mercy!" the gathering cried, the women among them shaking so hard that their hairpins came loose, letting their hair flow freely about their shoulders.

"God will have victory tonight!" Creffield cried.

"God will have victory tonight!" the gathering cried, each individual sounding as though he was trying to outdo the others in righteousness.

More time passed. Five hours, six hours, then seven. By then the gathering were no longer asking for forgiveness for their sins—they were *begging* for it. They were doomed to burn in

Hell if they didn't receive redemption now. They could practically hear the screeching of those who repented too late and were burning already.

"When you get God's best, you become unmanageable, irresistible; you're not afraid of clay faces any more," Creffield cried. "Fear of man is burned out, and all you see is the soul plunging into an everlasting, burning, seething Hell, and your cry becomes, 'Holiness or Hell.'"

"It is either holiness or Hell," the gathering cried, clapping and stomping. "The Scripture cannot be broken."

"Be ye holy!" Creffield bellowed.

After eight hours of prayer—or was it nine or ten or eleven? Did any of them know? Did any of them care? All were pleading for the Baptism of the Holy Ghost.

Creffield was still going strong. "God, have mercy! God will have victory tonight!" He said that anyone who believed he'd sinned—and who doesn't believe he's sinned at some point—needed to seek forgiveness by lying on the floor and rolling over and over until his sins had been atoned for. Some began to roll about the floor, beating it with their hands and feet and praying at the top of their lungs. On and on they rolled and prayed. And rolled and clapped and rolled and stomped and rolled. And rolled. And rolled until after twelve hours of this religious frenzy all were physically and emotionally spent, their bodies exhausted, and their minds unbalanced. Not just unbalanced, but spinning. They were glorying in heaven for their prayers were answered—God spoke to them. Personally. God Almighty spoke to them. Personally! To them. Ordinary sinners. Hallelujah!

Creffield told them they were now God's Anointed.

"It is not for us to judge whether one has the spirit of God," one of the newly anointed said. "The one seeking admittance will have to feel sure of that."

And they, God's Anointed, were now sure about the spirit of God. Not only that, they were now sure about Creffield's link to God. In Creffield, they now trusted. After all, hadn't he told them that with his help they too would be able to receive messages directly from God—no small feat—and isn't that exactly what happened? This man Creffield—no, not just a man, but

God's Elect—obviously he knew what he was talking about. And since he had been right about this, what else was he right about?

Had any of them received a message directly from God while they were with the Salvation Army? No. How could they have? The Salvation Army's people were not entirely of God—or so Creffield, God's Elect, had told them. So, all of God's Anointed deserted the Army.

> *The big drum of the Salvation Army is no longer in evidence about eight o'clock each evening and tambourines are very cheap in Corvallis. The army has gone to its religious 'Waterloo'—it met a body of Divine Healers, Army of Holiness, or something, and went over to the enemy. True religion of a respectable character, a religion that is reasonable, that commands at least the respect of the greatest thinkers and the better class of people, is the last thing on earth that should be treated in a contemptuous manner. But a "holy show" that is a burlesque on religion is a bad thing for any community as it is not taken seriously and consequently lays the foundation for the youth of the land to scoff at religion in any form. There should be reason and moderation in all things. There may be efficacy in prayer—who can say there is not?—but it must be the prayer of a sane mind and a reasonable being. The prayer of a religious fanatic cannot avail much.*
>
> Corvallis *Gazette*, December 5, 1902

Not only that, but get a dozen or more religious fanatics praying and rolling together, and you have a "Babel of weird sounds"—or so said those living near the services—"the effect to the uninitiated being extremely weird."

And extremely annoying.

So annoying that by the summer of 1903 city officials forbade Creffield from holding gatherings within Corvallis city limits. Undaunted, he told his followers that he had "received instructions from on high" to hold a camp meeting on Smith Island, a small, uninhabited island three miles out of town.

Bring family and friends, he told everyone, because there are a limited number of spaces on that Holy Roll in Heaven, and if your family and friends don't get their names inscribed on it soon, they will be doomed, doomed to spend an eternity in Hell.

Besides, it'll be fun.

We'll build wigwams and camp out.

It'll be sort of like a vacation.

It was on the island that things really started to get wild.

Oh travelers, where are you going? You seem to be not of this land;
You seem to be pilgrims and strangers, A happy victorious band.
O yes, we are seeking a city, Before us the prophets have trod,
A city whose walls are salvation, Whose builder and maker is God.

Reverend Knapp's *Bible Songs*
of Salvation and Victory

CHAPTER THREE

THE FLOCK

LOCAL LORE.
NEWS OF CORVALLIS AND VICINITY TOLD IN BRIEF.
The comings and Goings of People, Social Gossip,
Personal Mention and Other Items of Public Interest.
Regular feature in every issue of the *Corvallis Times* in 1903

So who were these people, these God's Anointed? It would be comforting to think all of them were a bit off. Who else would mistake hallucinations—they were hallucinations, weren't they?—for the voice of God, but someone who was a bit off? Or at the very least that they came from bad stock. Or had wretched childhoods. It could be disconcerting if they were *normal* people, people like the rest of us, intelligent, well-adjusted people from good homes, people of "a sane mind and a reasonable being."

If any of God's Anointed could be said to have had wretched childhoods, it would have been the Mitchell sisters, Donna and Esther. In 1894, when Donna was fourteen and Esther was six, their mother, Martha, died of typhoid, and their father, Charles, essentially abandoned them.

Charles Mitchell was described, on the one hand, as a "nothing," and, on the other, as "a man of strong peculiarities and eccentricities." He was a Quaker not known for his peaceful ways, a man who "could not argue, or debate, or reason with anyone without flying off the handle." After his wife died, he joined the Salvation Army, and soon it consumed his every waking thought. He was intoxicated with the Salvation Army, so much that his seven children would have been little worse off had he spent his evenings drinking at a saloon, and his days sleeping off a drunk. Nothing could keep him from his religious devotions—not even taking care of his children, five of whom at the time of his wife's death were between the ages of six and fifteen. Eventually, Charles Mitchell returned to Illinois, where the family had migrated from. He remarried, but he never brought any of his brood out to live with him.

Donna, now twenty-three, was married to Burgess Starr. Burgess, thirty-two, loved Donna very much, saying she was a "model wife and mother" to him and their children: Gertrude, two, and Rachel, a newborn. Burgess also believed in the tenets of Creffield's church, but he mainly went to Smith Island that summer to fulfill a wood-cutting contract. That was as close as many in Corvallis came to having a vacation—camping while cutting wood or picking hops. Burgess thought he could cut wood while his wife was off begging for forgiveness for her sins. What those sins could be, he couldn't imagine since, in his mind, she was "a good girl."

Burgess's brother, Clarence Starr, had no interest in Creffield's church, but was on Smith Island that summer helping Burgess fulfill the wood-cutting contract. Clarence's wife, Hattie Starr (née Hattie Baldwin), accompanied him, as did Una Baldwin, Hattie's niece.

Esther Mitchell, Donnas Starr's youngest sister, was on Smith Island, too. Esther, now fifteen, a piano player for the Salvation Army, was said to not be "in complete harmony with this wicked world." She was considered to be gentle and kind, but she rarely smiled, had "a far away look in her eyes," and "a dreamy, absorbed expression." She was also "given much to silent thought"—especially that summer on Smith Island.

Attie Bray, Burgess and Clarence Starr's niece, also came to Smith Island. Attie, twenty-two, was one of the first—if not the first—white children born on what had been the Alsea Sub-

Agency for the Siletz Indian Reservation. It wasn't discussed much—at least not in polite society—but Attie's mother's family, the Starrs, had been squatters on the Reservation. At the time the reservation was closed to non-Indian settlement. As soon as the area was opened to whites, though, Ira and Georgianah Bray (neé Starr), Attie's parents, were among the first settlers to begin legitimate homesteading on the central Oregon coast.

Ira Bray was a cruel man—especially around his five children. For example, he would eat candy in front them while telling them they couldn't have any because they were bad. So even as a child Attie was regularly told that she was a sinner even when she wasn't. Unlike her father, Attie was sweet and kind, and easily endeared herself to all she met. Some day she hoped to become a schoolteacher, but for now, she worked as a "servant girl."

Attie was on Smith Island with her friend, Rose Seeley. The Seeley children, like the Mitchell children, had also been abandoned by their father after their mother died. In the Seeleys' case, Rose Seeley, now twenty-seven, had assumed the responsibility of raising her younger siblings—not an easy task for someone with about a seventh-grade education who, like Attie Bray, worked as a "servant girl." Her father, Judson Seeley, a former justice of the peace, had abandoned his seven children when he—well nobody seems to know exactly what happened to Judson Seeley. He just wasn't there one day, and he certainly wasn't there when Rose and three of his other children—Edna, twenty-eight and a Salvation Army Cadet; Wesley, nineteen; and Florence, sixteen—went camping on Smith Island with Creffield.

If any of God's Anointed could be said to have been a bit off, it would be Maud Hurt. Twenty-three, five-foot-two, with jet black hair, large, expressive and deep blue eyes, Maud was said by Salem's *Daily Capitol Journal* to be a "comely looking woman" who talked "very intelligently."

She was also a "very peculiar girl and hard to understand long before the days of Creffieldism"—or so said her father, O. V. Hurt. He had always assumed her odd manner was somehow the result of the severe typhoid and scarlet fevers she had suffered from as a child. No matter, he still adored her. O. V. adored all of his children. His was "a happy family" he said, "of which love was the keystone."

"My daughter had always been of a very religious turn of mind," O. V. said, and "whenever a new religion was presented she invariably put all her soul into the teaching." *Religious turn of mind* sounded better than religious fanatic—which she clearly was. At the age of eight—*the age of eight!*—she was already referred to as "a child wonder" at religious work, an "energetic worker at revival meetings, going among the congregations and pleading with friends and acquaintances to seek the salvation so freely offered."

"Her chief aim was to become as nearly perfect as a Christian could be," a friend of hers said. And she wasn't one of those Christians who preached salvation, and then sinned on the side. "All her life Maud Hurt was kindly and generous, with an even temper and a good disposition," her friend said. Maud took the teachings of Christianity to heart and led a truly Christian life, always helping those in need. For instance, she could often be found in the homes of people who were ill, caring for their children, doing their wash, and helping with other chores.

When she was fourteen she joined the Salvation Army because she believed it would give her more opportunities to perform good works. But soon after meeting Creffield she left the Army because it was "teaching the Bible in a narrow manner" and she didn't like its methods for collecting donations.

"It is not right to hold ice cream socials and other special gatherings where money is taken," Creffield had told her. Might as well be holding out a tin cup while quaffing a few at the saloon or hooting at a burlesque show.

Wanting to insure a place on the Holy Roll in Heaven for her family, Maud invited them all to come to Smith Island. Her father, head salesman at Kline's Mercantile, stayed at home, but her mother, Sarah Hurt (neé Starr) went, as did her sister, Mae. Mae was sixteen and five years earlier had won a "fine guitar" for having the nation's second highest sales rate of *The War Cry*, the Salvation Army's newspaper.

Oregon Coast History Center, Neg. 440
The O. V. Hurt family. Front row, from left: Mae, O. V. and Sarah. Back Row: Maud, Roy Robinett and Frank Hurt.

Maud was engaged to James Berry. James didn't camp on Smith Island that summer, but, mostly out of curiosity, visited frequently. James, twenty-four, the son of a United Brethren minister, was a successful businessman who owned the Bicycle Hospital, a bicycle store and repair shop with the best selection of bicycles in Corvallis. Initially he was rather taken with Creffield's ideas and lent him money to get his church rolling.

It *would* be comforting to think that *all* of Creffield's followers were peculiar or had wretched childhoods, that they were *not* normal people—people like the rest of us. It's therefore disconcerting to learn that this wasn't the case. It's disconcerting because it means that normal people—people like the rest of us—*can* fall victim to someone like Creffield.

"Respectable, modest and refined women and girls," was the way Will H. Morris, an attorney who got involved in the Creffield case, described many of God's Anointed. "From old neighbors, who had known them from childhood, I learned that prior to their coming in contact with Creffield and his pernicious teachings and blighting influence, all of these women and girls were from families of good reputation, respected by all who

Alsi Historical & Genealogical Society
James Berry behind the wheel of an early airplane. Berry was engaged to
Maud Hurt when she joined Edmund Creffield's flock.

knew them, and that not a breath of reproach or a taint of suspicion had ever been directed toward their reputation for virtue
and womanly conduct."

And not all of God's Anointed were women. One of Creffield's
most ardent followers was Sampson Levins. Sampson, thirty-
five, the second youngest of nine children, had been a private in
the Spanish-American War, and was now a logger. He had had
"a deep interest in the Methodist Church," he said, but when it
failed to meet his "heart's desire," he joined Creffield's Church.
"Some people think ours [Creffield's] is a strange doctrine, but
John Wesley was attacked by mobs when he founded the
Methodist Church," Sampson said, adding, "of course, the
church is not now as he [John Wesley] left it."

Another male follower of Creffield was Lee Campbell. Lee
was engaged to Sophie Hartley, an attractive student at Oregon
Agriculture College studying history. Before going to Smith
Island, neither she nor Lee were known to have been of a "religious turn of mind." In fact, their previous religious affiliation
is unknown—Methodist, perhaps. Maybe Sophie's decision to go
camping on Smith Island that summer had nothing to do with

religious beliefs, but youthful rebellion. Maybe she was doing something wild and spontaneous to upset Papa. Papa was Lewis Hartley, one of the richest men in Corvallis.

Sophie's mother, Cora Hartley, came to Smith Island that summer too. Why is also not known. It was certainly a mystery to her husband. Why would his wife, forty-four, he wondered, choose to spend the summer living in a wigwam instead of the magnificent new ten-room house he'd just had built for her?

He certainly had no time to spend on Smith Island that summer as he was busy in the Bohemia Mining District managing his claim, the Hole in the Ground. It was different if *he* opted to live in primitive conditions—it was still sort of the wild west in the Bohemia Mining District—he was a man, after all. That's what men did. Make sacrifices and work hard to provide a good home for their wives and children.

And he, at forty-eight, provided better than most. He'd come far since 1892 when, en route to Alaska, he was shipwrecked off the Oregon coast. Now his company, Hartley's Great Eastern Mining Company, had just filed articles of incorporation with capital stock of $1,250,000. One million, two hundred and fifty thousand dollars!

While he was slaving away in the mines—so to speak—he expected his wife to be home taking care of their two children. Except that their two children—Sophie, twenty, and Warren, twenty-one—were grown-ups going to college. They were about to embark on lives of their own. What was Cora supposed to do from now on? Sit home alone and bored in their magnificent new ten-room house? Not if she could help it.

Another of God's Anointed who came from a well-to-do family was Mollie Sandell, one of the first of Creffield's followers to leave the Salvation Army to join his church. The Sandells were Methodists who owned considerable property in Seattle. Mollie, now twenty-two, a slight woman with gray eyes and light-colored hair, had left the Methodist Church two years earlier to join the Salvation Army. She had recently reached the rank of Captain when she resigned her commission to follow Creffield.

Mollie's twenty-six-year-old sister, Olive, another former Methodist turned Salvation Army soldier, also came to Smith

Island, as did Mollie's fiancée, Frank Hurt. Frank Hurt, Maud's twenty-one-year-old brother, was a friendly, tall, handsome, fair-haired, blue-eyed young man. He too had belonged to the Methodist Church until joining the Salvation Army—it's not known whether the Methodists begrudged the Salvation Army the members it wooed away. Frank was also a devoted follower of Creffield's before that summer, and left not only the Salvation Army to go to Smith Island, but his job as well. "Our religion [Creffield's religion] is to help one another," he said as explanation. He, like others in his family, wanted to do good works, and he felt he would have more opportunities to do so by following Creffield than by toiling as a shipping clerk at Ainsworth Dock in Portland.

"Our religion is to help one another," Frank Hurt may have said, but "our religion means the restoration of all things," is what Creffield said when everyone finally gathered together on Smith Island. "The restoration of the world will soon come," he said. "The seals mentioned in Revelation will soon be broken and curses and plagues will visit the earth. The world will be destroyed by fire and there will be a new world in which nothing but peace will reign. There will be no sin. It will be the same as in the Garden of Eden. Everything will be the same as at the beginning of the world."

As if that weren't news enough, Creffield also announced: "I am now Joshua, the Holy Prophet, and at some future time will become Elijah, the Restorer." His work, he said was "to lead the twelve tribes of Israel back to Jerusalem, where the restoration of all things will take place, and the millennium will dawn on earth."

"Creffield, our leader, is an apostle," Frank Hurt said in awe. "The same as those mentioned in the Bible." Frank may have thought Creffield was like an apostle, but Creffield thought of himself as being more like Jesus Christ.

Little is known about Creffield's early years—like Jesus Christ's. It's not known when he was born—probably sometime around 1873. Or where he was born—probably somewhere in Germany. Or to whom he was born—possibly to a well-off family. Or what his education was—possibly some studies for the priesthood. Or when he immigrated to America—probably around his twentieth birthday. Or why he immigrated—possibly to avoid military service. We do know that his legal name was Franz Edmund Crefeld (later anglicized by the press to Creffield) and that his father also was named Franz.

At the time he gathered with his followers on Smith Island, Creffield was probably in his thirties—about the same age Jesus Christ was when he began to gather his followers.

It was time to get the followers'—the flocks'?—heads spinning again before they began questioning his appointment as an apostle, before the remark "Joshua Creffield, our leader is an apostle" was changed from a statement of awe to a one of skepticism: *"Joshua Creffield. . .our leader. . . .is an apostle?!"*

❦

Have you ever felt the power Of the Pentecostal fire,
Burning up all carnal nature,
Cleansing out all base desire,
Going thro' and thro' your spirit,
Cleansing all its stain away;
Oh I'm so glad to tell you It is for us all today.
Jesus offers this blest cleaning Unto all His children dear,
Fully, freely purifying,
Banishing all doubt and fear.
It will help you, oh my brother,
When you sing and when you pray
He is waiting now to give it. It is for us all today.

From the Reverend Knapp's
Bible Songs of Salvation and Victory

CHAPTER FOUR

HOLY ROLLERS

And the LORD God planted a garden eastward in Eden; and there he put the man whom he had formed.—Genesis 2:8

W hat's an easy way to keep followers heads' spinning so fast that they can hardly think straight? Hold more record-length prayer services. That's what Creffield did.

For hours Creffield kept his flock in a state of frenzied excitement. He had them rolling, praying, rolling, wailing, rolling, groaning, rolling, singing, rolling, clapping, rolling, stomping, rolling, tumbling, rolling and rolling and rolling.

For hours on end he had them rolling—twelve hours if it was a short service, twenty-four hours if it was a typical service. All heads were spinning because they were glorying in Heaven.

Or were they suffering in Hell? They were too exhausted to know which, but they were pretty sure they were glorying in Heaven.

After the group had been on the island for several weeks, James Berry came for a visit and found something he thought almost impossible—the Holy Rollers even more frenetic and excited than they usually were. When asked why, they told him that God had answered their prayers for a new tabernacle and that it was to be erected immediately.

And—ever the business man—James asked exactly where they were expecting the funding for this project to come from?

"You," they said. Joshua had told them that God had said for him, James, to furnish the money.

And what about the loan he had already made Creffield—or Joshua, as the flock now called him? It was past due. When might he expect payment on that?

Creffield came out and solemnly informed James that the debt had been canceled, and that he should write a receipt showing payment had been received.

The debt has been canceled and I should write a receipt showing payment has been received? Is Creffield out of his mind?

Creffield wasn't out of his mind but was in direct communication with God—or so he said. Perhaps if James had spent more time on the Island, he would have been able to receive this message himself directly from God.

And God was now telling Creffield that James should quit work, sell his valuables—including his new automobile—give the money to Creffield, and devote himself to the church. The automobile, one of the first in Corvallis, was obviously goods received from "carnal" hands. Just look at the article about it in the *Gazette:*

> The *Gazette* man is indebted to J. K. Berry for his first spin in an automobile. He didn't ride far. The ethics of his profession do not permit of enjoyment to the point of satiety. But the exhilaration; the pulse quickening strange sensation of even a short excursion on an Oldsmobile machine beats the tintinnabulation of the sleigh bells and the—see how easy it is to lapse into poetry when there's inspiration.

Sell my new automobile, the one I just paid $690 for? Creffield is out of his mind.

"Either God or Creffield made a mistake," James said, telling God's Anointed that he wasn't going to give Creffield another cent.

Morning Oregonian

Creffield's flock at Smith Island in 1903. Front row, from left: Cora Hartley, Olive Sandell, Donna Starr, Coral Worrell, Mae Hurt, Maud Hurt, Edmund Creffield, Sara Hurt, Sophie Hartley, Attie Bray. Back row: Sampson Levins, Charles Brooks, Hattie Starr, Esther Mitchell, Rose Seeley, Florence Seeley, Mollie Sandell Hurt, Frank Hurt, Edna Seeley, Una Baldwin, Lee Campbell.

God was mad now—or so said Creffield, who said that God would "smite" James for this.

Not only that, God wanted Maud to call off her engagement to James—or so Creffield told her.

Creffield was God's Elect, Joshua, the Holy Prophet, an apostle, the same as those mentioned in the Bible. How could she say no to him? In Joshua she trusted.

So she called off her engagement, saying she was doing so because of "a command from God."

Personal purity now became a favorite theme of Creffield's, and he professed that he had a horror of all things carnal— "Flee fornication. Every sin that a man doeth is without the body; but he that committeth fornication sinneth against his own body"—1 Corinthians 6:18.

"Are you still in bondage to your carnal nature?" he preached. "Is the 'old man' still living in your heart? Have you still this man-fearing spirit, this something which hinders you from becoming a visitor at all times? Do not be discouraged. God wants to use you, to cleanse you, to purge you from your inbred sin, baptize you with fire, and enable you to come up to His commandment to live a holy life. . . . Claim the promise, stand firm upon it, and the witness of the Spirit will come, and will baptize you with His love and make you a holy man—make you victorious over the world, the flesh and the devil."

Creffield told Sophie Hartley and Lee Campbell to call off their engagement, proclaiming that "the relation of man and wife was unholy."—"Now concerning the things whereof ye wrote unto me: It is good for a man not to touch a woman"—1 Corinthians 7:1. So Sophie and Lee did as they were told, and called off their engagement.

One of Sophie's teachers, Ellen Chamberlin, was worried about her.

> *After a two days absence from the class, I asked her brother* [Warren Hartley], *also attending the College, what had become of his sister Sophie: his answer was evasive, unsatisfactory but I found out she was too taken up with those* [Holy Roller] *meetings to think or care for school work. One day she came to Dr. Gateh's* [the college president's] *office and asked if she might pray for him: He assented, called in his secretary, Prof. Crawford and one of the lady teachers for the prayer. Afterwards he told me how beautifully fervently she prayed for him to be more interested in the religious life of his students and do more for their Spiritual welfare. The next day she came at the noon hour to my room. I placed the sobbing girl in a chair, and tried to reason with her but all to no purpose, as before. . . . Glad enough was I to learn her mother from southern Oregon had come to be with her children. But alas, the mother too became a victim of the Satanic influence. . . . A pathetic thing indeed . . . especially so to those who saw and realized what was transpiring yet were unable in their efforts to control the obsession that became so deeply rooted and disastrous.*

Perhaps the timing was just a coincidence, but before Creffield had a chance to tell Mollie Sandell and Frank Hurt to call off their engagement, the two were married in a private ceremony in O. V. Hurt's home. Justice Holgate, not Joshua, administered the marriage vows.

This didn't prevent Mollie from being endowed with the grace of love. This was Joshua's latest direction from on high—

that he was to perform a ceremony with each and every woman in the flock that would "endow" them with the "grace of love."

This ceremony was performed privately in his tent, where he and the woman went to "retire" and "engage in a long prayer service." At the end of the service, Joshua would tell the woman to put her arms around his neck and kiss him.

If a woman refused? Joshua immediately denounced her and declared she was "carnal and of the Devil." And all of God's Anointed knew what happened to such.

> *All the company labored in vain to pray old Nick out of him. Salvation by that method was finally given up, and Prophet Creffield took the lad out into a private tent to "whip the devil" out of him, as the sect styles the process. Ed Sharp, who has since backslidden, raised the flap of the tent to see how the two were making it, so the story goes, and the apostle and his patient saw the act. In the dim light they took Ed for the devil and both took after him. Ed ran his best, but was overtaken according to the account, and given such a beating that he appeared in town next day with two black eyes.*
>
> The *Times*

Ed Sharp wasn't the only one to backslide. Burgess Starr told his brother, Clarence, that he too was beginning to have doubts about Joshua. Up until now he had believed in Joshua's teachings, had remained true to the tenets of the church, but now he didn't know. Some of Joshua's actions seemed to border on the criminal. Truthfully, Burgess wasn't sure whether Joshua—Creffield—really was an apostle.

Creffield couldn't risk dissent. He announced that God had revealed to him that Burgess was "insincere" in his faith and he should be shunned. And it wasn't just Burgess who was insincere in his faith. All of the men in the camp—all but himself, Frank Hurt, Lee Campbell, and Sampson Levins—were insincere in their faith and should be shunned. Anyone who was not a believer should be shunned.

And so Burgess, Clarence, and all the other men in camp

were shunned. And not just by Creffield, but by the whole flock!
Even their wives shunned them.

*Have they all lost their minds? Just like that, on the say-so of
some religious fanatic, kith and kin, people who've known us all
our lives, now believe we're "infidels"?*

In a sense, yes, everybody had gone mad. For weeks on end,
engaging in prayer services practically every waking moment—
frenetic sessions that would exhaust circus acrobats—all the
while living off of little more than peaches stolen from a nearby
orchard, no one in camp had the energy to resist. It was easier
to just go along with whatever Joshua dictated—no matter how
outrageous.

Joshua tells them to shun kith and kin and they shun kith
and kin. Joshua was God's elect, and they were God's Anointed.
It was either holiness or Hell, and they were opting for holiness—and holiness was whatever Joshua told them holiness
was.

"When he placed his hands on their heads they were
absolutely in his power and did anything he told them," a
despondent Burgess said. "He abused them and called them
names, but they never resented it, and had he told them to
jump in the river they would not have hesitated a moment, but
plunged in."

"This new order is apparently very devout," the *Times* said,
expressing concern for the Holy Rollers, "but their customs,
rites and formalities are so queer and unusual that the organization has been the subject of much comment from those who do
not enter fully into the idea of allowing persons to worship God
in the manner that seems to them best."

The first amendment—that one that mentions something
about making "no law respecting an establishment of religion"—be damned. It was their friends and families—and especially *their women*—who were the victims of "the Satanic influence." Something had to be done.

The Salvation Army sent in the cavalry in the form of
Captain Charles Brooks, a dedicated soldier for the past eleven
years. When he arrived at Smith Island, Brooks was confident
of victory, his spirits buoyed by recent meetings with General
William Booth, the founder and leader of the Salvation Army.

Within days of arriving on the island, however, Brooks cried that he was approached by the Devil who was covered in snakes, and that he himself felt as though he was covered in frogs, lizards, and other "hideous reptiles." "As a means of placating his devilish majesty," Brooks tore off his Salvation Army uniform, hurled it into a fire, and then—as they did in that day and age—swooned.

Not only did he join Creffield's flock, but he announced he was also "a prophet." Soon he became Creffield's most trusted disciple.

"Yes, the Captain has deserted us," a dejected Lieutenant Manness said. "In his talks on the street you no doubt have heard him declare how certain he was that he was saved in the Army. At last he concluded that he was not saved and affected to believe that he could be saved only through the Comeouters [as the Salvation Army called Creffield's group]."

"The boom of the bass drum" was hushed as the Salvation Army withdrew from Corvallis and the Corvallis Steam Laundry took over their building.

The fall rains were coming soon, and would make camping on Smith Island miserable, but lacking a tabernacle and still being barred from holding noisy meetings within city limits, Creffield wasn't sure what to do. And then Maud and Sarah Hurt answered his prayers. They invited him, Brooks, and eighteen others of God's Anointed to move into their family's home across Mary's River, just outside Corvallis's city limits.

O. V. Hurt didn't know what hit him. If there is a hero in this story, it is Orlando Victor "O. V." Hurt. Portland's *Morning Oregonian* paid him a tribute in 1906:

> *Any dissatisfied and unhappy citizen who thinks that he has a rough time in his daily life, and that the world doesn't treat him well, should pause long enough to consider the case of Mr. O. V. Hurt, of Corvallis. It is not necessary to enter into details as to the recent history of the Hurt family, for everyone knows it; and everyone feels that few men have deserved more and got less from the hands of fortune and providence, than Mr.*

Hurt. Yet he has complained not at all, but has met each new vicissitude with remarkable fortitude and rare devotion to his high conception of his duty. The members of his family have thought little of Mr. Hurt, but they have received much from him—far more than many another husband and father in like circumstances could or would have given. . . . His entire conduct throughout his terrible trouble, or series of troubles, has been something really beautiful and noble.

But this is jumping ahead, for in 1903 O. V.'s terrible trouble—or series of troubles—had barely begun.

*All life's summer now is ended, And its harvest too, is o'er,
I must reap what I have scattered, Reap in hell for evermore,
Self deceived, my soul was bartered, Oh the fearful cost;
Sold to sin and Satan's service, I am lost, forever lost.*
                    From the Reverend Knapp's
                    Bible Songs of Salvation and Victory

CHAPTER FIVE

HOUSECLEANING

My burdened heart was sad and sore;
The things that charmed me charmed me no more;
The pleasures that I once enjoyed
Have left a sting,—my peace destroyed.
I wandered very far away; In Egypt I'll no longer stay,
My Father's house has and to spare;
He offers still to me my share.
Coming home, yes, coming home,
To Father's house I'm coming home;
Jesus calls, I'm coming home,
To Father's house, no more to roam.

> From the Reverend Knapp's
> *Bible Songs of Salvation and Victory*

Step three in starting a new church: Have one's followers obey one implicitly. That's what Creffield did.

This isn't as hard as it sounds. At this point in starting a new church, even someone who began with the intention of duping people is probably beginning to believe his own message. *All these other people believe I am a special messenger from God—if not His exclusive messenger—so maybe I am. And if I am real-*

ly God's exclusive messenger, that surely must mean I am in possession of special insights that ordinary mortals lack. So why shouldn't I be telling people how to live their lives? I know better than they do.

Joshua knew better than God's Anointed—or so he and God's Anointed thought.

They believed he had been given "the authority to regulate the details of their daily life"—even small details. For example, he said that to lead a holy life, they must never use candles or other forms of artificial light—"everything except the light of day was eschewed."

As on Smith Island, Joshua said that it was necessary for them to frequently roll about the floor until their sins had been atoned for—and he alone would know when that was. And so God's Anointed obeyed, rolling and praying so loudly that neighbors said the noise could be heard a quarter of a mile away from the Hurts' house.

> *When they got together for the religious services, all would lie on the floor. Creffield would walk among them and sometimes he would roll about, too. While lying this way they were supposed to receive messages from God. Creffield would keep telling them to pray and shout with all their might or God would smite them. . .*
>
> *He would keep telling them that God would smite them unless they did as he said. He claimed to be the Savior. I have known Creffield to keep them rolling about on the floor in this manner for from twelve to twenty four hours at one time.* O. V. Hurt

Joshua established rules about how God's Anointed were to eat, how they were to sleep, practically how they were to think. In order to eat, Joshua had to "sanctify" all that was consumed by God's Anointed by touching it with his hands. This sanctification made what had been unfit, fit for consumption. For almost a week all he would sanctify was bread and water—so, according to Joshua, they would know hunger.

Then he sanctified nothing, not even bread and water: "And he caused it to be proclaimed and published through Nineveh,

Edmund Creffield with Bible

by the decree of the king and his nobles, saying Let neither man nor beast, herd nor flock taste any thing; let them not feed, nor drink water."—Jonah 3:7. Joshua said he had been directed to tell them that they that were to fast, or he would be taken away from them.

Joshua ruled that men, women and children were all to sleep together on the floor in the same room while wearing little clothing. They were to do this, according to Joshua, so they would know cold.

Joshua established rules about whom they could communicate with. If someone wasn't one of God's Anointed, or refused to accept the "spirit," Joshua told them to have no dealings with "the infidels"—even if the infidels were members of their own families. "Those of your own household may fight you," Joshua warned. "When you get baptized with fire your friends become few."

The flock may have been half starved, cold, and estranged from their families, but they were God's Anointed. They were special. Their names were inscribed on a Holy Roll in Heaven. Could naysayers say the same?

Which brought up the problem of O. V. Hurt. He refused to join Joshua's church, but living in his home, God's Anointed were having regular dealings with him. They now referred to him as the "Black Devil," and repeatedly warned him that God would "smite" him unless he made peace with God. Meanwhile, O. V. tolerated the Holy Rollers' presence in his home because he loved his wife and children dearly and hoped that by having them near him—instead of being off on some island doing God knows what—they might come to their senses.

He and Sarah, forty-two, had been married for twenty-three

years. They had met on the Oregon coast, where Sarah had
grown up. When her family, the Starrs, including her brothers
Burgess and Clarence and her sister Georgianah, had first
moved to the coast in 1873, they squatted in an old Indian hut
on the Siletz Indian Reservation. The reservation was created
at a time when the government was trying to "civilize" Indians.
"Civilized" people were Christians who tilled the soil, wore cotton or wool clothing, and spoke English. The government
parceled out reservations among Christian denominations, and
the Methodists—those infidels—were given the Siletz Indian
Reservation.

When they were first married, O. V. and Sarah lived at the
Starrs' homestead on the Yachats River. It was there that their
three children were born—a forth child, Mary Edna, had died in
infancy. Later the Hurts moved to the reservation school, where
O. V. worked as a teacher and Sarah as the matron. Because of
disharmony among the Methodists working for the Indian
Agency, the Hurts left the reservation in 1893. They moved to
Corvallis where they had since lived peacefully and happily.

Now, when Sarah Hurt's brother, Burgess Starr, came to see
his wife, Donna, at the Hurts' home, she refused to so much as
shake hands with him. Joshua had warned her to not touch
anyone who had "relations with the wicked world," even her
husband: "Be ye not unequally yoked together with unbelievers:
for what fellowship hath righteousness with unrighteousness?
and what communion hath light with darkness?"—II
Corinthians 6:14.

At first, when Warren Hartley went to the Hurts' to try and
persuade his mother and sister, Cora and Sophie, to go home,
they lay on the floor in something like a trance and showed
almost no signs of recognizing him. When they finally did
acknowledge him, they said they weren't about to leave the
"holiest of holies." Warren then wired his father to return
posthaste from the Bohemia Mining District.

Lewis was aghast when he heard about the goings-on back
home. He'd attended a few of Creffield's meetings when he'd
first started preaching in Corvallis, but thought the man was
harmless—Lewis was one of those who summed up his opinion
by tapping a finger on his forehead. Why wasn't his wife home

Sunday Oregonian Magazine, 1953

Creffield's marathon prayer services brought out a different side of many of the female members of his flock.

taking care of their magnificent new ten-room house? This was 1903 and that's what women were supposed to do in 1903—especially proper women, women who were the wives of respected men, women of high character and standing, God-fearing, decent women.

For heaven's sakes, if Cora was bored and wanted to join some group why didn't she join one of the many fraternal organizations that flourished in Corvallis, organizations such as the Oddfellows, the Masons, the United Workmen, or the Good Templars? Then again, the Good Templars, a temperance group, was the only group that accepted women as members. And how would it have looked if Cora had joined them when it was known her husband drank—not to excess, mind you, but still he was known to have a drink or two on occasion.

When Lewis arrived at the Hurts' to collect his wife and daughter, Cora told him to go away. Joshua had enlightened her about marriage, how it was "unholy," and how "eternal damnation" was what awaited "wives and children who did not separate themselves from unbelieving husbands and parents."

Lewis could not contain himself. Were the rumors true? he asked Cora. Were orgies taking place in the Hurts' home? Cora, who had never lied to him before, said they were not.

How O. V. Hurt managed to live in this chaos and still maintain his job for as long as he did was a marvel to people. It was an extraordinary man who could come home from work daily, find twenty-some people rolling about his living room floor beseeching, "Oh, God, oh, Jesus," and return to work the next morning as though life at home was normal. But finally the "Babel of weird sounds" took its toll.

On Wednesday, October 28, O. V. succumbed to Creffield's will, or saw the light. He resigned from his position at the mercantile, sent a note in with his keys that said he had "been living in sin" and that hereafter he intended to devote himself "to the work of God." Signs were posted on the Hurts' porch and door: "Positively no admittance except on God's business."

"Instead of the neatly dressed man of a few weeks ago," the *Telegram* reported, "Hurt now wears the poorest kind of clothes, and his face is partly hidden behind a sprouting beard of several days' growth. He wears a soft shirt and a slouch hat, and his general appearance betrays a heavy mental strain."

> *I believe all those who are followers of our faith are sincere and honest in their belief. I have not so much faith as have they, but I justify them in their belief, and trust that since their views are but slightly in advance of what has been the foundation of many new sects, they are not unlike many who have preceded them and are therefore not justifiably the subject of contempt and ridicule. They preach the faith of John Wesley. They believe no more than many another sect has taught, the difference being that other sects after gaining ground and followers have begun to pander to the worldly.*
>
> O. V. Hurt

The day after O. V. quit his job, a housecleaning took place at his home. People in Corvallis usually did a thorough housecleaning twice a year—once in the spring and once in the fall. During a typical fall cleaning, people took their carpets outdoors and beat them with a carpet-beater. The carpets were then laid back down on a padding of fresh straw, and tacked to the floor. Curtains, most of which were white lace hanging on brass rings from walnut or white poles, were washed, boiled, blued, and starched. While still damp they were pinned to a curtain frame to dry. While the curtains dried, the windows were washed until they sparkled.

Any items one didn't want, Jake Bloomberg took off one's hands. Jake drove a team and wagon about the county collecting things for his junk shop. "Any rags, any bags, any bottles today?" he would yell as he approached a house. "The junk-man is coming your way." Outgrown clothing was given to those with smaller children or made over. Garments no longer usable were cut into strips, the strips were sewn end to end, and the long strip was wound into a ball. Balls of this sort were then given to a woman with a hand loom who wove them into rugs and carpets. Nothing was ever wasted.

The Hurts' housecleaning that fall, though, was in no way typical. On Joshua's orders, the flock took all of the Hurts' furniture outside. . . and set it on fire! The flock then took bric-a-brac, kitchen utensils, mandolins, heirlooms, photos and other goods received from "carnal" hands, and put them on the fire.

"When God sets us a-going, we will be like King Asa," Joshua preached, "cut down the groves, not stopping at that, but go right up, with drawn sword, and smash the idols of our own household, and make the inmates come down, down, down, until God can lift them up. Hallelujah! This is love divine. Have you got it? 'Buy the truth, and sell it not,' says God's Word."

Frank Hurt took his Cleveland bicycle, the one he rode from Corvallis to Oregon City in record time, and put it on the fire. He watched it burn alongside Mae Hurt's fine guitar, the one she won for once having the nation's second highest sales of the Salvation Army's *War Cry*.

Shotguns, dishes, baby buggies, and a stove were destroyed. Outside, wooden walks were torn up, and flowers, shrubbery, grapevines, and fruit trees were uprooted and added to the fire. Finally, a score of chickens, a cat, and a dog were added to the blaze.

Cora Hartley, and her daughter, Sophie, went to their house, smashed their heirloom china, and hauled what possessions they could manage to the fire at the Hurts'. Not that there was much left in the Hartleys' new ten-room house. The two women

Benton County Historical Museum
Baby Martha Hurt

had already sold most of their valuables and furniture to raise money for Joshua.

They then stripped Warren Hartley's place of photographs of his friends and other goods received from carnal hands, and added them to the fire at the Hurts'.

When Warren Hartley discovered what Cora and Sophie had done, he got a gun and started on a "Holy Roller hunt." Had his friends not intervened, there would have been, he said "several 'apostles' knocking for admittance at the golden gate that night."

Una Baldwin, Sarah Hurt's niece, went to her home and packed her clothing and other belongings in a trunk. She put it on the porch for a drayman to have it transported to the Hurts', where it was to be added to the fire. Word was sent to her father, Edwin Baldwin, and he arrived in time to prevent her carnal goods from being taken to the Hurts'. But he was too late to prevent his daughter's return.

A second fire was started at the Starrs'. Their neighbors were awakened by a bright light and, assuming a house was on fire, jumped out of bed. When they got outside, they saw it wasn't a house on fire, but the Starrs' household idols—furniture and other household goods—going up in flames.

Everyone in Creffield's flock now claimed to be in constant communication with God—not directly in communication with God, mind you, but in communication with God through Joshua, God's exclusive messenger on Earth. Anyone who couldn't comprehend such an idea didn't understand Joshua's great overriding mission—whatever that might be. He hadn't filled the flock in on all the details yet, but he would. Soon.

God's Anointed also may have had a new prayer, one they prayed silently to themselves:

Please, God, don't let Joshua be wrong.

What fools they would look like if Creffield was wrong . . . so he couldn't be wrong.

Please, God, don't let Joshua be wrong.

Creffield no longer had to press God's Anointed to trust that he was having one-to-one chats with the Almighty. They provided the pressure all by themselves. They needed him now as much as he needed them. Now his goals—whatever those were, he would tell them soon—became their own.

Please, God, don't let Joshua be wrong!

The newspapers had a grand time with the story.

"Rules of etiquette have been discarded," the *Telegram* reported. "The members apparently are drifting back to the mode of existence of people upon whom the stamp of civilization has not yet been placed."

> *The Indians of the Quinault Agency are typical "Holy Rollers." Under the influence of religious excitement they roll from side to side until exhausted. There is no record, however, that they have broken up their furniture, roasted dogs and cats alive, or performed other sacrificial rites which lately made the Corvallis contingent conspicuous as physical demonstrators of "religion." But then the poor Indian is but recently civilized.*
>
> The *Oregonian*

Many of O. V. Hurt's friends went to his home and pleaded to see him. Creffield or Brooks, however, met all callers, and wouldn't let anyone enter the premises. O. V. was "seeking God," they always said, and could not be disturbed. They themselves never stayed outside long because their presence was needed inside to receive the latest "message from the Holy Ghost."

Almost no topics other than the goings-on at the Hurts' were discussed on the streets of Corvallis the next day. The walks between the Hurts' house and Mary's River Bridge were lined with the curious. There are some estimates that as many as 2,000 of the city's 3,000 citizens came to do a little prurient prying that day.

What had been whispered about before was now talked about openly. Were things other than religious services taking place among the Holy Rollers? Would Creffield and Brooks, "two huskies" really live in a locked house with a number of young girls, and do nothing but pray all day? Was Creffield taking advantage of the "weak minded"? Was Creffield preaching more than love—was he preaching "free love"?

And what about Martha, the baby the Hurts' had recently adopted? Had she really been burned along with the dog and cat?

I came to Jesus long ago all laden down with sin,
I sought Him long for pard'ning grace,
He would not take me in.
At last I found the reason why as light came more and more;
I had a shelf with idols on just in behind the door.
That shelf behind the door—don't use it any more;
But quickly clean that corner out from ceiling to the floor;
For Jesus wants His temple clean, He can not bless you more,
Unless you take those idols out from behind the door.

From the Reverend Knapp's
Bible Songs of Salvation and Victory

CHAPTER SIX

COMMUNITY CONCERNS

I tore it down and threw it out and the blessing came;
But e'er I got the victory and felt the holy flame.
Beelzebub came rushing up and said with awful roar,
"You cannot live without a shelf right here behind the door."
From the Reverend *Knapp's*
Bible Songs of Salvation and Victory

The Hurts were such a loving family, that when O. V. and Sarah realized that their children were soon going to be leaving home to embark on lives of their own, they adopted more—Roy Robinett, fourteen, and Martha, a baby. Now with the rumor of Martha's demise, Sheriff M. P. Burnett finally had some legal reason to intervene in the doings at the Hurt house—human sacrifice stretched the limits of the right to freedom of religion.

In the company of Deputy Henderson and Deputy Attorney E. R. Bryson, he pounded on the door and demanded to be let in.

"Well, I will consult God about it," Creffield said when he answered.

"Thereupon," the *Times* reported, "he began to walk backward and forward across the porch with a faraway look in his eye and his face turned to the sky, as though he were penetrating the mysteries beyond."

The officers were able to get O. V.'s attention, and, after exchanging greetings, O. V. invited the men in.

The sheriff found most of the Holy Rollers lying on the floor in one bare room. Some were lying on their faces, others on their backs, and others were crouching. Some were praying, some were laughing, and others were weeping. All had haggard faces, hollow eyes, and pallid complexions.

In the center of the room lay a young girl who appeared to be in a trance. Who she was is not known because her face was covered with a cloth. Creffield lay down beside her with his head almost touching hers and said she was "receiving a message from on high," and that some of the others were writing down the communication. When Deputy Henderson attempted to remove the cloth, the rest of God's Anointed shouted: "Don't touch her!"

And then Sheriff Burnett saw baby Martha. She was very much alive. She even smiled at him.

What was the purpose of these fires? the sheriff wanted to know.

The fires had been set because it was "God's will." God, through Joshua, had told them, God's Anointed, what to destroy and what to preserve. This had all been done, they said, in order to "fully sanctify" the Hurts' house and premises. The things destroyed had "acted as hindrances" to their conversion. Loving worldly things more than they ought, and living in a house with such things, was not "acceptable to God."

"We burnt the furniture at my father's house," Frank said. "We did, but only old pieces in order to secure more room for the meetings. Some trinkets and goods of no particular value were destroyed because we do not believe that those saved and having their names inscribed in heaven should enjoy luxuries."

Too many people when asked, "What is the Tenth Commandment?" answer: "'Thou shalt not covet other folks' things—but get Sears and Roebuck catalog and buy them for thyself." Such people would never have their names inscribed on a Holy Roll in Heaven as God's Anointed did.

Was it true a dog and cat were burned?

Evening Telegram

The O. V. Hurt home in Corvallis

"We killed a dog and a cat, I admit," Frank said, "but did so because we wanted to get rid of them but failed."

Were they sacrifices?

No, God's Anointed assured the sheriff.

"We have no laws except the Bible," Frank said. "You find nothing like that in the Bible."

"The dog that was killed," O. V. said, "was an impertinent little canine on which sentence of death had been pronounced many times before and which ought to have been carried out." This didn't sound like the kind, patient, and loving O. V. Hurt Sheriff Burnett knew.

"The ground was hard and dry and it was difficult to bury the remains, so we threw them on a bonfire," Frank said. "It was purely for sanitary reasons. The burning of the animals had no connection with our religion."

The burning of household pets was nothing to worry about because "you find nothing like that in the Bible." "It was purely for sanitary reasons." And the burning of children in the Bible? Well, Abraham was ready to slay his son, Isaac, but didn't as God intervened in time. So there you had it. Nothing to worry about.

The sheriff didn't think the concerned populace outside would find these explanations terribly reassuring. He had a problem on his hands—there was no law against burning cats and dogs. People, however, didn't care about the letter of the law. "It was generally conceded that Creffield and Brooks, the acknowledged high priests of the sect, should be required to quit the community," the *Gazette* reported. "It is the universal opinion that they are fanatical to a degree bordering on mental unsoundness."

So Burnett exercised the only legal option open to him—taking Creffield and Brooks into custody to have their sanity examined. If they proved to be a threat to either themselves or others, he could rid the community of them by having them committed to the insane asylum—the loony bin.

Please, God, don't let Joshua be wrong! God's Anointed silently prayed as the men were led away.

Creffield's and Brooks' sanity examination was conducted by Doctors Pernot and Cathey, with County Judge Watters and Deputy Attorney Bryson in attendance. The two said their stopover at the Hurts was merely a "tarrying" while they prepared for and awaited "God's final order" for them to go out and preach their version of the "gospel to foreign lands." Creffield said he was an "apostle, just like Christ's apostles," and that his was "a revival of the old order of religion as Christ taught it and practiced it in his time."

Creffield said that his creed was "to do nothing, however trivial, without querying Heaven and receiving directions from above, to do nothing for money, to read the Bible early and late," and finally "to commit no sin." Of the last one, committing no sin, he added that in fact he was incapable of sinning.

If God were to direct him to kill a human being, Creffield was asked, would he follow the command?

Yes, he would "make a burnt offering of a child," he replied—but *only* "if the Lord bade it."

When Brooks was asked the same question, he was silent for a moment, then quoted a passage of Scripture in which it was declared that "the law of God must always be supreme."

When asked whether "God was likely to command the destruction of any person," Brooks replied that God had never commanded him to do anything of that kind—yet. He, however, did "not consider such a command likely."

Several Holy Rollers came to the courthouse to support Creffield, including O. V. Hurt. Edwin Baldwin, who'd lived near him on the Siletz Indian Reservation, cornered him. Didn't he see the similarity between the Indians' "savage manifestations" and Creffield's religious practices? Compare Creffield's current secrecy, his friend pleaded, with the way the medicine men would not permit white men to be present when they performed their ministrations. They hadn't been sure what the shamans were doing behind closed doors, but hadn't they always assumed they were having "orgies"?

O. V. said he wanted to be left alone, that he had "withdrawn from the world for all time," and that hereafter he planned to devote himself "to the work according to the new faith."

Edwin told him that many of his friends sympathized with his plight.

"I don't need their sympathy," he murmured. "It is they who need sympathy."

Please, God, don't let Joshua be wrong!

Creffield's and Brooks' minds, although not found to the soundest, were not found to be unsound enough to permit their being committed to the insane asylum against their will. It was assumed that neither man would hear God asking for a human sacrifice in the near future.

Deputy Henderson informed "the apostles" that, although by law they were free to do as they chose, they should know that there was still strong public sentiment against them. The words *tar, feathers, and vigilantes* were now peppering many conversations in Corvallis. Because of this, the deputy advised Creffield and Brooks to leave town—while they could. Creffield flared and told the deputy to not talk to him anymore, that "the Lord would take care of his own."

As the Holy Rollers prepared to return to the Hurts, Edwin Baldwin seized the opportunity to grab his daughter, Una. With the help of friends, he dragged her kicking and screaming from the courthouse to a waiting carriage. Creffield bellowed that God would "smite" him unless he returned Una to him, but Edwin wasn't about to do that. Instead he drove Una, twenty-two, home and confined her to her bed.

That night, others in Corvallis also took matters into their own hands. Their town was becoming a laughing stock. People were beginning to receive letters from friends elsewhere asking whether they too had joined Creffield's church.

It was bad enough that the Portland papers had picked up on the story, but now dispatches about these goings-on were literally being sent around the world by the Associated Press and special correspondents.

And some of these reports weren't even accurate. Just look at the article in Edinburgh's *Scotchman*. "'John the Baptist' reincarnated, is preparing to offer to the altar's flames one of his most devoted followers, a young girl, Miss Matilda Johnson." Creffield had claimed to be many things, but he had never claimed to be John the Baptist. And who was this Matilda Johnson they were writing about?

Something had to be done before Corvallis's reputation was permanently marred by a group of religious fanatics.

As a group of men banged on the Hurts' door, Joshua announced he had an important message from God: The end of the world was in "immediate view," and they, God's Anointed, now "The Holy Ones," should be "prepared for glory."

As the pounding on the door continued, the Holy Ones prayed.

Oh, God, oh, Jesus.

Someone broke the door's window, but the Holy Ones did not stop their praying.

God have mercy.

Boys threw rocks on the roof.

God will have victory tonight.

Boys threw rocks at the house.

Be ye holy!
Boys threw rocks through the house's windows.
It is either holiness or Hell!
Finally, in disgust, the malcontents overturned the outhouses and left.
Oh, God, oh, Jesus—don't let Joshua be wrong!

The next day, Halloween, most people in town condemned the stoning. At noon Brooks addressed the spectators who once again had gathered. Asked whether the Holy Rollers planned to prosecute those who had done the damage, he said that that wasn't Joshua's way. If a "man dragged him through the streets by the hair of the head, he would not prosecute him."

O. V. Hurt and his son, Frank, did go to the sheriff's office and ask for protection. O. V. said that if the county authorities would not protect those in his home, he would appeal to the governor. O. V. had friends in high places as he had once been Republican Party state committeeman. Sheriff Burnett said that he would provide what protection he could, but noted that if Creffield and Brooks left the house, there wouldn't be need of it.

The next day it looked as though the apostles took the sheriff's advice and left town. Creffield was seen fleeing south in a buggy, and Brooks was seen on a bicycle "pedaling for all his life was worth."

"Creffield and Brooks, two apostles of the 'Holy Rollers' who have created a sensation here during the past few days, took flight," the *Eugene Morning Register* reported. "It is thought that now the fanatical displays will cease."

They thought wrong.

⚬⟞⟝⚬

Some go away from the house tonight, Purified from sin;
Others reject the precious light, And go away unclean;
Lovingly still the Savior stands, Pleading with thy heart;
Patiently knocks with his bleeding hands, Unwilling to depart.

From the Reverend Knapp's
Bible Songs of Salvation and Victory

Chapter Seven

Esther: The Chosen One

What can wash away my sin?
Nothing but the blood of Jesus.
What can make me whole again?
Nothing but the blood of Jesus.
Oh, precious is the flow
That makes me white as snow;
No other fount I know,
Nothing but the blood of Jesus.
From the Reverend Knapp's
Bible Songs of Salvation and Victory

B rooks sought shelter in a house in Wren, a small village fifteen miles west of Corvallis. "The Lord sent me here," Brooks said, startling a woman in her kitchen. Mud-splattered and rain-soaked, he threw himself onto the floor by the fire, and loudly thanked the Almighty that he had at last found a "friendly refuge." He told the woman that he was "an apostle from God" and asked whether she would kindly cook him dinner.

"All right," she replied. "Just wait a few minutes." She'd need to get some items at the village store—you can't serve just any dish to an apostle from God, after all.

When she got to the store she told five "stalwart backwoods-men" who were hanging about that she had one of the Holy Roller apostles at her house.

Would they mind getting rid of him for her?

With pleasure!

They went back to the woman's house and pitched Brooks "into the rain and darkness, with an emphatic 'git.'"

Within days, though, both Brooks and Creffield were back at the Hurt home, brought there by Frank Hurt. To Frank and the rest of the flock Creffield was still God's Elect, Joshua, the one who could communicate directly with God and tell them, the Holy Ones, what to do next. With the end of the world in imme-diate view, they needed him now more than ever. Who else could receive the necessary instructions telling them how to prepare for glory?

"The Hurt family had the sympathy of the community for being a prey to such fanaticism," the *Telegram* said, "but now that they followed up Creffield when he took to flight, and brought him back and are now harboring him in their home, another chapter has been opened up in the scandal that has made Corvallis the subject of much ridicule."

"We do not care what the newspapers have to say," Maud Hurt said. "In fact we expected them to misrepresent us. We have not taken the trouble to read their accounts of us and our sect."

When a reporter asked whether he could speak to her father, Maud said he was busy seeking God. "He has not as yet spoken to anyone of the world," she said, "and I could not disturb him at present."

When O. V. Hurt then did come to the door, Maud shooed him away, telling him she didn't think it was necessary for him to answer any questions. "Judging from the humble way in which the man of the house obeyed this admonition," the *Telegram* said, "he is under complete control of the fair members of the Rollers, who in turn seem to center their utmost faith on Creffield, the apostle."

The Hurts' phone was disconnected. Through Joshua, the Holy Ones had a direct line to God. What more did they need?

In mid-November the Holy Rollers began to enlarge the Hurts' house, turn it into a fit tabernacle for Joshua. While the work was being done, the neighbors were given a respite from the Babel of weird sounds that had emanated from the house for months.

And O. V. Hurt was also given a respite. His head stopped spinning enough that when James Berry suggested they go to Portland he didn't reject the proposal out of hand.

And in Portland O. V. had an epiphany.

"Removed from the influences that biased his better judgment here," the *Gazette* reported, "and out of the reach of the emotional excesses that surrounded him in his home, Mr. Hurt's mind returned to its normal condition."

"I studied his [Creffield's] proposition for an entire week," O. V. said, "looking at it from every point of view, and then decided that I would have nothing to do with it as his religion was nothing more than hysterical sentiment."

Hallelujah!

SNAP SHOT OF FRANK HURT.

This man appears to be sincere in his convictions, and believes he has found the only true religion.

Evening Telegram
Frank Hurt

On his return from Portland, O. V. told Creffield he was no longer welcome in his home. "He took all his things and left," a relieved O. V. said. "The same in regard to Brooks."

Sam Starr, whose wife Hattie had been held under Creffield's spell, declared that if he ever again saw Creffield, "the latter will do as much rolling and tumbling in five minutes as he has been doing all summer."

O. V. Hurt may have rejected Joshua, but the rest of his family hadn't. His son, Frank, took Creffield west in a one-horse buggy through the Alsea Valley. November wasn't the time of year to travel through the Coast Range—not that there really was a right time of year. The road—more of a trail, really, than a road—after one rain was a muddy trail, and after two rains was an almost impassable muddy trail with streams crossing it. A week before a trip smart travelers on it had made inquiries about the weather and road conditions, and brought with them a bedroll, plenty of food, shovels, saws, axes—and dynamite. Really smart travelers stayed home.

But Frank and Creffield weren't just any travelers. Frank was one of the Holy Ones and Creffield was God's Elect, Joshua, God's Holy Prophet. So off they went, crossing into the valley via Preacher Creek Mountain.

Could they have found a more fittingly named route? Surely another sign that the Holy Ghost was looking out for them.

They headed down to Five Rivers, but when they tried to ford the swollen waters, their buggy overturned. Not only did the two men do more rolling and tumbling in five minutes than they had done all summer, they were baptized as they, along with their horse, were swept downstream about 200 yards. Eventually all three managed to scramble safely ashore, but the buggy was destroyed.

Frank returned to Corvallis and he and his wife, Mollie, rented a house on the east bank of the Willamette River. Like O. V. Hurt's house, it was just outside Corvallis's city limits, thus outside of where Creffield had been legally barred from holding services. The house—the barest of necessities—became Creffield's new tabernacle as he and about a dozen other of the Holy Rollers moved in to it.

Joshua told the group that God had again spoken to him, told him of some new teachings, new ways of cleansing themselves of sin, of attaining purity. Wesley Seeley contemplated what he was hearing, what it took, according to Joshua, to be purified. He knew he didn't have it in him to perform the necessary rituals. He risked eternal damnation and having his name stricken from the Holy Roll in Heaven, and left Creffield's church. Two of his sisters, Florence and Rose, however, stayed. Wesley, already having risked God's wrath, didn't tell anyone outside of the flock what his sisters and the others were about to do.

Joshua made another astonishing announcement that evening: he was going to marry Esther Mitchell, now sixteen.

Like Hell he was.

Before any such thing had a chance of happening, Esther's older sister, Phoebe, committed her to the Boys' and Girls' Aid Society, an institution for homeless and abused children in Portland. She would have committed her to the state insane asylum, but Esther was too young to be sent there.

Seattle Post-Intelligencer
Esther Mitchell

"Hallelujah! Glory to God!" Esther shouted over and over while being admitted. "Hallelujah! Glory to God! Hallelujah! Glory to God!"

Joshua was "God"—not just God's Holy Prophet—she said, and that Joshua had command over her. She shouted and shouted until she fell in a faint.

"Bright, but deranged," the physicians at the Aid Society wrote. "Mind almost unhinged by religious fanatics called the 'Holy Rollers' in Corvallis."

When Perry and George Mitchell, Esther's brothers, went to see her at the Aid Society she said she didn't recognize them. George, eighteen, who had doted on Esther since their mother had died and their father had abandoned them, pleaded with her, telling her she *had* to recognize them, that he and Perry were her brothers.

If that was so, she said, they were her brothers "in name only."

George was devastated.

"I had my own living to make," he said, "and you can't make enough in a lumber mill or a lath factory to give up all your time to such things"—such things as pleading with your bright but deranged sister.

George couldn't eat or sleep. Perry, twenty, told him that if he didn't quit worrying about Esther, he "would soon be as nutty as the Holy Rollers."

In the Aid Society, Esther wouldn't associate with the other girls. Almost around the clock, she rolled on the floor, her Bible clasped in her hands, while she shouted "Glory to God." When forced to go to bed by Mary Graham, the matron, Esther would go, but at the first chance would get up and begin rolling again.

One night Esther told the matron that she had been receiving messages from God. After that, the matron said she was afraid to allow Esther to stay at the Aid Society lest she receive a message from God telling her to kill some of the other children there. What had Brooks and Creffield said at their sanity hearings when asked whether God was likely to command the killing of a human being? God had never commanded them to do anything of that kind . . . yet.

But what *if* God did make such a command?

Yes, they said, if the Lord bade it.

Would He now make such a command to the bright but deranged Esther?

Something had to be done about Creffield.

That was all that was discussed on Main Street Monday night, January 4, 1904. Well, that and James Berry's wedding. James, having recovered from Maud's rebuff, had earlier in the day married Clara King, of Salem. "Both are young people of high character and standing," said the *Times*.

Of more immediate interest, though, to those gathering on the street were rumors that someone had reported seeing on Smith Island a naked Creffield surrounded by a bevy of women. Not only that, he—or was it a she? Exactly who the someone was, wasn't known. But it didn't really matter. This someone, it was said, had not only seen a naked Creffield surrounded by a bevy of women, but had also taken a photo of this . . . this . . . outrage. "Adam and Eve were put into the world without clothing," Creffield had said. "That is the way we should live."

And *what* exactly was to be made of the story of that young woman "prominent in society circles," the one who said she was "held prisoner" by Creffield in the old Capitol building while she was "in a trance"? She, whoever she was—did it *really* matter—refused to discuss what had gone on between her and Creffield while she was in this compromising situation.

Which is as it should be.

Young women of high character and standing do not discuss the more intimate details of their lives. But it was safe to assume something indecent had taken place.

The law be damned. Something had to be done about Creffield. These were their wives and their daughters being led astray under some hypnotic influence, women of high character and standing, God-fearing, decent women. Most important, these were *their women.*

By nine o'clock, a plan was settled upon. Twenty men calling themselves the "White Caps" boarded the ferry.

> *There was not a boy or hoodlum in the party. "In the main, they were persons who have felt the results of the strange spell that the apostles have seemed to exert on the members of families, often in a way to bring sorrow and trouble. It is believed that their purpose was not for motives of revenge, but an effort to get Brooks and Creffield out of the community, hoping thereby to secure a rest from the religious agitation which has dethroned the mind of one young woman* [Esther Mitchell] *of its reason, at least temporarily".*
>
> The Times

The ferryman let the White Caps off about 200 yards from Frank Hurt's house. The group quickly surrounded the perimeter, cutting off all avenues of escape, and broke down the door. In the house, Creffield and Brooks sat amid about a dozen barefoot followers. They looked as though they had been expecting something like this for some time.

"They killed Christ, killed the apostles and stoned the disciples to death, and we expect them to do anything with us," one of the women cried. "It is either Heaven or Hell, and I am for Heaven."

The male Holy Rollers who were in the room—Creffield, Brooks, Levins, and Campbell—were ordered to put on their shoes and hats. While the men complied, the women sang—all but one who stared intently at each intruder's face.

The four men were bound with rope, ordered out the door, and were marched directly to the ferry. Once across the river in Corvallis, the White Caps didn't bother to take the back streets. They knew that no one—not even the sheriff and his damned adherence to the letter of the law—would interfere with their plan. The light of a winter moon shone clear and bright in the eastern sky, and the men passed directly under streetlights as they walked from the ferry to Main Street. From there they went to the first bridge past the sawmill and ordered Creffield and Brooks to take off their clothes.

"Let us pray," Creffield said.

"We have heard too much of your prayers already," a White Cap growled.

"Lord, forgive them for they know not what they do," Creffield said.

Jesus, my Lord, to Thee I cry,
Unless Thou help me I must die;
Oh, bring Thy free salvation nigh,
And take me as I am!
From the Reverend Knapp's
Bible Songs of Salvation and Victory

Chapter Eight

Tar and Feathers

Will our lamps be filled and ready,
When the Bridegroom comes?
And our lights be clear and steady,
When the Bridegroom comes?
In the night, That solemn night (that solemn night),
Will our lamps be burning bright,
When the Bridegroom comes?
O be ready! O be ready!
O be ready when the Bridegroom comes!

From the Reverend Knapp's
Bible Songs of Salvation and Victory

While Brooks was stoical, Creffield "trembled like an aspen." Once stripped, the two men were coated with a thick layer of pine tar. The mob, being partial to Creffield, gave him a second coat. Afterwards, the two were bedecked with enough feathers to "make the biggest bird known turn blue with envy."

"Well you would make a fine old Santa Claus now," one man said to Creffield as he proudly surveyed his work.

After tar and feathers had been applied to Creffield and Brooks, the White Caps turned their attention to Campbell and

Levins. On the top of the head of each, a gob of tar was poured and in it feathers were stuck, making the men look like "Indian chiefs." It gave Campbell, who was bald, "a dashing appearance."

The White Caps then commanded the Holy Rollers and their Holy Prophet to put their clothes back on and warned that if they ever came back to Corvallis they would "wake up some morning dangling from a telegraph pole."

"Whether the feathers aided them in their flight we cannot say," the *Gazette* commented, "but the first 100 yards was made by Creffield in 10 seconds flat and if we had him on our track team in the spring, honors would all fall to us as his speed is something marvelous."

Frank Hurt, who wasn't home when the White Caps came, witnessed the tarring and feathering from a distance. Afterwards he caught up with Creffield, took him back to the house, and spent the rest of the evening removing as much tar as possible with linseed oil.

The next day the two men and Maud and Mollie Hurt went to the Albany courthouse. They weren't there to file a complaint against the vigilantes, but so Creffield could get married. Creffield's original bride of choice, Esther Mitchell, still being locked in the Boy's and Girl's Aid Society, Creffield married his second choice—Maud. Judge H. M. Palmer performed the service in a room where "the odor of tar was noticeable."

After the ceremony, Creffield announced that "criminal methods" would not drive him away from "God's work" and he would return to Corvallis.

Not if O. V. Hurt had anything to do with it. For the first time ever, O. V. publicly denounced Creffield. "The 'apostle' has not only the wrath of the community to contend with if he returns," he said, "but also that of Mr. Hurt."

Assuming that Creffield had returned to Frank Hurt's house, the White Caps made a return visit themselves. Under a moon dim behind the fog, they spied three "desperate looking characters" lurking in the shadows.

"Who's there?" one of the White Caps said. "Stand and unfold yourself!"

"Frank." "Bob." "Willie."

Three voices merged into one as three men made their way up the bank.

"Here they are," said one of the White Caps. "The little fellow is Creffield."

"And the big mustached man is Levins," said another.

"And the other is Brooks," said a third. "We've got the whole gang, let's string them up at once."

"Anything new, boys?" one of the desperate looking characters stammered. It turned out the three of them were reporters looking for a scoop. The White Caps rolled their eyes, left them and barged into Frank's house. They knew Frank wasn't there. He'd been seen earlier leaving with two women.

Those inside ignored the intruders, barely missing a beat in their prayers, as the men looked for their Holy Prophet.

Damn. One of the women leaving with Frank must have been Creffield dressed in woman's clothes. The coward! Did the man have no shame? No self-respect?

The White Caps cornered Frank at the livery stable when he went to drop off his buggy. Local sentiment had been against him for some time since he was the one who brought Creffield back to Corvallis. It was thought that if he had left well enough alone, Corvallis would have been spared the most recent ordeals.

The White Caps worked much more secretly than they had the previous night because, as big an ass as Frank had made of himself, he was still O. V. Hurt's son. O. V. Hurt had suffered enough already.

The men took Frank to the spot where Creffield had been tarred and feathered and ordered Frank to undress.

But he refused to do so.

What could they do? He was O. V. Hurt's son.

They told him, as sternly as possible, that he had to promise to leave the Holy Rollers and "desist from the late manifestations" or he too would be tarred and feathered. Frank stated that he would never give up his religion, but that he would "hereafter live within such regulations as would put an end to the Holy Roller troubles."

The White Caps let him go.

What else could they—not a boy or hoodlum in the party—do?

We sincerely hope that the happenings of the last few days will forever close the Holy Roller fame in Corvallis. While we do not approve of Monday night's fray, we feel that the end could only have been brought about by some violent measure and no easier method could have been adopted than the one resorted to.

The Gazette

Though every person who participated in the affair that drove them away is guilty of a misdemeanor and liable for prosecution under the state law, there is no enforcement of the penalty. The reason is that the two men had committed offenses against the people of the vicinity that the laws could not reach. . . . The act of violence is deplored, but the departure of the men is welcome."

The Times

Maud moved back in with her parents and, after having "a number of serious talks" with her father, said she had "about made up her mind to have nothing more to do with him [Creffield]."

In March, 1904, after three months of calm, the *Daily Journal* felt confident enough to say : "The Holy Rollers seem to have rolled out of view, much to public satisfaction."

As before, the papers were wrong.

Creffield had rolled out of Corvallis, but he didn't change his ways, didn't "desist from the late manifestations." He merely changed locations, moving the whole spectacle to Portland. It was just as easy for the Holy Ghost to talk to him there. And while there he said that the Holy Ghost informed him that he, Joshua, had been elevated from God's Holy Prophet to "Second Savior"—"And there came a voice from heaven, *saying,* Thou art my beloved Son, in whom I am well pleased"—Mark 1:11.

Joshua, the Second Savior, told the Holy Ones they were only tarrying in Portland, "pending the annihilation of material things," and making plans to go to China, South Africa, and other "foreign lands" as missionaries.—"And he said unto them,

Go ye into all the world, and preach the gospel to every creature"—Mark 16:15.

Burgess Starr put a halt to any such plans when he filed a complaint with the district attorney's office alleging that Creffield had had adulterous relations with his wife, Donna—a criminal offense punishable by two years in the state penitentiary.

A quick refresher on who's who: Donna Starr, the woman Creffield was charged with having adulterous relations with, was

Morning Oregonian

Edmund Creffield in better times

his wife's aunt by marriage. Creffield's wife, Maud Creffield (née Hurt) was Sarah Hurt's daughter. Sarah Hurt (née Starr) was Burgess Starr's sister.

As if that weren't confusing—or base—enough, Donna Starr (née Mitchell) was the sister of Esther Mitchell, Creffield's original bride of choice, the young women sent off to the Boy's and Girl's Aid Society in November.

Donna, like her sister Esther, hadn't willingly left Creffield's tabernacle in the Hurts' home. Burgess had forced her to come with him to Portland. There he said she soon reverted to the model wife and mother she had once been. Now she was "a good girl," Burgess had said. A good girl, that is until Creffield came to Portland.

Donna quickly fell under his influence again, once more refusing to so much as touch Burgess because he belonged to "the wicked world" and was, as the *Telegram* said, "outside the pale of the select sect of the Creffield contingency."

After Burgess took the bold step of risking humiliation for his wife and for himself by charging Creffield with adultery, twelve others—others also "outside the pale of the select sect of the Creffield contingency"—went to District Attorney John Manning and asked "permission to lodge a charge of the same nature against Creffield."

Manning said, alas, he couldn't issue a warrant for Creffield's arrest unless he had some proof that these accusations were something other than assumptions. He'd accept the say-so of one of the husbands as proof, however. Had any of them caught Creffield in the act, *in flagrante delicto?*

No, none of them had.

None? Not even Burgess Starr?

Not even Burgess Starr.

And none were willing to lie and say *yes, I caught that fiend, Creffield, committing unspeakable acts with my wife.*

Why? Was it that they were God-fearing men, so none were willing to lie under oath—do you swear to tell the whole truth, nothing but the truth, *so help you God?*

Possibly.

It is more probable, though, that if any of these men—decent and as God-fearing as they might have been—if any one of them had actually caught Creffield in bed with his wife, he would have pummeled him—if not killed him outright. And *everyone* knew this. Since Creffield was alive and well, awaiting the annihilation of material things, it was pretty obvious that no husband had actually seen him *in flagrante delicto.*

Without their testimony, Manning could do nothing. Unless? Could Burgess, perhaps, somehow, some way, persuade Donna to come into his office and admit to having had adulterous relations with Creffield?

Of course. What could be simpler? All I, a man of the wicked world, needed to do is ask my wife, one of the Holy Ones, to be Judas, so that Pontius Pilate, in the form of District Attorney Manning, can crucify Joshua, the Second Savior, and Donna, my good girl, will come down to the District Attorney's office at once and give a statement for a few pieces of silver. Is Manning as crazy as the Holy Rollers?

This task proved to be easier than expected. When Burgess brought Donna to the police station, Manning had no problem getting her to sign an affidavit stating that, yes, there had been "improper relations" between her and Creffield. The reason she signed so readily? She didn't know what she was signing.

Furthermore, she thought she was required to sign anything put in front of her. She was a *good girl*, after all, had never been in a police station before. Not under circumstances like this, at any rate.

By the time Donna realized what she had done, it was too late. A warrant had already been issued for Creffield's arrest.

And within days he was found guilty—by the press, at any rate.

"The details of the case of this low-lived Gospel-imitating rascal are revolting in the extreme," the *Gazette* reported. "In fact the penitentiary is too good for a varmint of this caliber and the worst prisoner there would be degraded by having to associate with him."

It would be some time before the courts could determine Creffield's guilt because he vanished before he could be arrested. Detective Hartman and two other officers were assigned to work full time looking for Creffield. Hartman, starting on the east side of Portland, made a house-to-house canvas in that city, another officer worked in the vicinity of Corvallis, and a third worked in eastern Oregon. All the roads in and out of Corvallis were patrolled and barricaded, and the sheriff and a posse of private citizens searched every house in which they thought Creffield might be hiding. No one found a clue to his whereabouts.

Lewis Hartley offered a $40 reward for Creffield's capture. Within a day, another $60 had been collected, and more was constantly being added to the purse. It was now a race between the officers and the posse. The former were after the $100. The latter would simply settle for Creffield's hide.

Circulars were sent to all county officials and towns in the state with railroad depots:

> *Creffield's given name is Edmund instead of Joshua, which latter he adopted when pronouncing himself a Holy Roller. Edmund Creffield is described as being about thirty years old, very light complexion, white hair,*

white whiskers, unless smooth shaven, which he is very likely to be at present; weight about 135 pounds, height five feet six inches, wears No. 5 1/2 shoe; has good black suit, but may be wearing blue-colored blouse with belt run through it; also wears brown leggins. He is sure to have a Bible under his arm or in his pockets.

When two weeks passed with no sign of Creffield, the April 1st *Daily Journal*, not intending an April Fool's joke, said: "There is no doubt but that Holy Rollerism in Corvallis has ended."

Then the madness began.

❦

Thou shalt not commit adultery.—Exodus 20:14

CHAPTER NINE

SANE PEOPLE
DON'T GO BAREHEADED

*For I testify unto every man that heareth the words of the
prophecy of this book, If any man shall add unto these things,
God shall add unto him the plagues that are written in this
book:*

*And if any man shall take away from the words of the book of
this prophecy, God shall take away his part out of the book of
life, and out of the holy city, and from the things which are written in this book.*

Revelation 22:18-19

Creffield may have vanished, but the Holy Ones didn't
"desist from the late manifestations." If anything, the
manifestations got stranger. Seventeen of the flock now
crowded into Frank and Mollie Hurt's house where they spent
entire days and nights lying flat on the floor, face downward,
"praying to the Lord for further light."

"We received messages direct from Him," Florence Seeley
said, and He commanded that they interpret the Bible literally.

Literal interpretation of the Bible was not uncommon in the
Victorian age. To close readers of it, it was often a liberating
thing during a time where many a father thought his daughters
and his daughters' bodies belonged to him until they and their

bodies belonged to their husbands. The Holy Ones just took their interpretations to an extreme.

They now believed that the Lord commanded that they not work: He would "care for his children"—a literal interpretation of Matthew 6:34: "Take therefore no thought for the morrow: for the morrow shall take thought for the things of itself. Sufficient unto the day *is* the evil thereof."

"As there seems to be a disposition on their part to allow the Almighty to do all the providing," the *Daily Journal* said, "it is believed they will starve." And soon they did look as though they were about to starve. At the command of the Lord, they stopped eating meat and cooked food because cooked food was sinful. "Fire [has] not been brought into the world by the creator," they said, "but [is] the invention of man." Apparently it was one thing to use this "invention of man" to burn their possessions—not to mention a dog and a cat—but another thing to use it to cook with.

The Holy Ones said they were now "learning to eat what food nature had provided, just as it was prepared by the Creator"— a literal interpretation of Matthew 6:26: "Behold the fowls of the air: for they sow not, neither do they reap, nor gather into barns; yet your heavenly Father feedeth them. Are ye not much better than they?"

Eventually, at the command of the Lord, the Holy Ones wouldn't mix their fare, eating only one type of food at a meal— a literal interpretation of Numbers 11:6, 19-20: "But now our soul is dried away: There is nothing at all, besides this manna, before our eyes. . . . Ye shall not eat one day, nor two days, nor five days, neither ten days nor twenty days; But even a whole month, until it come out at your nostrils, and it be loathsome unto you: because that ye have despised the LORD which is among you."

Elsewhere, other Holy Ones were acting equally strange.

Cora Hartley, a woman who loved sunshine and flowers, was spending all her spring days in her ten-room house praying on her knees in a dark closet—a literal interpretation of Matthew 6:6: "But thou, when thou prayest, enter into thy closet, and when thou hast shut thy door, pray to thy Father which is in secret; and thy Father which seeth in secret shall reward thee openly."

Maud Hurt, back at her parents' home, seemed to do "anything that came into her mind," her father said, "saying that she had received a message from the Lord to do so." Saying the Lord told her to do so, she refused to call him "Father," instead, calling him "that old man Hurt"—a literal interpretation of Matthew 23:9: "And call no *man* your father upon the earth: for one is your Father, which is in heaven."

Saying the Lord told her to do so, Maud turned pictures to the wall. The Lord told her to do so because pictures "partook of vanity and the world."

Saying the Lord told her to do so, Maud would run into a crowded room, kneel down in the middle of the floor, and pray for the salvation of those present.

And like the other Holy Ones, Maud would fast for days at a time. When she did eat, she refused to eat in her father's presence—saying the Lord told her to refuse.

At the command of the Lord all of the women of Creffield's flock went "parading" about in public with "their hair unbraided and unkempt, flowing in tangled masses over their shoulders"—a major breach of societal norms.

Were the Holy Rollers mad? Public opinion varied.

"It is admitted by all that they are not crazy," said Salem's *Daily Oregon Statesman.* "Any one conversing with them can tell that their minds are as well balanced on general subjects as those of ordinary mortals."

Meanwhile, the *Albany Democrat* declared: "Sane people don't go bareheaded."

Sane people don't go bareheaded?

Even for 1904, this seems a bit extreme. What were they afraid of? That people who went around bareheaded one day might go around naked the next? Maybe.

"They [the Holy Rollers] can be easily recognized at sight as members of the sect, by their peculiar manner of dress," the *Statesman* said. "Although they have not yet adopted the original human habit of attiring themselves in a fig leaf, at least not in public."

The peculiar manner included going barefoot—something

HOLY ROLLERS TO PUT WORLD WHERE ADAM ENTERED IT

Evening Telegram

Florence Seeley in a Mother Hubbard

else the *Democrat* said sane people didn't do—and the women wore nothing but Mother Hubbards, thin, brown, collarless dresses with a drawstring around the neck—a literal interpretation of I Peter 3:3: "Whose adorning, let it not be that outward adorning of plaiting the hair, and wearing of gold, or of putting on of apparel; But let it be the hidden man of the heart, in that which is not corruptible, even the ornament of a meek and quiet spirit, which is in the sight of God of great price."

In time we will be restored to innocence and purity such as marked the condition of Adam and Eve, but in order to reach that state we must put away all that is sinful. To do this we must conquer our pride and everything that tends to make us proud, and this includes the destruction of clothing and ornaments. When the world is restored to its original condition of innocence, we will be as were Adam and Eve, and there will be no use of clothing or raiment of any kind. Then the world will once more be innocent and God will dwell with us here on earth and we will be like him. . .

Adam and Eve were put into the world without clothing. That is the way we should live. When Adam fell the world was cursed, and now there is death. There would have been no death if Adam had not sinned. All things

will be restored, and we can bring the world back to
that condition by living like the Lord wants us to.

Florence Seeley

In the end it didn't really matter whether the Holy Rollers weren't actually crazy. They were driving everyone else around them crazy—so something had to be done. "There is a strong sentiment in favor of stopping the practices of the Holy Rollers," the *Gazette* said, "even if heroic measures have to be adopted."

And the heroic measures? "It seems to be the opinion of those who have come in contact with them that the only way of breaking up the movement, which threatened to undermine a certain element in society, is to send them to the asylum," the *Statesman* said.

Either that—or find Creffield. Few doubted that he was somehow behind all these antics, that he was "the Lord" making commands, instructing the Holy Rollers from some secret hiding place to interpret the Bible literally. But no one had any idea where he was. "Had the earth opened and swallowed him, he could not have disappeared more completely," the *Daily Journal* noted.

So, the only way to break up the movement was to send the Holy Rollers one by one to the Oregon State Insane Asylum in Salem.

On April 28, Edna Seeley filed a petition with Judge H. M. Palmer asking that her sixteen-year-old sister, Florence Seeley, be taken from the Holy Rollers, and, being too young to be committed to the asylum, be committed to the Boys' and Girls' Aid Society.

Edna was one of the few souls the Salvation Army was able to recapture from Creffield. She had been with the group on Smith Island but now charged that "the Holy Rollers are a depraved, demented, disreputable people, the members of which lie around on the floor without regard to sex or other conventionalities and are totally unfit for a girl to associate with."

When Deputy Munkers served the warrant that Judge Palmer issued, he said that all those in Frank Hurt's house "appeared to be dazed or on a verge of insanity."

When Florence was brought into court for a sanity hearing the *Telegram* described her as "more than 'passing fair,'" and having the expression of one older than sixteen. She was "bareheaded and her luxuriant growth of hair hung down her back uncombed and confined by neither ribbon nor comb." Edna asked permission to comb her sister's hair. The judge told her not only to comb her sister's hair, but to buy the girl a hat! He also ordered that Florence be committed to the Aid Society.

She was soon joined there by Mae Hurt, O. V. Hurt's sixteen-year-old daughter.

Sophie Hartley was soon thereafter committed to the asylum, declared insane because she was a "religious fanatic" who claimed to be "an apostle."

Rose Seeley was committed, declared insane because she claimed that Joshua's church, the Second Savior's church, was "*the only church*," and Creffield was "a child of God."

Attie Bray was committed, declared insane because she believed "in the restoration of all things and as an indication of some of her beliefs, regarding dress, she goes about with her head uncovered and hair streaming down her back."

Maud Creffield was committed, declared insane because she believed "in not wearing any covering for the head and the destruction of all the unnecessary articles of apparel."

During Frank and Mollie Hurt's sanity hearing, Frank was asked whether he didn't know he had been hallucinating and he was acting foolishly.

"No, I know when God talks to me," he said. "We believe that any person can get messages from God by first preparing themselves to receive them. God always answers prayer, and we pray so that we will be able to get our direction from him."

And why was he parading about town barefoot and bareheaded?

Because God commanded him to, and he always obeyed God. Frank then proceeded to use the invention of man—a fire in a stove—to burn the new shoes and straw hat his father had just given him for the hearing.

Had going bareheaded and barefoot ever before caused such a stir?

Frank said he would rather spend years in the asylum than

return to the "worldly ways" that preceded the arrival of Joshua. "I am satisfied and will remain until they get tired of keeping me," he said. "My father expects me to get weaned away from my views, but he will never accomplish what he expects to do."

He and his wife Mollie were committed, declared insane because they "lie upon their faces upon the floor and pray day and night, claiming to receive messages directly from God; go upon the streets bare-headed, in the thinnest of raiment; destroy clothing and valuable and useful property belonging to themselves, injuring their mind and health by continuation of these practices which they claim are the commands of God."

The doctors also said the two were "not destructive except as above stated, not violent and have not been restrained." But as soon as Frank arrived at the asylum—bareheaded and barefoot, of course—he began praying loudly for its destruction. Little short of an act of God *could* have destroyed the institution, a group of massive yet graceful brick buildings that loomed on a hillside over Salem. The asylum housed about 2,000 people, nearly one of every 200 Oregonians. It took at least thirty minutes of fast walking to visit all the wards where patients were segregated by sex and condition—mild patients, violent patients, and "imbeciles."

Much to their frustration, the Holy Ones were not given their own ward, so were forced to mingle with those "outside the pale of the select sect of the Creffield contingency."

The last to be committed was Sarah Hurt, O. V. Hurt's wife. O. V. now declared that Sarah had been ready to allow Martha, their adopted baby, to be sacrificed in October along with the dog and cat. Now Sarah would have nothing to do with the baby.

> *She wouldn't even take care of the adopted child. I cared for it in the morning, dressed it and looked after it until I left the house. Then I took it to a neighbor's and left it there until I returned home.*
>
> *My wife and my daughters refused to wash the child's clothing, or to wash its body. They refused to feed it, or to wash the dishes in which the baby's food was*

prepared. They declared that God would be displeased with them if they had anything to do with the child. Creffield had told them so. . . .

My wife and daughters came to believe that I was defiled, and that this little one was defiled. At the suggestion of that viper, they talked of making sacrifice of the child; they would have burned her along with their clothing, their furniture and the cats and dogs which they declared to be of this world and unfit to live. They were all crazy—yes, all crazy. . . .

I was pleading, threatening and trying all in my power to bring my wife and daughters back to sanity, but without avail.

O. V. Hurt

On June 27, when the sheriff came to take Sarah to the asylum, she put up a fight and tore off all her clothes. O. V. struggled to get a union suit—long johns—on her, and it was wrapped about her neck as she was carried from the house screaming at him, "I hate you, but I love Creffield!"

She was declared insane because she "claims her husband is not related to her, and that God is her husband." O. V. was not a violent man, but now he said he "would like to hurt Creffield with a bullet."

"Under the present plan the state of Oregon will have the settlement of Holy Rollerism," the *Democrat* said. Only a few of Creffield's flock weren't under lock and key, but those that weren't, weren't rolling about free either.

Una Baldwin was still under her father's watchful eye in Corvallis.

Cora Hartley was with her husband, Lewis, in the Bohemia Mining District. Thinking that cooking for six men would keep her mind off of Creffield, Lewis took her there—despite her complaints that she suffered constantly from a buzzing in her head.

Esther Mitchell was released from the Boy's and Girl's Aid Society and shipped to Illinois to live with her father.

Donna Starr was with her husband, Burgess, in Portland,

but at least now she wasn't as cold toward him as she had once been. She would even eat pork, pickles, and other "forbidden fruits" that Creffield's creed hadn't allowed. She still adhered to the belief, however, that Creffield was Joshua, the Second Savior, that she and all of the Holy Ones would one day "have the power to cast out devils and perform other miracles reputed of fact in Scriptural story."

Meanwhile, the search was still on for Creffield. He had told his flock before he went into hiding: "Fear not for me as the Lord is my keeper and will not let me famish or deliver me into the hands of my enemies." He assured them that it would be impossible for the officers to arrest him. Now, having eluded capture for three months, Creffield's prophecy appeared to be true. This only enhanced his stature in the minds of the Holy Ones. To them, Creffield was God's Elect, the Second Savior, their Lord. In Joshua they now trusted more than ever.

The reward for Creffield, whom the *Democrat* described as "the dirtiest scrub who ever menaced the peace of a community," was up to $350, almost half a year's wages for a working man.

The reward was never collected.

⚬⚬⚬⚬⚬

If some say we are peculiar, and don't do things just "their way,"

They cannot understand us, neither what we do or say;

There is One above who knows us, And he keeps us pure within,

When we "sing and shout, and leap for joy," he knows just what we mean.

From the Reverend Knapp's
Bible Songs of Salvation and Victory

CHAPTER TEN

"MORE BEAST THAN MAN"

And he was there in the wilderness forty days, tempted of Satan; and was with the wild beasts; and the angels ministered unto him.—Mark 1:13

On July 29, over a month after Sarah Hurt's committment, Creffield was found. He'd been under O. V. Hurt's nose all the time—literally. Roy Robinett, the Hurt's fourteen-year-old adopted son, digging for "corks"—worms used for fishing bait—turned up Creffield.

> *There are always a lot of corks under the house, and I crawled under there to look for them. After I got a considerable distance under the house, I noticed something white back in the northeast corner. The thing looked like a big pillow, but it was so dark that I could not tell what it was. . . . I went around the corner, and with a stick, pushed a piece of cement out of the foundation. When I did that, a voice from from under the house spoke to me in broken English saying something that I could not understand. I made up my mind at once that the voice was that of Creffield. I had heard it lots of times, and after he spoke to me I was sure.*
>
> Roy Robinett

Roy ran and told his father that he wouldn't *believe* what he'd found under the house.

> *I shouted for the man underneath to come out. He said he was too weak to move. I told him I would come under and move him in a way that he would not like if he did not crawl out. . . .*
>
> *As he crawled towards me from under the building he was the most frightful looking human being I ever beheld. His white hair stood out from his head in all directions, as did also his long white beard and both were filled with dirt. His body was nude, his nails long, and his whole person filthy. I had to grit my teeth to keep off of him, but what could a man do? If he had been well and a man—but if a dirty, sick dog came and crouched at your feet you could not kick it, and I could not kick him.*
>
> O. V. Hurt

When Creffield came out from under the house he looked like a "semi-human creature," the *Gazette* said, "more beast than man." He was ghostly pale, hollow cheeked, emaciated, trembling, and barely able to stand. He looked to be about sixty years old, though he was probably thirty-one. He straightened up, rolled his eyes, stretched out his arms and said: "I am Elijah." It was almost laughable. Jesus, after he'd been dead for three days, probably looked better than Creffield looked now—although one police officer on the scene did remark that he was "most wonderfully endowed by Mother Nature."

The hole under the Hurt house where Creffield had lain all those months was only six feet long, eighteen inches deep, and two and a half feet wide.

> *If he never got out from under the building at night to shake out his plumage and drink in a breath of fresh sea breeze, he must not, during the long period of his sneak, have once been able to raise himself to the full of his majestic stature. To have lain so long on his back, on one side or the other or on his face with but twenty odd*

Creffield was described as "more beast than man" when discovered hiding by
Roy Robinett.

> *inches of space between earth and floor to operate in, is*
> *illustration in itself of the manly character of this latest*
> *and funniest of all the Elijahs. Probably no other man*
> *on earth, whether one in complete touch with the*
> *Almighty or just an ordinary sinner, would have devot-*
> *ed so much time to so noble a calling, to-wit: hide under*
> *a man's house, be fed by foolish women, in avoidance of*
> *a simple, plain charge of adultery. Any man with the*
> *spirit of a seven-year-old boy in him, would have quit*
> *the spot any dark night, and have fled to some other*
> *place where at least he could stand on his pins and look*
> *the world in the face.*
>
> The *Times*

And why had he risked starvation by staying hidden long
after all of his followers had been committed? "I went under the
house because I was told to hide away by the Lord," Creffield

said. "I was crucified while I was there. God came to me. I was to suffer for my people. I was to die from hunger and from the cold."

O. V. now understood why Sarah had to be forcibly dragged out of the house when she was about to be taken to Salem. It wasn't that she was afraid of institutionalization. She was afraid that Creffield, her Lord, might starve to death. In the hole O. V. found two old bed quilts, a pillow, a pair of drawers, a shirt, a knife, a spoon, a small tin cup with some butter in it, and eighteen jars. Most were empty. One had a bit of sugar in it, another a little flour, and in several there were the decayed remains of fruit. These may have contained all the food Creffield had had to eat in the thirty-two days since Sarah had been sent away.

Also in the hole, O. V. found a dirty and crumpled letter that Creffield had written to Maud. In it Creffield scolded her for depending on her father. "You are looking to Hurt to get you out of the asylum," Creffield wrote, "but you must have nothing to do with him. Look to God for help. Hurt is a fiend."

Shortly before Sarah was committed to the asylum, she and O. V. had visited Maud there. O. V. had hugged her tightly and she had hugged him back with what appeared to be genuine affection. No doubt Sarah had relayed this fact to Creffield, and that was what had prompted his missive. Creffield had intended for Sarah to deliver the letter to Maud, but Sarah was committed before he had a chance to give it to her.

Creffield had wanted Maud to act more like O. V.'s younger daughter, Mae, who was in the Boys' and Girls' Aid Society. "Under Creffield's influence my little daughter grew so she would have nothing to do with me," O. V. said. "She believed that I, her own father, would defile her by my touch."

Neighbors began recalling that on numerous occasions they had seen some of the Holy Rollers bending as though they were picking flowers at the northeastern corner of the Hurts' home—just across the brick foundation from Creffield's hole. It was now supposed that they were actually taking instructions from their Lord, instructions that when carried out, made them seem strange—if not downright crazy. At the same time, Creffield was also adding martyr to his list of titles.

GOD WILL BE HIS LAWYER

Evening Telegram
Roy Robinett Hurt, left, and Creffield,
right, as he appeared in a photograph
shortly after his arrest.

Creffield was taken to the Benton County Jail. When he first arrived he was very weak. He spent much of the day lying in what looked like a semi-comatose state, stirring occasionally to mutter something about Jesus. "Oh, I feel so good; Jesus is so near me," he would say. "Jesus told me last night, this would happen."

Doctor Pernot, one of the two doctors who examined Creffield's sanity in November, was summoned to examine him again.

"It is not a doctor that I want," Creffield informed him. "The Lord is my doctor."

"When did you have your last meal?" Pernot asked, trying to

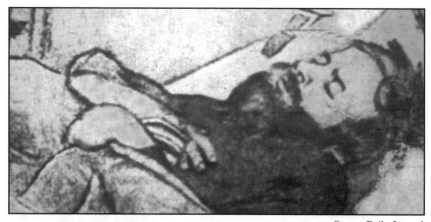

Oregon Daily Journal
A half-starved Creffield rests in jail shortly after his capture.

get Creffield's attention. "What did you have for your last meal?"

"A little flour," Creffield said hesitantly.

"Wouldn't you like some food?"

"Yes, if there is no hog meat in it," Creffield whispered, after some more ramblings about Jesus. "Jesus don't want us to eat hogs, you know."

Pernot suggested he have a little mush, bread, and milk.

"And a few eggs?" Creffield asked. "Can I have a few eggs?"

Pernot's diagnosis this time around? Creffield was "demented." As the *Times* noted: "Three months or more under the floor of a house, always in a reclining position, naked all or most of the time, half-starved all the day long, hunted by the law and hated by men—all this is enough to craze."

As news of Creffield's capture spread through town, crowds gathered, asking officials for details and a peek at the "semi-human creature." Creffield wasn't available for public viewing, though, as he was locked securely in the jail's innermost cell— a steel cage. As an added precaution, Deputy Sheriff Wells locked the keys to this cell in a safe. He wasn't worried that Creffield might try to escape, but that an unruly mob might try to lynch him.

Portland authorities had notified him that the Starr brothers were heading to Corvallis and that they intended to kill Creffield. But Deputy Sheriff Wells was told not to worry. Detective Hartman, the Portland officer originally assigned to Creffield's case, and the officer who had now been assigned to transport Creffield back to Portland, said he would make sure everything went smoothly.

For four months the only thing Detective Hartman had been able to tell reporters was about his repeated failures to find a single clue as to Creffield's whereabouts. It had been humiliating. Now that Creffield had been captured—no thanks to him—Hartman was determined to get some positive press for his heroics in bringing Creffield back alive, no easy feat . . . at least according to Hartman.

The night after his capture, "Creffield was saved from certain death at the hands of the mob at Corvallis," Hartman told reporters. "Deputy Sheriff Wells and an armed force of guards stood the mob off."

Hartman told reporters that the day after Creffield's capture he had "made arrangements with the railway people to completely fool the would-be lynchers." When the train arrived at Corvallis, Hartman said, he had it stop not at the station, but two blocks north, where he had Creffield concealed. "Deputy Sheriff Wells hustled him on board before there was any time for trouble," Hartman bragged. "Creffield was badly frightened. The mobs that attempted to take him were made up of representative citizens of Corvallis and vicinity. There were men, women and children. A second mob gathered at a railroad crossing just this side of the town, but the train did not slack up, and it was cheated."

Most of the story was of Hartman's fabrication. It's true that when the Starr brothers had hit town they were angry. But before going to the jail, they went to O. V. Hurt's home. There they discussed whether the punishment Creffield was likely to receive would be adequate. Probably not. But O. V. said, even though he hated Creffield, he wanted "peace at all cost." He wanted to "allow the law to take its course." And that was that. If O. V. Hurt was willing to allow the law to take its course, so were they.

And what of the $350 reward for Creffield's capture? Did O.

V. and Roy have any plans for it? Absolutely not! "It was Creffield that we wanted; not money," O. V. said. "Several of those who are contributors to the reward fund have expressed to me their willingness for the boy to have it, but I do not want him to have it." Roy agreed with his father, and refused to accept a cent for his deed.

It was also true that, when Creffield was escorted from the jail, more than a hundred people—"representative citizens of Corvallis and vicinity . . . men, women and children"—were waiting outside for him. But they had gathered not to lynch him, but to catch a glimpse of the man the *Times* referred to as "the champion sneak."

Although still pale and emaciated, he wasn't as wild looking as the day of his arrest. His six-inch beard had been shaved off and he had taken a bath. He walked with difficulty, and needed help from Deputy Sheriff Wells and Detective Hartman; but when he saw a photographer, he threw up his hands and shouted: "Glory to God!"

It was also true that Hartman had made plans to have the train pick Creffield up two blocks north of the station. But it didn't take people long to find that out. This was Corvallis, after all, where everybody knew everything about everyone else in town. A large crowd gathered, but was peaceful. Creffield paid no attention to it as he waited for the train while sitting on the curb singing in a low voice. Most of his words were unintelligible, save once when he was heard to say: "Jesus hath the victory."

At every station between Corvallis and Portland, great crowds appeared to get a look at "the champion sneak." Creffield often drew the curtain next to his seat, but Hartman always reopened it so that Creffield might "be identified more readily should he escape." Detective Hartman taunted Creffield, telling him that they were likely to be met at the station in Portland by an angry mob.

"I expect to be killed," Creffield said. "Men who are not understood are always killed. If the Lord commands it, I shall be killed."

When the train pulled into Portland, Creffield was supported by Hartman and Wells as he was escorted through a crowd of a thousand people to the back room of a nearby saloon. "Being the leader of a religious sect is not much fun, is it?" a bystander said to Creffield while he and the officers waited for a patrol wagon. Creffield didn't bother to look up at the man.

"You are pretty faint and weak, ain't you?" inquired another. Creffield gave an almost imperceptible nod.

Creffield was taken to the Multnomah County Jail where he was given a cell by himself. Once settled in, all he asked for was a drink of water and to be left alone. He fell asleep quickly, perhaps feeling safe for the first time in months.

<hr />

Once a sinner far from Jesus, I was perishing with cold,
But the blessed Savior heard me when I cried;
Then He threw His robe around me and He led me to His fold,
And I'm living on the hallelujah side.

From the Reverend Knapp's
Bible Songs of Salvation and Victory

CHAPTER ELEVEN

"GOD WILL PLEAD MY CASE"

I KNOW NO SIN"—APOSTLE CREFFIELD
Headline, Portland *Oregon Daily Journal,* August 4, 1903

"I am not crazy; I am Elijah!" Creffield said to the ministers of the Gospel who visited him at the jail.

"Get that notion out of your head that you are one of God's pets," the Reverend J. Vertteig said. "It is that idea which has brought you where you are, and the sooner you are rid of it the better for you."

Raising himself from the cot he was lying on, Creffield propped his head on one hand, and in the strongest voice he had used since his capture said again, "I am not crazy; I am Elijah."

But what of the other Elijahs? the ministers of the Gospel wanted to know. What of men like John Alexander Dowie of the Christian Catholic and Apostolic Church in Zion? Dowie said he too had advanced to the position of prophet, was now "Elijah the Restorer," and he too believed that God had given him the authority to ordain and direct apostles. Dowie was claiming that at any time—perhaps even now as they spoke—he was about to be promoted to "Prophet of the Restitution of all things."

Can't these ministers see that John Alexander Dowie is a fake while I am not? Are they soft in the head?

"I am not crazy; I am Elijah," Creffield repeated. "There are many impostors"—"For false Christs and false prophets shall rise, and shall shew signs and wonders, to seduce, if it were possible, even the elect"—Mark 13:22.

"To every new Elijah, every other one is an impostor," the *Daily Journal* commented. "To this extent they are right."

When Sheriff Word came to take Creffield to court on Monday, Word found him lying on his cot studying a Bible, a Bible that had just been given to him by—of all people—O. V. Hurt. O. V. had been on his way to see his daughter Mae at the Boys' and Girls' Aid Society and decided to stop and check in on his son-in-law. Creffield had wanted a Bible, so O. V. gave him one. It was the Christian thing to do, and O. V. was a Christian in all senses of the word.

"How are you feeling this morning?" the sheriff asked Creffield.

"I feel better than I did when they found me under the house," he said. "I think that I shall get well. Of course, if I am to die, I shall die, but I feel better this morning than I have for a long time."

Creffield leaned against the jail bars and gripped them to steady himself. When he spoke, he spoke without his usual fire. But this enhanced his current status as martyr.

"Are you surprised to find yourself in this place?" he was asked.

"I am in God's hands. He will protect me from this poor benighted people. Let His will be done."

For his arraignment he donned not only a blue serge suit—O. V.'s Bible visibly sticking out of one of the pockets—but shoes, black ones. He did go hatless, however.

He was so weak that when he didn't have Bailiff Goltz propping him up as he walked, he had to support himself against a wall. He looked pitiable. Spectators in the crowded courtroom could but wonder what there was about him that made people follow him. How could such a pathetic-looking man gain so much control over people—people like the rest of them, intelligent, well-adjusted people from good homes, people of "a sane mind and a reasonable being"? How could he cause them to forsake their families and be locked up in the loony bin? He didn't look like anyone's idea of Elijah. Hell, he didn't even look like a street preacher who could distract you for more than an instant.

Not able to stand unaided, Creffield leaned against a desk while Deputy Prosecuting Attorney Haney read the charges against him: "Edwin Creffield is accused of the crime of adultery . . ."

Edwin Creffield? Not *Edmund* Creffield? Although his legal name probably was *Franz Edmund Crefeld, Edmund Creffield* is the form most often found in newspaper accounts. *Edwin Creffield* is the name that appears on his court and prison records, but four other agencies that kept records on him listed his name four other ways: Edmond Crefeld, Franz E. Crefeld, F. E. Crefeld and Edmund Crefeld. He never seems to have corrected anyone about what people called him. Maybe it didn't matter to him. These were temporal names. History would remember him as God's Elect, Joshua the Prophet, the Second Savior, or Elijah.

Anyway, the charges against "Edwin Creffield" continued:

> *The said Edwin Creffield, on the twentieth-eighth day of February, A.D. 1904 in the County of Multnomah and State of Oregon, then and there being, did then and there unlawfully and feloniously commit the crime of adultery with one Mrs. D. Starr, a female person, she the said Mrs. D. Starr then and there being a married woman and the wife of one B. E. Starr, and he the said Edwin Creffield not being then and there the husband of said Mrs. D. Starr.*

"How do you plead?" Creffield was asked.

"Not guilty," he whispered.

He spoke so softly that Haney had to repeat the answer to Judge Hogue.

With a slight wave of his hand Creffield added: "God will plead my case. I need no lawyer."

"You had better secure someone on earth to defend you—I'm

Daily Oregon Statesman
Doctor. J. F. Calbreath, superintendent of the Insane Asylum

afraid I can't hear God," Judge Hogue quipped. "Do you realize that this charge is a serious one; that there is strong feeling against you and that if the allegations made are true you will go to the penitentiary?"

"I understand it."

"And you want no attorney?"

"No, God will not justify me to have one."

"How do you expect to receive justice without a lawyer?"

"God will be with me all the time. If he desires to have me found guilty, I shall receive it joyfully."

Creffield said that, according to the promises in the Acts of the Apostles, the Holy Spirit would tell him what to say in court— "And they were all filled with the Holy Ghost, and began to speak with other tongues, as the Spirit gave them utterance"—Acts 2:4.

And if he were found guilty and sent to the penitentiary?

"God wills it so, of course," Creffield said. "I shall wait patiently His commands, and do whatsoever He says. I am ready to lay down my life for Him."

Did he know that many people believed he was insane, and that he might be examined by the sanity commission?

This apparently was news to Creffield. "God usually tells me everything that is going to happen, and this is the first time He has failed to inform me," he said. After a bit more reflection he concluded: "If God had wanted me to know, He would have told me."

"I do not think there is a bit of doubt that Creffield is insane," Deputy District Attorney Haney said. "I am of the opinion that the case will never come to trial, but that he will be sent to the asylum."

"Poor, poor people! They are in the dark," Creffield said of those who thought he was not right in the head.

Creffield waived his right to a hearing, wanting to take his case before a grand jury.

When brought before the grand jury, Creffield again pleaded "not guilty." Bail was set at $2,000, and since he was penniless—God was his lawyer, but not his bail bondsman—Creffield had to stay locked up for six weeks while he awaited trial.

He quickly adapted to jail life—not surprising for someone who had spent four months in a small hole under a house. When he first arrived, every other prisoner within shouting distance of his cell yelled curses, accusations, and sarcastic jibes at him. Soon, though, Creffield's charisma came into play and he charmed them all—even his jailers, who considered him a "model prisoner."

"I have no feeling of animus toward anyone," Creffield said. "I love all men with a divine love. Not as the world loves, but with a divine love. If they were to sentence me for life, hurt or kill me, I would still love them. All hatred has left me, but the world cannot understand this."

Creffield didn't charm them as he had charmed God's Anointed—folks at the jail didn't think he was the Second Savior, by any means—but within days he went from being one of the most reviled men in the jail, not to mention all of Oregon, to one treated with respect—and even good humor.

They all had a good laugh when a company in San Francisco sent him a letter asking him to try their nerve tonic. The company had read that after Creffield was first arrested, he "was a complete wreck, both physically and mentally," and his "nervous system was shattered." Their tonic, they assured him, was "the best in the world and will cure anything." Everyone agreed that if any one didn't need nerve tonic, it was Edmund Creffield.

On account of his physical condition, if not his peculiar position in the world as Second Savior, Creffield wasn't put to work while he was in jail. He was allowed to remain in his cell during the day reading his Bible and holding conferences with his attorney, the Lord.

He rose every morning at half past six and ate a breakfast of potatoes, beef, gravy, and coffee. At noon he ate a light lunch of tea and bread, and for supper he, like all the prisoners, ate pork and beans.

Ten days before his trial Creffield asked Jailer Grafton questions about the penitentiary at Salem. Were preachers permitted to visit convicts? Were Bibles and religious tracts allowed?

"What do you want to know all this for?" Grafton asked. "Do you expect to go there?"

"Well, if God so wills it, I suppose I must accept my fate," Creffield said.

Besides, if he were sentenced to the penitentiary, he would in a sense be nearer to his flock who were still locked in the asylum. The penitentiary and asylum were situated close to one another, and the brick walls of both institutions were visible to the inmates of each.

> *My people are being persecuted: they have been unjustly imprisoned in asylums for the insane. They were not given fair trials, and the physicians who examined them for their sanity were not competent to judge. It is persecution, 20th century persecution, if you will, but persecution just the same. They are as sane as I am . . . .*
>
> *The reason my followers are insane, as people say, is because they are being sanctified for Jesus' sake. They are not crazy—they are bound up in the spirit of God for a purpose. People who are in darkness cannot comprehend the things of the light of the spirit; that is impossible.*
>
> Edmund Creffield

And back at the asylum, the authorities were currently dealing with a plan of theirs that had misfired. They had decided not to tell Creffield's flock—his people who were being persecuted unjustly—about their leader's arrest. The authorities assumed that since his people didn't trust them anyway, they wouldn't believe them—they would think it was some sort of trick. Better for his people to hear the news from other patients. The doctors also thought that Creffield's arrest would be taken by them as proof that their leader, Creffield, was not God's exclusive messenger.

But insane people do not act in predictable ways—that's one of the reasons they're considered insane. Not only did Creffield's capture not cause disillusion among his people, his people were now more resolute than ever. "Stick fast to the faith!" was their mantra. They credited God with Creffield's timely rescue from a seemingly inevitable death from starvation, once again showing Creffield's personal connection to the Almighty.

J. F. Calbreath, the asylum's superintendent, also now informed O. V. Hurt that his wife, Sarah, was hopelessly insane.

For many shall come in my name, saying, I am Christ; and shall deceive many.—Matthew 24:5

CHAPTER TWELVE

SCANDAL

*For out of the heart proceed evil thoughts, murders, adul-
teries, fornications, thefts, false witness, blasphemies:
These are the things which defile a man.*—Matthew 15:19-
20

On Friday, September 16, Creffield was tried in Circuit
Court before Judge Alfred F. Sears. The case for the state
was presented by Assistant District Attorneys G. C.
Moser and H. B. Adams. Creffield—with God presumably in the
ether nearby—represented himself. As it was expected that
some of the testimony would be indecent, Judge Sears ordered
the courtroom doors closed.

The prosecution called only five witnesses.

Burgess Starr testified that as soon as he heard of the illicit
relations between his wife and Creffield, he made the complaint
against him.

Donna Starr testified—her baby sitting in her lap—that she
had committed adultery. She said she was inspired by God to do
so "for the purging of my soul of devils." She said she did not
regret it in the least, she knew she was right, and she had acted
of her own free will and volition.

John F. and Coral Worrell testified that both had been Holy

Rollers "until Creffield made an improper proposal." John testified that he then "notified" Creffield to keep away from his wife
and his home. Coral said she had seen Creffield and Donna
Starr "kiss each other," that she had seen "them in a room
together," and that they had had "relations" in her home. She
said the public called the sect "The Holy Rollers," but the members called themselves "The Brides of Christ."

Lewis Hartley testified that his wife and daughter were
Brides of Christ and that, in consequence, his daughter was in
the insane asylum.

After Lewis testified, the prosecution rested its case.

That was the state's case? disappointed spectators wondered.
*Where was all the tawdriness? No juicy tidbits to whisper and
gossip about? Why bother closing the courtroom doors?*

The state could have produced more salacious testimony—
could have had witnesses elaborate on the improper proposals
Creffield had made, could have had witnesses tell why the Holy
Rollers called themselves the Brides of Christ, could have
explained why being a Bride of Christ was enough to drive some
hopelessly insane. But the state chose not to. They didn't want
to shame Creffield's most innocent victims—shame them more
than they had already been shamed, that is.

"The acts of that man Creffield were so terrible," William
Gardner said, "that to those who did not actually know the facts
it is hard to believe. The newspapers have not printed half.
They cannot, for the story is too revolting for print."

Gardner, superintendent at the Boys' and Girls' Aid Society,
had cared for three of the sixteen-year-old girls who were Brides
of Christ—Esther Mitchell, Mae Hurt, and Florence Seeley.
They had told him that all the things Creffield had been
accused of had happened. They spoke of "Creffield's lust," and
the "criminal relations" he had had with them—and worse.

"Many things have come to light through confessions of former followers never even imagined by those who placed the
worst construction on his motives and acts," the *Telegram*
reported. Alas, those interested in the lurid details—and who
wasn't?—were disappointed in that none of the most scandalous
acts were revealed at that time.

The revolting story the girls told Gardner was about what

had happened in Frank and Mollie Hurt's house in December of the last year. At that time Joshua told his flock that God had again spoken to him, had given him some new teachings, new teachings that he now desired to be revealed to the Holy Ones.

"But," Joshua said, "it is not for me to tell you what these teachings are. You must ascertain them for yourselves through prayer."

Seattle Daily Times
William Gardner, superintendent of the Boys' and Girls' Society

He preached about David and Bathsheba, the Hittite's wife. David, upon seeing Bathsheba washing herself, "sent messengers, and took her; and she came in unto him, and he lay with her; for she was purified from her uncleanness: and she returned unto her house. And the woman conceived, and sent and told David, and said, I *am* with child"—II Samuel 11:4-5.

Joshua kept the Holy Ones in constant prayer so that they perhaps wouldn't think beyond what he preached to them, wouldn't think about the rest of the story, wouldn't think about what happened to Uriah, Bathsheba's husband. After Bathsheba was with child, David sensed that embarrassing questions might be asked in nine months, since Uriah was away in battle.

David called Uriah back home, told him to go to his wife. Uriah, however, wouldn't leave his soldiers. So David set Uriah up in a situation where he was sure to be killed. Uriah was slain, "and when the mourning was past, David sent and fetched her [Bathsheba] to his house, and she became his wife, and bare him a son. But the thing that David had done displeased the LORD"—II Samuel 11:27.

Joshua didn't speak about this. Instead he proclaimed: "Holy people need not wear clothing." Drawing the curtains, Joshua undressed—exposing how he was "most wonderfully endowed by Mother Nature." He said that "clothing was intended to cover up sin and shame, and if the heart was made pure there was no sin, therefore should be no shame." So all the Holy Ones undressed.

He started to chant, swaying his arms and body.

Soon everyone in the room was chanting, swaying, and crying loudly.

He rolled on the floor, and the Holy Ones rolled with him.

"When one is living in the Holy Ghost he cannot sin," Joshua cried. "He lives a pure life. We are told in the Bible that the Apostles lived without sin. They lived by faith. I can live the same way."

He spoke of cleansing oneself of sin, of attaining purity, of love, and of Jesus.

> *What must I do to be holy? Let us turn to Romans 12:1. Paul says, "I beseech you, therefore brethren, by the mercies of God that ye present your bodies a living sacrifice, holy, acceptable unto God, which is your reasonable service." Paul was speaking to the converts. Their sins were washed away, but they had not taken the next step, and that was to make their consecration complete. The apostle urged them to give up all to the service of Christ, who had redeemed them, so that they might receive the Holy Ghost and become holy men. A sacrifice. There is a condition—a complete one. Have you made it? . . .*
>
> *Do not be discouraged. God wants to use you, to cleanse you, to purge you from your inbred sin, baptize you with fire, and enable you to come up to His commandment to live a holy life. If you are willing to meet the conditions, give yourself a living sacrifice, holy unto God. Put yourself on the altar, fully given up to do His bidding, to follow Him wherever He leads. Claim the promise, stand firm upon it, and the witness of the Spirit will come, and will baptize you with His love and make you a holy man—make you victorious over the world, the flesh and the devil. . . . The man or woman who is not willing to pay the price to become a soldier of*

Mae Hurt and Attie Bray.

Jesus Christ will fall sooner or later, for "without holiness no man shall see the Lord." Take time to be holy.

After hours of exhausting prayer one of the Holy Ones approached him and said God had spoken to her.

She said that she believed that He—Joshua, God's Elect, the Second Savior—like Christ, could purify her.

She wanted to give up all in the service of Him.

She wanted to make a living sacrifice to Him.

She wanted to be put on the altar by Him.

She wanted fully to give herself up to His bidding.

She wanted to follow Him wherever He led her!

Hallelujah! Creffield must have thought.

He told the Holy Ones that this woman was right, that this was what God had desired be revealed to them. Creffield said that he could now reveal what God had wanted them to know all along—that his true mission as Joshua was to find the woman who was going to be "the mother of the second Christ." This is why he had been sent to them.

"Christ would come again as He did before," Joshua said, "a babe born of a virgin." Joshua said he didn't know which woman was to be the mother of the second Christ, but that he knew it was to be one of the Holy Ones—now to be known as "The Brides of Christ."

Which one of us? they all wanted to know

Joshua didn't know. It could be any one of them.

Any *one of us?*

Yes, any one of them could be the mother of the second Christ.

How is this possible? How can all of us be candidates to be the next Mary if the second Christ is to be "a babe born of a virgin"? Plainly not all of the women in the flock are virgins. Some at this very moment are lying on the floor next to their offspring. How can these women be virgins?—women such as Sarah Hurt, here with her three children; or Cora Hartley, here with her daughter.

Once sanctified, Joshua said, they were all virgins in the sight of the Lord—"Unto the pure all things are pure: but unto them that are defiled and unbelieving is nothing pure; but even their mind and conscience is defiled"—Titus 1:15.

Creffield said that God had told him that like "Mary of old," the next Mary would need someone like "Joseph of old" to protect her. God had told him that he, Joshua, was to take on this role as the new Joseph. And as this new Joseph, he was to play a more active role than the first Joseph had played in the first Christ's birth. The new Mary would be purified and be ready to be the mother of the second Christ *only* after she had made love to him, Joshua.

God had told Him who the new Joseph was to be, but not who the new Mary was to be? Why?

Because, Creffield said, it didn't matter who the new Mary was because God had also instructed him that he, Joshua, was to lay his hands upon all of the Brides of Christ to purify them. This was because the other women in the flock, those not destined to be the mother of the second Christ, were still destined, according to their dispositions, "to be goddesses of love or duty"—"Having then gifts differing according to the grace that is given to us, whether prophecy, *let us prophesy* according to the proportion of faith"—Romans 12:6.

They would all be considered Brides of Christ.

"Jesus Christ, I tell you," Joshua said, "has chosen me to

purge the flesh from sin of all those who are willing." He assured them that what he was about to bid them to do—"free love"—did "not partake of the quality of lust," but was "the will of God." He assured them that no matter *what* he did, because of who he was, Joshua, God's Elect, the Second Savior, he was incapable of sin. And so were they.

And why shouldn't there be enjoyment in glorying for God? Were they expected *always* to be suffering for God, exhausting themselves by praying and rolling for days on end, sleeping on bare floors so they would know cold, fasting so they would know hunger, estranging themselves from their friends and families? They had done their penance. Now it was time for the reward God had always wanted them to have, for them to become Brides of Christ.

And so orgies—in the name of God and purification—were held in Frank's house during the Christmas season of 1903. Mothers were "debauched in the presence of their daughters," and daughters were debauched in the presence of their mothers.

And after all had been debauched—purified—Joshua instructed the women and girls to submit "themselves to the lust of other men." The only other men left in the flock were Frank Hurt, Charles Brooks, Sampson Levins and Lee Campbell.

All of Creffield's flock—young and old—gave up all in the service of Him, Joshua, God's Elect, the Second Savior.

All of them made living sacrifices to Him.

All of them had themselves put on the altar by Him.

All of them fully gave themselves up to His bidding.

All of them followed Him wherever He led them.

All of them, that is, but Sarah Hurt. She refused to submit to him—to make love to him. Joshua finally said that if Sarah would not submit to him, he would drive her out of the church and God would smite her. All she would see in the hereafter was her "soul plunging into an everlasting, burning, seething Hell."

So, rather than risk eternal damnation, Sarah risked Hell on earth and became a Bride of Christ by making love to her son-in-law in front of her children, just as they had made love to others in front of her. Very Old Testament this business of mothers being seduced in front of their children and their children being seduced in front of their mothers. Is it any wonder that Sarah Hurt was now considered hopelessly insane?

After Joshua had made love to all the women in his flock in Corvallis he said God finally revealed to him who the new Mary was going to be. First of all, he said, despite what Esther Mitchell had told officials at the Boys' and Girls' Aid society—and perhaps what some of them believed—he himself was not God. God was the head of their church. He was merely the "visible head" and Maud was their "spiritual mother." Despite this error, Creffield said, Esther had found favor with God, that she was a saint, and was now their church's "spiritual God." She was also going to be the mother of the second Christ.

Since Esther, sixteen-years old, was still locked up in the Aid Society, she was also the only virgin—by the usual definition of the word—left in Creffield's flock.

Donna Starr had kept in touch with Esther by secretly meeting her in the Aid Society's cellar. It was during one such clandestine meeting that Donna relayed the wondrous news to her, that she had found favor with God and was to be the mother of the second Christ. "Glory to God," the sisters shouted while embracing each other. "Down with the devil. Victory!"

Superintendent Gardner—unaware of Esther's meetings or of her new status with God—worried about Esther's mental health, noting that for some unexplained reason she was suddenly getting worse. "Her case is one of the most pathetic I ever knew," he announced publicly. "Unless she changes for the better soon we will ask to have her consigned to the insane asylum. She would pray all day, kneeling by her bedside if permitted so to do."

Donna Starr and Frank Hurt were detailed to abduct Esther from the Aid Society, but their attempts failed. Officials there didn't know why the Holy Rollers so desperately wanted Esther, but they feared that unless they did something, Esther would eventually be abducted—and that certainly wouldn't help her sanity any. So, they put Esther on a train with her brother Perry, and shipped her to Blueford, Illinois, to live with her father, Charles Mitchell—"a man of strong peculiarities and eccentricities."

After Esther was sent to the Midwest, Joshua continued to "purify" the other members of his flock. Just because the mother of the second Christ was trapped in Illinois didn't mean they shouldn't fulfill their destinies to be goddesses of love or duty. Nothing would stop him from helping them purify themselves— not tarring and feathering, not getting married to Maud Hurt, not even there being a warrant out for his arrest.

While Creffield had been hiding under the Hurts' house, he had gone on purifying. "There were prayer services and purification services almost daily," O. V. said. "When I was away at work he would come out from under the floor and hold his orgies in my home." Creffield made love to all of the women of his flock. Even Mae, O. V.'s "little girl." Mae may have been sixteen, but she would always be O. V.'s "little girl."

"I learned from her lips all that had been going on," O. V. said. "As I held her on my knee, she told me the story."

"The only thing that kept her father from prosecuting Creffield," Gardner said, "is he did not want the publicity which would probably be detrimental to his daughter hereafter."

Had Creffield been found guilty of having sexual relations with teenage girls, he would have been sent to prison for a very long time—possibly for the rest of his life if he somehow were to meet an untimely death in prison.

O. V. felt the worst had already happened. His wife was hopelessly insane and nothing could undo what had been done to his little girl. Why go through more public humiliation by revealing it all in court?

It was a decision he regretted.

And the king loved Esther above all the women and she obtained grace and favour in his sight more than all the virgins; so that he set the royal crown upon her head, and made her queen instead of Vashti.—Esther 2:17

CHAPTER THIRTEEN

A CALM BEFORE THE STORM

Have you heard of the appointment which we all must surly meet,
When the final court assembles, with the Judge up on His seat?
You have certainly been summoned, for the Bible tells me so,
And whatever your engagements, you must to judgment go.
Oh what weeping and what wailing, as the wicked turn away
To their awful doom eternal, on that great and awful day.

From the Reverend Knapp's
Bible Songs of Salvation and Victory

Creffield called no witnesses in his defense at his trial. All
he asked was for the jury to listen to his plea. After
affirming—rather than swearing—to tell the truth, he
said that the laws of the country were founded on the Ten
Commandments, and he had never violated one of those
Commandments. His defense, he said, was founded on the Holy
Bible.

Creffield quoted from Corinthians, from Genesis and from
Mark. He asked the jury to turn to the passages he had designated. Judge Sears did his best to keep up with Creffield, barely scanning one verse before having to jump to another.

"God called me to preach His will," Creffield said. "I was
threatened by mobs, but I stayed there [in Corvallis] until God

told me to go to another station. Among my converts was this woman [Donna Starr]. It was all an individual matter, a matter of conscience, as she has told you. God teaches that one must have direct connection with him before he can be saved."

"You don't claim to be God, do you?" Judge Sears asked.

"No, but one to have had direct connection with Him," Creffield said. "God called me to do all I have done and I am obeying Him. The gospel He put on me was to purge the body and I have done so. Jesus Christ, I tell you, has chosen me to purge the flesh from sin of all those who are willing."

"You admit this crime, then, according to the law of the land?" Judge Sears asked.

"Yes, in the eyes of the world, I am guilty. But God is on my side."

"How do you reconcile the two?"

> *When Christ came on earth the first thing he did was to break the Sabbath, and the Jews crucified him. I have broken the laws of the land, and I don't expect to be understood any better than the Jews understood Christ. If I were a court in a case of this kind, I would act just as you are about to act, I would convict. I don't expect to be freed. I know the prison cell is staring me in the face, but I am not ashamed of God's command, and I will do what he has told me to do. This is why I did not want a lawyer. . . .*
>
> *In the eyes of your law, yes, I am guilty. In the eyes of God I am innocent. I know He is on my side. And while you may lock me in my prison cell, I can still cry 'Glory to God!' and rest secure in the knowledge that when my time comes God will plead my case!*

At 11:05 the case was submitted to the jury. The only questions to be determined under the charge of Judge Sears was whether Creffield was insane or whether, under the evidence, he had been proved guilty.

Not wanting to sway the jury, Judge Sears didn't state his personal opinion—that Creffield was quite mad.

It only took the jury twenty minutes to reach a verdict, about

The Oregon State Penitentiary in Salem

as long as it took them to go to the jury room and back. While the verdict was read by jury foreman Jacob Spiegl, Creffield stood erect.

"Guilty," Spiegl said. Creffield broke into a smile.

Did he have anything to say before his sentence was pronounced?

"Nothing," Creffield answered.

Judge Sears sentenced him to two years in the state penitentiary in Salem, the longest sentence allowed by law.

"God bless you," Creffield cried. "Glory to Jesus, glory to God."

His example is an extreme case of depravity, robed in the livery of Heaven, posing as a saint and mouthing of sacred things while secretly playing the libertine [the Times pronounced]. His like in perfidy and dishonor would be hard to duplicate on the face of the earth. The man who lies in wait and shoots his victim down is a gentleman compared to this man-shaped reptile. The fire-bug is one of the lowest and most despicable of offenders, but he is even more respectable compared to this rotten Creffield. The ordinary libertine who enters a home and contaminates it is vile beyond compare, but this offense is trivial in contrast with that of him who

*does the same thing on a false pretense of Christianity
and with the name of Jesus and God on his dirty lips.
In vileness, diabolism and all-round deviltry, Creffield
is unmatched, and matchless as his own avowals and
the desolate condition of his asylum victims so faithful-
ly prove. In his brazen confession, there is full and sat-
isfactory explanation of why those he had wronged
drove him, tarred and feathered from Corvallis, and a
wonderful exhibition by them of self control and respect
for legal authority, in that they did nothing worse.*

The *Times*

And the *Times* didn't even know the whole story.

Seventeen months passed, and on Wednesday, December 13,
1905, an unrepentant Creffield was released from the state penitentiary—his sentence was reduced seven months for good
behavior and working on the road gang. While in prison he
avoided being drawn into conversations, even ones about religion, and especially ones dealing with his past. No one had any
idea what was going through his mind.

No one knew that he was now the new Christ. While he may
not have spoken to anyone while he was in prison, God had continued to speak to him. Soon after his release Creffield said that
God had told him that Christ wasn't to be reborn, but that he,
Joshua, God's Elect, was now the new Christ risen from the
dead, his imprisonment paralleling Christ's crucifixion and
three days in the tomb. After Christ's resurrection Christ went
to Galilee. After Creffield's resurrection Creffield went to
Seattle and tarried with Frank and Mollie Hurt and their new
baby daughter, Ruth.

By now all of Creffield's flock had been released from their
various institutions. After Frank and Mollie had been released
from the asylum, Mollie's parents convinced them to move into
a cottage they had built for them on the shore of Lake
Washington. Frank got a job as an engineer on a steamship and,
at about the time Creffield arrived, was appointed deputy
assessor of King county.

Once Creffield settled in Seattle, he sent for his wife, Maud.

Oregon State Archives, Penitentiary Records
Edmund Creffield upon arrival at the Oregon Penitentiary

She wasted no time in coming. Maud told Joshua that while he was in the penitentiary, she had divorced him. She hadn't wanted to, but her parents had forced her to. And now, ever since his release, she said, she had felt "called" to him, had felt his presence with her continually.

Right after his conviction she had gone into a trance at the asylum. When she came out of the trance, she went into such hysterics that she was put into a straitjacket and tied to a bed. Eventually she seemed to get better so the asylum released her "upon six months leave of absence in care of her father, O. V. Hurt."

In other words: She wasn't "cured," but they thought she was stable enough to live at home, thereby saving the state the cost of housing her.

Back in Corvallis Maud was fine—most of the time. Only occasionally, according to her father, did she break down in "melancholy, weeping spells and when over the effects of one of these spells would destroy her clothing and proclaim to all who knew her that 'God will protect me.'"

Now in Seattle, she and Creffield remarried on April 3—"What therefore God hath joined together, let not man put asunder"—Matthew 19:6. Newspapers falsely reported that they applied for their marriage license under the names "Franz E. Carefield" and "Ida M. Hunt", to insinuate they were trying to hide their true identities.

Creffield wrote O. V. Hurt: "Hurt: God has resurrected me. I have now got my foot on your neck. God has restored me to my own. I will return to Oregon and gather together all my followers. Place no obstruction in my way or God will smite you. Creffield."

O. V.'s wife, Sarah, then announced that she had never lost her faith in Joshua's "perfection—his divinity." An exasperated O. V. said: "It is almost impossible to believe the power he exerted over some of his followers."

Joshua told Frank and Maud that he had decided that they should create a new Eden on the Yachats River near where the two of them had been born. Besides, it'd be fun. They'd build wigwams and camp out. It'd be sort of like a vacation. It'd be like Smith Island all over again.

Word must be sent to the Brides of Christ, for those who didn't immediately go to this new Eden were in danger. "I have called down the wrath of an angry God on these modern Sodoms of Seattle, of Portland, of San Francisco, of Corvallis itself," he said.

San Francisco? Creffield had on a few occasions tarried there. He had also been upset when that city's papers ridiculed him when he burned everything in the Hurts' house. Then again, almost every paper in the northwest had ridiculed him at that time. Whatever the reason for his displeasure with San Francisco, on Wednesday, April 18, 1906, just days after he had put a curse on it, the city was nearly leveled by an earthquake.

Creffield took full credit for the devastation. Only a hardened skeptic could now doubt that he had a direct connection to God, that he was God's Elect, the new Christ. His flock, more devoted than ever, prepared to go to the Oregon Coast.

"A God-forsaken region of floods, foul weather and loneliness," H. R. Dunbar, an early teacher at the Siletz Indian Reservation School, had written of the area Creffield had chosen to create his new Eden in. "No one that thinks anything of his family and that has never stepped in such a hole as this with his family absent from him, can realize what it is to stop in this lonesome, wicked place."

But many of Creffield's flock—including the Hurts, the Starrs, the Seeleys, Una Baldwin, and Attie Bray—did know what it was to stop in this lonesome, wicked place. Their families had homesteaded there, and many of them had been born there.

Frank Hurt took $300 from his savings, quit his job, and told his brother-in-law, Louis Sandell, that he was ill and was going to the Oregon coast for his health. He was taking along his wife and daughter, Mollie and Ruth; his sister, Maud; and Mollie's sister, Olive. "Merely a summer camping trip," Maud said of the expedition, going places where she and her brother had "spent many childhood days."

"I had a talk with Frank," O. V. Hurt said, "in which I told him he was crazy to quit his job and leave his home, to go out on a career such as that on which he was embarking. He got mad and threatened to have nothing more to do with me."

The night Donna Starr sneaked off to join the flock on the coast she was unusually affectionate to her husband, Burgess. Burgess had thought Donna had come to terms with Creffield. "My sister [Donna]," George Mitchell said, "told her husband that she was sorry for what she had done, that she hadn't meant to do anything wrong and that she didn't know why she had done as this man bade her. She said she realized it all now and that she would never again do these things he had led her to do. Her husband forgave her and life for all of us seemed to be worth living again."

Burgess said Donna seemed happy and there was peace in their home after Creffield's conviction—save for an occasional moment when Donna would "roll" on the floor in the middle of the night and disturb his slumbers.

Then late one evening, soon after the San Francisco earthquake, Burgess woke and found Donna missing. She had left him a letter: "I cannot wait until daylight because the babies would cry to go with me. I have taken about $3.50 of your money, but I guess I have been worth that much to you. It is not enough to pay my fare, and I will have to walk to the place I am going."

Donna took a train from Portland to Corvallis. From there she hiked through the Coast Range Mountains, up towards Mary's Peak, and through terrain heavily populated by bears and cougars. She went along the Alsea River through a lush primeval forest of thousand-year-old trees that were hundreds of feet high and tens of feet thick. In some places the vegetation was so dense that it was dark even under a bright midday sun.

When she reached the Pacific in Waldport, she walked along the water's edge. There were no roads or bridges on the coast, and there were river crossings where, during high tide, she had to wait hours before going on. There were rock outcroppings where, even at low tide, she had to sprint ahead of waves to avoid being swept out to sea. All along the beach she had to avoid sinkholes that acted much like quicksand, and had been known to swallow horses. She walked almost eighty miles from Corvallis to reach the site of Joshua's new Eden, the Yachats River. But what's eighty miles when you're going to rendezvous with the new Christ?

Burgess couldn't go looking for Donna because he now had no money. Also, someone had to look after their three children—five-year-old Gertrude, three-year-old Rachel, and seven-month-old Clifford. Donna had written, " . . . He said that Christ will take care of them," "He," with a capital *H,* being Joshua. But Burgess didn't have as much faith in divine assistance as she did, and wasn't about to leave his children motherless *and* fatherless.

Esther Mitchell, now eighteen, also was making her way to the coast. In 1903 she had been sent to live with her father, Charles Mitchell, in Blueford, Illinois. Together Esther and her father were miserable. Esther refused to call him "father," saying her only father was "God," and she had "no father on earth." In her father's view this was all Creffield's doing. "To my mind there is no doubt that when my daughter returned to her home in Illinois," he said, "she had lost all her filial affection and seemed to be almost a stranger at the home of her childhood."

Home of her childhood? Her father had abandoned her and her six brothers and sisters in Oregon when she was six, moved to Illinois, remarried, and never sent for her, and now he was surprised that she "had lost all her filial affection and seemed to be almost a stranger?" Well, he had been described "a man of strong peculiarities and eccentricities."

Much of Esther's misery, though, was caused by her fear that she'd never be able to fulfill her destiny to become the mother of the second Christ. She heard nothing from any of the other Brides of Christ. Had they forgotten her? Had someone else found favor with God?

No. Esther's sister Donna had written her often, telling her the flock would soon be reunited, to "keep up her faith and hurry back to Creffield." Esther's father, however, intercepted these letters and destroyed them.

After Esther heard nothing from the flock for a few months, "she got more sensible, and we thought she was cured," her brother Perry said. "We let her go back to Oregon after Creffield had been put in jail."

But Esther hadn't been cured of her belief that Creffield was the Second Savior and that she was destined to be the mother of the second Christ. She got a job as a tailor at the Oregon Woolen Mill, in Oregon City, biding her time until she too could be purified. Esther was, therefore, overjoyed when shortly after Creffield's release her sister Donna told her she was still "the virgin" and now her duty was "to bring forth the Christ to take up His work when he was killed."

After hearing this, Esther left work one noon, never returning, not even to collect the wages owed her. She was on her way finally to fulfill her destiny.

Meanwhile, Esther's brother, George Mitchell, believed he was receiving messages not only from God but also from his dead mother. While Creffield was in prison, George became a spiritualist, and now he thought his mother's spirit was telling him that Esther was going to have trouble with Creffield and that God was commanding him to "deliver up the spirit of Creffield." Now he believed he was the only man living who possessed the power to rid the world of Creffield.

He was receiving these messages while sick with the measles and delirious from a high fever. For two weeks in the Good Samaritan Hospital in Portland he raved about how he worried that Creffield would get his hands on his sisters—especially Esther, "the one great object of that fiend's lustful desires."

Even though his doctor said he was still "in a weak condition, mentally and physically" George left the hospital when he heard his sisters were on their way to the coast to join Creffield.

"He was going to find Creffield," George's brother Perry said, "even if he had to walk from place to place in order to get him."

"I am God's agent," George announced. "I am chosen by God to hunt Creffield down and I am going to do it."

George Mitchell went to Donna and Burgess's home, hugged his little nieces and nephew, and wept while telling them that he would go and bring their mother back. "The more I thought of it," George said, "the more angry I got and I resolved at the first opportunity to meet Creffield and secure my revenge."

<hr />

But when they persecute you in this city, flee ye into another.—Matthew 10:23

CHAPTER FOURTEEN

GIVING UP THE GHOST

BY THE ROLLING SEA. HOLY ROLLERS
Headline, *Corvallis Gazette*, May 1, 1906.

Most of Creffield's flock traveled to the coast by train, getting off at the Yaquina City depot, the closest one to the site of Creffield's new Eden. People in Yaquina City and in nearby Newport began to wonder why so many women were walking through their towns, heading south. They hadn't heard that a new Eden was to be established thirty miles away on the Yachats River.

When Cora and Sophie Hartley boarded a train for Yaquina City, Sophie was just days away from graduating from college. Forget graduation, Joshua told her. All learning was the work of the Devil, and unless she left school, God would smite her. "The professors try to kill you," he said, "and lash you to death with their foul tongues; but you have grown strong and healthy. Hallelujah!"

How could Sophie doubt the word of Joshua, God's Elect, the new Christ, a man who, in the words of her mother, "condemned the city of San Francisco and brought the earthquake"? Sophie ripped up the graduation dress that she had been working on all winter and left with her mother for the new Eden.

Sophie also left behind a gold watch for her father to find—a watch he had given her, and Creffield had taken a hatchet to. "Now they do not treat him as good as they would a dying dog," Aileen Hartley said of her father-in-law, Lewis Hartley. They "can't call him father, say he is an unnatural father, a very demon, and try to drive him to suicide or to fill a drunkard's grave."

Cora Hartley knew how to deal with the likes of Aileen—a woman who was going to become a Christian Scientist, no less—a woman whose name was not inscribed on a Holy Roll in Heaven. She'd "damn everlastingly" Vernon LaMar, Aileen and Warren's new baby. No matter that he was also her only grandchild.

> *Creffield, the Holy Roller, is accumulating another stock of lunatics who sooner or later will have to be taken care of by the state. The capture and care of his misguided followers cost the state several thousand dollars two years ago, and from the start he is making, it is not improbable that there will be another big bill of expense to foot in the near future. The husbands or brothers of these misguided women who run after this fakir seem to have something lacking in their make-up, or the Holy Roller would long have been given a treatment which would have prevented him from carrying out a portion of the religious rite which he is accused of practicing on his victims.*
>
> The *Oregonian*

Lewis Hartley learned of his wife and daughter's plans in time to catch the train they were taking; but the women saw him and, without his knowledge, got off in the small town of Blodgett. From there they walked the remaining fifty miles to the coast.

Lewis was irate when he realized the women had eluded him. Time to be a man. Time to do what a man had to do when his women were being threatened. Time to show that he wasn't lacking in his make-up. Time to buy a gun.

In order to get to the Yachats River, Creffield was going to

Sunday Oregonian Magazine, *1953*
Lewis Hartley attempts to kill Edmund Creffield at
the Newport, Oregon ferry dock.

have to cross Yaquina Bay; and since there was no bridge, it meant he'd have to take a boat. Knowing this, Lewis, with his new revolver, lay in wait on Newport's bay front. As Creffield and some of the flock were boarding a ferry, Lewis spotted them, approached them, drew his weapon, held it within inches of Creffield's head, and, in front of witnesses, fired.

The gun snapped harmlessly.

Lewis fired again, and again the gun snapped harmlessly.

He fired again.

And again.

And again.

He fired a total of five times, and all five times the gun snapped harmlessly. Lewis stared, mouth agape, at the gun in his hand. Sophie said that if her father had succeeded in killing Joshua, she would have killed him.

"You see," Creffield said as he and the flock crossed the bay, "no man can kill Joshua."

"He walked in a cloud and it was impossible to kill him." That's what the Brides of Christ now said of their leader. If any of them had lingering doubts about Joshua's divinity, they had been eradicated. Only a fool would now question that Creffield had a direct connection to God, was God's Elect, was the new Christ.

It wasn't divine intervention that had saved Creffield, however, but Mr. Ingalls, the storekeeper whom Lewis had bought the gun from. Ingalls knew Lewis was going to go gunning for Creffield but, not wanting Lewis arrested for murder, sold him the wrong kind of ammo. The gun Lewis bought used center-fire cartridges, but Ingalls gave him rim-fire cartridges.

After failing to kill Creffield, Lewis went back to Corvallis and sued for a divorce from Cora. The complaint made sensational reading, although its inept legalese had the unintended effect of turning the whole affair into a farce.

> *That the defendant* [Cora Hartley] *in total disregard of her marriage duties has been guilty of cruel and inhuman treatment and personal indignities toward this plaintiff* [Lewis Hartley] *for the past three years rendering his life burdensome in this: That without the knowledge and against the will of this plaintiff in the early summer of 1903 and at all times until the fall of 1903 covering a period of many months the said defendant deserted the home of this plaintiff and took herself to Kiger's Island* [Smith Island] *in said County and went into camp with one Creffield known locally as "The Joshua" or "New Christ," and the head of what is known as the Holy Rollers; and said defendant remained in camp with sundry women and men and more particularly the said Creffield; the said defendant said Creffield and other women being engaged in wild orgies on the earth together in almost a nude condition rolling on the earth together in a promiscuous way during unusual hours of the night and day separated from the balance of the world, and the said defendant conforming to certain ritualistic or sensualistic practices prescribed and ordained as coming from Heaven by and through the mediation of the aforesaid Joshua—said defendant divesting herself of her under clothing for the purposes of conforming to the revelations claimed to be received in some occult way by said Creffield and consenting to certain acts and practices with The Joshua in conflict with the fundamental laws of the State of*

Sunday Oregonian Magazine, *1953*
Creffield's flock bound for the new Eden.

Oregon; . . . that the said Camp and its followers left said Island in the fall of 1903 and established themselves immediately South of Corvallis at what is known as the Hurt residence and the defendant deserted her home and at said Hurt residence again took up her abode with said Creffield and his band of Holy Rollers in the same manner and form substantially as to acts and doings as on said Island, and there engaged in wild and unknown practices during whole nights with said Creffield; and burnt furniture, clothing, ornaments, watches, jewelry and generally every thing necessary to the comfort of a well regulated household; besides making burnt offerings of domesticated animals such as dogs and cats. . . .

That after the confinement of said Joshua in the Penitentiary . . . this plaintiff became advised of the whereabouts of the said Creffield and did immediately commence to evince the same dispositions as had before actuated her. . . . That this plaintiff in order to avoid further annoyance deemed it proper to assist the said Creffield to leave this mortal earth in a speedy manner, but owing to the fact of rim cartridges instead of center fire cartridges that happy event was avoided by the flight of the said Prophet: . . . That defendant refuses to

*live with this plaintiff and it is impossible for this
plaintiff longer to live with her as his wife or otherwise
live with her—that she pronounces him unclean-unsac-
tified* [sic] *and reprable* [sic] *and will not countenance
him for having endeavored to assist the prophet to that
happy country beyond this mundane sphere of tears and
sorrows.* . . .

*Wherefore Plaintiff prays a decree of the Court dis-
solving and annulling the marriage contract now existing between plaintiff and defendant and decreeing this
plaintiff his costs and disbursements in this suit.*

W. S. McFadden, attorney for Plaintiff

Creffield and the flock continued on to the Yachats River,
twenty-two miles south of the Yaquina Bay. The trek was ardu-
ous, but the Holy Rollers survived it relatively unscathed, led,
after all, by none other than the new Christ. But this Christ
wasn't able to walk on water. Creffield waded to the south side
of the Yachats River. Although the north side was where Maud,
Frank, and Mae Hurt had been born, the flock opted not to
tarry there as the property now belonged to another family, the
Hosfords.

Creffield's flock may have thought he was invincible—and
for a while he may have believed this too—but he was beginning
to have his doubts. Why else would he have now instructed his
flock that should someone succeed in killing him, they were to
eat his flesh and drink his blood—"Whoso eateth my flesh, and
drinketh my blood, hath eternal life; and I will raise him up at
the last day"—John 6:54.

Once their camp was set up, Creffield said that, as this was
their new Eden, they should live as Adam and Eve had lived in
the original Eden—sans clothing. Joshua told his flock that God
had revealed to him that they were to burn all their garments
and wear nothing but the thin cotton robes—robes that, fortu-
itously, he had brought with him.

One of the Hosford girls on the north side of the river, using
a makeshift spyglass, couldn't believe what she was seeing—
naked men and women burning clothes in a bonfire. Excitement
of any sort didn't happen very often around the Yachats River,

and excitement like this was almost unimaginable on this lonesome, not to mention chilly, coast. A day of seventy-degree weather was considered a hot spell. The girl ran and told her father, Erwin Hosford, what was happening. Erwin had no use for this sort of excitement, and ordered the Holy Rollers, in no uncertain terms, to leave.

Creffield and the Holy Rollers went south. Three miles after the Yachats River, they had to get around Cape Perpetua, the highest point on the Oregon coast. Locals joked that when the good Lord made Oregon, He found He had too much material on hand, and so, to get it all in, He had to stand part of it on end.

The wind sometimes gusted so hard around the Cape that the mail carrier, Art Carpenter, routinely dismounted his horse before rounding it, and, while hanging on to his horse's tail, would crawl along the narrow ledge blasted out of the basalt . . . until the day his horse fell off the trail, plunging into what was known as the Devil's Churn.

Near Ten Mile Creek, Creffield told his flock that he was going to leave them temporarily to go find an even better location than the Oregon coast for their new Eden—maybe on one of the islands off of Queen Charlotte Sound in British Columbia. He would come back for them soon.

He told Maud to go north to Seattle, that he would meet her there. It might take him a while since he planned to go a very circuitous route on foot with no provisions—continuing south then hiking through the Coast Range. But he would meet her there. God would make sure of it. Wasn't he God's Elect, the new Christ? She wasn't to worry. God would look out for him.

For now, Creffield said, see if Ira and Georgianah Bray would give the rest of them shelter at their nearby homestead. Surely they would offer assistance to a group of cold and hungry women, most of whom they were related to. But Ira Bray was a hard-hearted man and turned them all away, even his daughter, Attie. There was to be no room in his manger for the virgin who was to be the mother of the next Christ—Esther, Ira's relative, by marriage.

It was a good thing Creffield left when he did, because Ira, like Lewis Hartley, would have gone gunning for him, might have even gone so far as to fire three times—a real sacrifice on his part. Ira was well known for grousing about how the makings of gun shells had to be ordered from the east. When his sons would go hunting, he would only give them three shells and he would then belittle them if they didn't come home with at least one for future use.

The Holy Rollers left the Brays', walked eight miles north and set up camp at Cummins Creek, a very remote and inaccessible beach south of Cape Perpetua. The only nearby protection from the elements was a cave accessible only at low tide. Here they waited for word from Joshua.

Maud made it on her own to the Albany train station, the one nearest Corvallis. There she was spotted by George Mitchell and Edwin Baldwin, who were searching for Creffield in every freight and passenger train that passed through. While they were searching, Edwin tried to talk George out of killing Creffield, to let Edwin do it.

Edwin told him about how his eldest daughter, Una Baldwin, had been led astray by Creffield. "By force I had taken this daughter away from the Holy Roller camp; had carried her home, weak and emaciated, and had nursed her back to health," Edwin told George. "When the law gave up its claim on Creffield and he came back to Oregon, he reestablished his influence over my daughter and I was forced to use force to keep her from going to him. . . . I decided that I would remove her from the earth, rather than permit her to ever again get under his control. I decided that I had raised them [my son and my four daughters] honorably thus far, and that it was my duty to continue to protect them. . . . I am an old man and the honor of my family is dearer to me than life itself."

Edwin pleaded with George to let him be the one to kill Creffield. "I told [George Mitchell] that he was a young man with his life ahead of him, and with every opportunity offered to upright young men. . . . I tried to show Mitchell how much better it was that I, in my old age, with but, at best, only a few more years to live, should find Creffield, and remove him from the earth. . . . I had a family to protect and I could afford to give

Seattle Star *newspaper photo*

Quick Drugstore, Seattle

my life for that of Creffield, if in so doing, I should remove the danger to my family.

George thanked Edwin—who at forty-eight probably had more than a few years to live—but said he had been chosen by God to do this, and he and he alone held "the power to put a stop to the wrongs for which Creffield's influence was responsible."

George learned that Maud had a train ticket to Seattle, so he went there in search of her husband. Once in Seattle, George went to Louis Sandell, brother of Mollie Hurt and Olive Sandell. George asked Louis whether he'd seen Creffield, and said that he, George, had had a message from God to kill Creffield. "I could see at the time that [George] Mitchell was crazy as a loon," Louis said.

Neither of them knew where Mollie or Olive were, that at that moment they and other Holy Rollers were waiting for word from Creffield while camped on a beach, subsisting upon mussels, and huddling together at night under four cotton blankets, the only protection they had from cold rains and winds.

George walked the streets of Seattle for five days. And then on Monday, May 7, 1906, he spotted Maud and Creffield in the heart of the retail district. When George saw them, they were walking leisurely up First Avenue, near Cherry Street, arm in arm, on their way to buy a new skirt for Maud. The couple had on all the clothes they owned—on Maud a tattered shirtwaist, skirt, and worn shoes, and on Creffield a cheap black suit.

When they stopped in front of Quick Drugstore, for Maud to weigh herself, George stepped close to the building to allow them to pass without seeing him. He had never carried a revolver before in his life, and had only fired a gun a few times as a youngster. With no hesitation, however, he now raised his weapon, aimed it at the back of Creffield's head, and fired once.

Creffield, who may have been thirty-three, the age Christ was when crucified, fell dead at Maud's feet.

And when Jesus had cried with a loud voice, he said, Father, into thy hands I commend my spirit: and having said thus, he gave up the ghost.—Luke 23:46

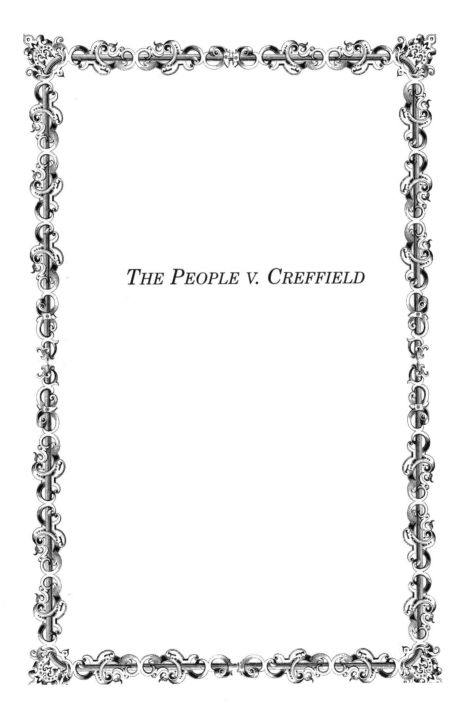

THE PEOPLE V. CREFFIELD

CHAPTER FIFTEEN

"I'VE GOT MY MAN"

For God so loved the world, that he gave his only begotten Son, that whosoever believeth in him should not perish, but have everlasting life.—John 3:16

Maud yelled at George and flailed her hands about, trying to strike him. She grabbed his arm to hold him until help came but, seeing blood flowing freely from Creffield, let loose her grasp. She knelt by the body, an arm under his neck and her face pressed against his. For the longest while she stayed like that, kneeling in total silence.

"He can't die," she finally whispered, "You cannot die, Joshua." She looked up into the faces of those who had gathered round and said: "He can't die. He can never die. He did no harm."

Emil Bories, the first doctor to reach the scene, lifted Maud to her feet. Misunderstanding her, thinking she had said it was all a "josh," he said: "Madam, this is no josh. This man is dead." Within moments a transformation came over her. She became the *Widow Creffield*. All emotion drained from her, and her large deep blue eyes were now those of an automaton.

She discussed the shooting with a nonchalance that police officers found disconcerting. She refused to answer most of their questions, even refusing to divulge her or her husband's real names. "I'll tell anything I have to tell at the proper time," she said to Detective Corbett. "But the man had absolutely nothing to shoot my husband for."

George made no attempt to escape. When Officer Ernest Le Count and Deputy Sheriff Sam Huth arrived, they found him standing beside the body calmly smoking a cigar. He handed his revolver to Le Count, who then put him under arrest. He was taken to jail where—short of fluffing his pillow and giving him a key—officers showed him every courtesy. Many openly admitted that they thought the killing was justified and predicted that no jury would ever convict their new hero. He was allowed to talk to reporters in the visitor's cell.

Sitting on a stool, George, a shy, twenty-three-year-old mill worker with sandy hair, freckles, and a boyish, innocent-looking face, twisted his big browned hands in a nervous clutch. He said he wasn't used to the limelight, and this, not having just killed a man, was what was making him nervous.

> *Well, I just shot the man for ruining my two sisters. That's all there is to it. . . .*
>
> *I am, of course, sorry that I have been called upon to take any man's life, but there is no one among you who can appreciate my feelings. No brother could love his sisters any more than I. . . .*
>
> *They were good Christian girls, until this man came along. . . . They believed in him and thought he was a godly man. I guess they believe in him yet. In spite of the fact that he has ruined them and disgraced the rest of us. I tried to make them see it like we and everybody else saw it, but it was no use as long as he was around. Well, he ain't around now. . . .*
>
> *It was willed that I meet him today and Creffield suffered the end that he was entitled to.*
>
> George Mitchell

George asked that a telegram be sent to O. V. Hurt: "I've got my man. I am in jail here. George."

"I feel that a less violent way of dealing with the man would

Morning Oregonian *newspaper photo*
First Avenue and Cherry Street, Seattle. The "x" indicates
the spot where the shooting occurred.

have been a blessing," O. V. said—as only O. V. would have. He was one of the few men whose daughter had made love to Creffield who wasn't running around with a gun, ready to blow the Second Savior away, should their paths cross.

Still, O. V. said: "I will spend the last dollar I have in the world to defend George Mitchell if necessary." He went to Seattle and hired Morris, Southard, and Shipley, one of the best law firms in Washington. At the time, Will H. Morris was perhaps the most renowned criminal lawyer in the state, with a record of eleven acquittals in eleven first-degree murder cases—among them were two brothers who killed a Seattle police chief, a wealthy Klondiker who shot his wife three times, and a man who killed the seducer of his daughter on a public thoroughfare in Seattle. Morris's partner, Silas M. Shipley, was one of the most effective advocates in the country.

George had $2.50 to his name, not even enough to cover the expenses of a day for the likes of Morris, Southard, and Shipley. He didn't need to worry, though. Besides O. V. Hurt, others in Corvallis rallied to his aid. Notices "For the defense of Mitchell" were posted all over town:

> *Everyone should assist and double the donations*
> *already made, for this case is not of the ordinary, and*

that young Mitchell was justified in committing the deed seems to be the general opinion of everyone familiar with the unholy teachings and practices of the slain Creffield. Everyone can donate at least a small amount towards the Mitchell fund and this should be done within the next few days, as the time is limited. Donations can be left at the Gazette office, or handed to Roy Raber, on the street.

None of this would have been necessary if George—or, as some now referred to him, young Mitchell—were to have been tried by the press instead of by a court of law.

According to legal bookworms, the killing of "Joshua" Creffield by George Mitchell yesterday morning was murder in the first-degree. According to fathers with families and to brothers with defenseless sisters it comes within the same category of the law as the killing of a mad dog. It is, perhaps, proper that in cases where human life is at stake there should be some such difference of opinion in order to discourage too hasty judgment by individuals.

His work was to take a life for the removal of which the law did not provide the means. It was not lynch law—this is usurpation of the functions of the courts. In such cases as this, the courts are powerless. The old, primitive, animal law holds, and this was its fulfillment.

It may not be technically correct to take the life of such a scoundrel—but if there were more men like George Mitchell there would be fewer human beasts and still fewer broken, ruined women in insane asylums and on the streets. The verdict will be largely a matter of public opinion.

The *Seattle Daily Times*

Morris and Shipley soon began receiving telegrams and letters from all over the country offering assistance. "The reasons which actuate these proffers are of course understood by all," Morris said.

All, that is, but by King County's prosecuting and assistant prosecuting attorneys, Kenneth Mackintosh and John F. Miller. "It seems strange that if public opinion in Oregon is in the mood it is represented to be," Miller said, "that these people could not have done their killing down there without picking one of the most prominent corners in Seattle as the wash-line for their dirty linen."

"The killing of Creffield by George Mitchell was the most cold-blooded case of murder in the first-degree that has occurred since I have occupied this office," Mackintosh said. "I will prosecute him, and believe he will be convicted. The popular opinion which opposes the enforcement of the law will not be considered. I see no reason why Mitchell should not be hanged. . . . I fail to see why the people of this county should not support their officers in the enforcement of the law."

Poor Miller and Mackintosh. They were about to become almost as reviled as Creffield for simply doing their sworn duties as officers of the court. They got an indication of what lay ahead of them when Multnomah County's district attorney in Portland, John Manning, sent them a letter offering his assistance, an offer Mackintosh described as "the most remarkable thing I ever heard of."

> *Dear Sir:*
>
> *I notice by the press that there was a man killed in your city the other day by name, Creffield, of religion, Holy Roller, so I hasten to say to you that I have had a great deal to do with this man Creffield, in his lifetime, and the outrageous crimes committed by this brute, in this state, on simple-minded girls and women were many. I had him arrested for the crime of adultery, committed with Mrs. Starr, sister of George Mitchell, the man who killed him. He was convicted, sentenced, and served a term of two years in the penitentiary at Salem, Or.*
>
> *Creffield broke up many families in Oregon by leading them astray on his fake religion. I investigated many, many charges against him while he was on his Holy Rolling tour in Oregon, the character of which*

were perfectly awful, in so far as being low, degenerate and brutal, and if permitted, I would like an opportunity to testify before the grand jury, before Mitchell is indicted, or the trial court, as to the low degenerate character of this man, and the outrages and brutalities practiced by him, in Oregon, upon ignorant and unsophisticated girls.

Our officers chased this man all over the state of Oregon, and finally found him hidden under the floor of a house at Corvallis, Or., he having ruined the family and broken up the home.

Now, Mr. Mackintosh, I do not want you to understand that I would not uphold the majesty of law, but when a man infringes upon the common decency of society to the extent that this man did, and there is no statute under which he could be prosecuted, and he has so grossly debauched families, I think the taking of the law in one's own hands, under such circumstances, to mete out summary justice is almost excusable.

Yours very truly,
John Manning

Mackintosh was appalled. *I think the taking of the law in one's own hands, under such circumstances, to mete out summary justice is almost excusable? This from Multnomah County's district attorney! Was everyone in Oregon crazy? Even the prosecutors?*

"I shall answer the letter as civilly as I can under the circumstances," Mackintosh said, "but I consider it the most remarkable thing I ever heard of, that a man whose duty it is to prosecute criminals should offer such advice as is contained in his letter."

Mackintosh answered Manning:

Dear Sir:

I am in receipt of your letter of May 8 in regard to the case of State of Washington vs. George Mitchell. . . . As your testimony in the trial of the case in Superior Court would be inadmissible, being merely of a hearsay

Seattle Post-Intelligencer
George Mitchell and Maud Hurt.

nature . . . your suggestion is . . . impracticable. . . . I wish nevertheless to thank you for the interest you have manifested in the matter and for your offer of assistance.

As citizens of this country, you and I realize that the enforcement of our criminal laws is entrusted to our courts, juries and public officers, and that lynch and mob law and anarchy are the natural and only results of the efforts of individuals to personally avenge real or fancied injuries. There is no security to life or property if the individual can act as attorney, judge, and jury, and take the execution, not of the law, but of his passions, into his own hands and kill anyone who he may determine has wronged either himself or his family, and this, whether his determination is the product of a sane or demented mind, and whether his wrongs are real or merely delusions.

As officers of the law, sworn to prosecute crime, you and I realize that it is our duty where we are satisfied that a crime has been committed and that there is suffi-cient evidence to prove the act, to honestly and vigor-ously prosecute the offender, and that the moral well-being of the community which we represent is vitally affected by the vigor or laxity with which these efforts to enforce the criminal laws are made.

The defendant Mitchell, with deliberate and premed-itated malice, shot Edmund Creffield in the back and the laws of this state constitute that act murder in the first-degree, and do not accept as a justification for it the facts and circumstances which Mitchell and his friends allege up to the shooting, even if such facts and circumstances are true as reported by those people. Being sure that this act was done, and that the witness-es to it are available, it became my duty to file an infor-mation charging Mitchell with murder, and this I have done; and it will become my further duty to prosecute the defendant fearlessly and vigorously, which I shall do. I cannot and will not presume that a jury of twelve men of the citizens of this county will do other than observe honestly the oaths which they take when they are sworn to try the case, and, observing these oaths, return a verdict in accordance with the law and the evi-dence, which in this case should mean a verdict of con-viction. . . .

Thanking you again for your kind offer in this case, I remain, yours truly, Kenneth Mackintosh

In the five days before young Mitchell was brought in to court for arraignment, over $30,000 in securities had been offered for his bail. Bail, if granted, was expected to be set at between $5,000 and $20,000. One man, someone George had never met, offered to mortgage his house if it would help—although the typical contribution was one dollar, all that most could afford.

None of this mattered to Prosecuting Attorney Mackintosh. He rose before Judge Archibald Wanless Frater and said bail should be denied because of a statute: "All accused criminals shall be bailable *except* in a capital crime where the proof is evident and presumption of guilt is great." He maintained that since the defendant didn't deny killing Creffield, this wasn't a bailable offense and urged the court to disregard all sentiment in the case.

George's attorney, Morris, admitted that if one wanted to get technical, yes, the statute applied to his client "so far as proof or presumption was concerned." However:

> *We have in addition* [he said] *a divine law and a human law which admits beyond all cavil the right of a man to protect the honor of his family. This boy who had seen his sisters debauched by the man whom he killed and driven frantic with the knowledge that the influence this man exercised over them had led one of the women who is dear to him to desert her husband and children, acted in the full knowledge that unless he acted as he did there was no salvation for the misguided woman.*
>
> *I appeal to you as a judge and as a man, I ask you if the slaying of a human leper, killed as you would kill a dog, is a deed to make this man a criminal, to make a desperate murderer, a man too dangerous to be at liberty in this community on bail. Can you call this boy, but 23 years of age, a criminal when he, a green country youth, has arisen in his manhood and taken the vengeance of nature upon the lustful viper who had stolen the honor of his sisters.*

Archibald Frater was a judge in Washington, which, for the moment, wasn't like Oregon, where, according to some hard-nosed prosecutors, "lynch and mob law and anarchy" ruled. Accordingly, Judge Frater responded to Morris's appeal: "The law seems clear and is not questioned even by the attorneys for the defendant and there is nothing to do but refuse the motion for bail."

"Mitchell will know he has been tried, at least, when he gets through with this," said Assistant Prosecuting Attorney Miller.

Thou shalt not kill.—Exodus 20:13.

CHAPTER SIXTEEN

THE WIDOW CREFFIELD

CREFFIELD IS DUE TO RISE TODAY
Headline, *Seattle Daily Times* , May 13, 1906

Detective Adams went with the Widow Creffield to the small attic room where she and Creffield had been living. The room was furnished with two chairs, a rickety table, and a camp cot. She gathered their few belongings: a Bible, of course; some writing paper; a few pens and pencils; combs and a couple of hair ribbons—no more publicly parading about with hair unkempt, flowing in tangled masses over her shoulders; a package of tobacco—indulging in sinful pleasures?—and a pistol. The Widow Creffield said she had carried the gun constantly—until the very morning her husband was killed. That morning she somehow left the room and forgot it. The cartridges for it were still in her pocket. "If I had a gun at the time," she lamented, "Mitchell would never have escaped death."

She wrapped these—all of their worldly possessions—in a newspaper. "We were going out to look for work," she said to the detective, as if embarrassed by her and her husband's evident poverty. Since she was penniless, but was needed as a witness, she was put in the care of Police Matron Kelly—who promptly confiscated the pistol.

While in Seattle arranging for George's defense, O. V. Hurt went to see his daughter at the matron's. "My daughter seemed to be afraid that I would scold her," he said, "so I tried to console her as much as possible. She can always come to my home and live, if it is her desire. She is my daughter and as such will always find a place there."

He declared he loved her as much as ever and that Creffield's flock should be sympathized with, not condemned. "It is my belief that each one whom he attracted and compelled to obey his commands complied in the sincere and honest belief that they were doing right and it never entered their heads that their actions were wrong," he said. "When a man is dead we are supposed to overlook his wickedness and speak in softer tones. . . . This much of criticism against him I will make—he was a dangerous man to the community. He was dangerous because of his power and because of the ill-use to which he employed it."

O. V. left money with the matron to buy whatever was necessary to make his daughter comfortable. "I told her distinctly that I was ready to take care of her and do everything possible for her," he said, "but at the same time, I would do all in my power to aid and assist George Mitchell."

Creffield's funeral was two days after his murder. His widow—who hadn't slept since the shooting—arrived at the Bonney-Watson Funeral Company leaning on Matron Kelly's arm. She wasn't wearing mourning attire. Why should she be? She wasn't in mourning since, according to her, her husband wasn't dead. She didn't care what the autopsy report said.

The Widow Creffield gazed silently for a few minutes at the body of the Second Savior. He wore a white shroud, what she had thought would be suitable resurrection attire. She was allowing his body to be consigned to the ground because she firmly believed that he would rise from the dead.

At the Lake View Cemetery, Creffield was buried in a cheap county-provided coffin upon which were the words "At Rest." Only the Widow Creffield, Matron Kelly, and an employee from the Bonney-Watson Funeral Company were in attendance.

Oregon Daily Journal
The widow Creffield

Maud shed no tears, offered up no prayers, sang no hymns, laid no flowers, and asked that no religious service be given.

The Widow Creffield said it was pointless to do any of those things. "He is not dead and will be here again to confound his enemies and obtain vengeance upon those who have wronged him," she said. "In four days 'Joshua' will again be in our midst, and Satan will again be rebuked. My husband cannot be killed. He is not dead now. He is only sleeping. Next Sunday he will arise and become the reincarnation of 'Elijah the Restorer.'"

"The girl buried Creffield in Seattle alone," O. V. said. "She would permit no one else. I admire her grit."

"No guard has been placed at Creffield's grave," the *Daily Times* quipped on the Saturday before Creffield's supposed resurrection, "and the authorities have taken no steps to provide for the unusual event."

Others may not have taken this rising-from-the-dead stuff seriously, but the Widow Creffield did. She pleaded with Prosecuting Attorney Mackintosh to allow her to go to the cemetery on Sunday so that she could witness her husband's resurrection. Risking the wrath of God—or at least the wrath of God's Elect—Mackintosh denied her request.

The Widow Creffield then begged Matron Kelly to take her to the cemetery. If she wasn't there to greet her husband when he arose, she declared, her soul would be lost and she would be punished for her infidelity—one can only imagine what she feared Creffield's punishment for infidelity might be.

Matron Kelly told the Widow Creffield that this was ridiculous, Creffield wasn't going to rise from the grave, and so there was no point in going to the cemetery. The Widow Creffield refused to be reasoned with, all the while groveling and crying hysterically. Matron Kelly, who had seen a lot sad sights in her work, said that the Widow Creffield's condition was the saddest she'd ever witnessed. This breakdown was in marked contrast to what had been her demeanor since her husband's death. Except for the first few minutes after the shooting, she had exhibited no grief or other emotions since Monday.

Taking pity on her, Matron Kelly relented and took her to the Lake View Cemetery on the designated day. It was late in the afternoon, and Matron Kelly was distressed that she couldn't buy flowers to lay on the grave. Flowers were the least of the Widow Creffield's concerns. She was sure that by the time they got there, they'd find the grave empty and her husband would have already arisen—come and gone, so to speak, off "to confound his enemies."

Upon finding the dirt over Creffield's grave undisturbed, the Widow Creffield tried to think positively. "I have got a message from Joshua telling me to worry no more about that poor old earthly body of his," she said. She said that her husband had previously told her he might actually return in spirit, not in body. Maybe that's what had happened. He'd returned in spirit. Spiritual love and spirit relationships had been part of his teachings, she said. She would now live in hope that she might recognize his spirit somewhere.

And where were the rest of the Brides of Christ? Why weren't they at Creffield's grave awaiting his return to earth? No doubt they would have been if they hadn't been having problems of their own. As it was, they weren't even aware of the pending resurrection as they were awaiting not Creffield's return to earth so much as his return to the Oregon coast. They were still camped at Cummins Creek, subsisting on clams, mussels and crabs. Timber cruiser George Hodges would have been no more surprised to see someone rise from the dead than he was when he stumbled across this group of emaciated, haggard, and scantily clad campers.

Sunday Oregonian Magazine, *1953*
Creffield's flock found by George Hodges

When Hodges told them their leader, Creffield, was dead they said that was impossible. "Creffield is the Second Messiah," one of them said, and he "had gone to Queen Charlotte Sound to select a location for a colony on one of the many islands there."

There was no persuading them to quit camp. "He [Creffield] had told them to remain where they were until his return, and they refused every offer that I made to see them safely back to civilization," Hodges said. "They would rather starve to death than disobey his instructions."

Hodges gave them all of his provisions, such as they were— sea biscuits and condensed milk—and went to seek help from the nearest homesteaders, the Hosfords. Erwin Hosford, however, wasn't about to lift a finger to help the women, wasn't about to risk having an outbreak of Holy Rollerism practically in his front yard. He almost refused to let Hodges spend the night because Hodges had acted as a Christian should act, had given aid and comfort in the form of food to starving women.

The next day Hodges got similar responses from every other homesteader he contacted. When he reached Waldport, he sent word to O. V. Hurt that he had found his missing relatives, including his five-month-old granddaughter. Alas, no one in the immediate vicinity would come to their aid, he said, even though "these women will starve to death or expire from exposure."

I am watching for the coming of the glad millennial day,
When our blessed Lord shall come and catch His waiting
Bride away;
Oh, my heart is filled with rapture as I labor, watch and
pray,
For our Lord is coming back to earth again.
Our Lord is coming back to earth again,
Yes, our Lord is coming back to earth again.

From the Reverend Knapp's
Bible Songs of Salvation and Victory.

CHAPTER SEVENTEEN

KILLER OR HERO?

**PROSECUTION AND DEFENSE
SEEK PROSPECTIVE JURORS' OPINIONS
REGARDING REPORTS OF ORGIES
CONDUCTED BY DEAD MAN**
Headline, *Seattle Daily Times,* June 27, 1906

George Mitchell's trial was expected to be one of the most sensational ever held in Washington. Also one of the most expensive, possibly costing as much as $2,500. The fees alone for the forty-six subpoenaed witnesses, most of whom were coming from out of state, were expected to run around $1,200. If Creffield had fled to British Columbia and George had chanced upon him in Victoria, Victoria would now be the site of this judicial spectacle. But young Mitchell hadn't chanced upon Creffield in British Columbia, so the trial was Seattle's lot.

Even though the first few days of the trial would be devoted to nothing more than jury selection, hours before the proceedings began on Monday, June 25, the courtroom filled and spectators flowed into the corridors.

The crowd for the most part is made up of long haired and bald headed men with unusual phrenological bumps prominent in their features, men of abnormal mental development or inclinations. Of the 160 or more persons in attendance, of whom some 20 were women, there were at least 30 bald headed men. One spectator is so completely bald and has such a striking resemblance to pictures and cartoons of John D. Rockefeller that it was the cause of much remark in the courtroom. Another spectator was adorned with Elbert Hubbard hat and hair, while there was a general tendency on the part of the male spectators to that kind of slovenliness in dress which so many persons appear to associate with habits of plain living and high thinking. The women for the most part are less noticeable for individual characteristics than the men, though there were several among them who were marked by some of the same striking general characteristics.

The *Seattle Star*

As George took his seat behind the rail, he shook hands with his attorneys and asked whether his brother, Perry, could sit next to him during jury selection. His request was granted. The brothers, described by the *Statesman* as being "alike as two peas," didn't just look like each other: They had both hated Creffield. Given the opportunity, Perry said he too would have killed Creffield on the streets of Seattle—or any other city he chanced to find him in.

From questions asked of prospective jurors by George's attorneys, it was obvious that his defense would be temporary insanity—a relatively novel plea in that day and age. Morris and Shipley also didn't want anyone on the jury who might have believed in Creffield's religious doctrines. Morris repeatedly asked: "If it is shown in the course of this trial that the deceased Creffield was a religious teacher, professed in fact to be a second Christ, will that fact have a tendency to influence you against the defendant?"

The attorneys for the prosecution, meanwhile, asked prospective jurors whether they could tell the difference

AN INTERESTED SPECTATOR –

ATTORNEY SHIPLEY FOR THE DEFENDENT –

GEORGE MITCHELL –

AN OREGON SYMPATHIZER –

– ONE OF THE JURYMEN –

Seattle Post-Intelligencer

Sketches from the trial

between "real insanity" and an excuse fabricated in order to escape punishment. They asked what states the prospective jurors had lived in. Anyone who had lived in Oregon—where "lynch and mob law and anarchy" ruled—was rejected. Miller also repeatedly asked: "Are you a believer in the right of personal assassination?"

Are you a believer in the right of personal assassination? How often had prospective jurors ever before been asked something so outrageous? What sane American citizen would admit on the stand, under oath, that "Yes, I do believe in the right of personal assassination"?

More amazing than the question was that many did admit that they could envision a state of affairs arising "which would justify one man in going out and taking the life of another."

One—a former police magistrate and justice of the peace, no less—said that he "would have acted just as Mitchell did."

As the *Seattle Daily Times* said, these were men who followed "that unwritten code of human law which is headed by the old injunction, 'An eye for an eye,' and which in its more modern form resolves itself into the doctrine that a wrong committed against the womenfolk of a household is punishable by death at the hands of the ablest male relative."

Mackintosh and Miller must have wondered: *Why couldn't George Mitchell have chanced upon Creffield in Canada?* Was this "the wrath of an angry God" Creffield had called down on Seattle in April? Perhaps they consoled themselves that at least Seattle wasn't having to dig itself out from under an earthquake the way San Francisco was.

A striking feature of the examinations was that *all* the prospective jurors had read about the case in the newspapers. Most had also discussed it with others and had already formed opinions as to the defendant's guilt or innocence. About the only way anyone in Seattle could have missed hearing about the murder would have been if they had been hiding in a hole under a house for the past three months—and things like that happened in Oregon, not Washington. The most unbiased man in the jury pool was a Siwash Indian, but the principal reason he didn't know much about the case was that he wasn't fluent in English. He was excused for cause.

One man said he was afraid to serve on the jury because his friends told him that if he came home without acquitting young Mitchell, he ought to be tarred and feathered. Two others were excused because their wives had told them to be sure to acquit young Mitchell.

Throughout most of the jury selection George sat quietly in his chair with his hand upon his chin, attentively looking on. References to him didn't appear to move him in the slightest, and even though he knew that every eye in the crowd was upon him, he didn't look self-conscious . . . until the brigade of gray-haired ladies descended.

On the second day of jury selection, after the prospective jurors had already been seated, but before Judge Frater had arrived, a group of gray-haired ladies—at least fifteen of them—walked up to the side rail and grasped young Mitchell by the hand. With tears pouring down their faces they all declared that he had done the right thing and prayed the jury would acquit him. George, a tear or two in his eyes, blushed beet red and thanked them.

Prosecuting Attorney Mackintosh looked on in frustration. Why weren't the bailiffs doing something? Because the bailiffs had been trained to deal with the rabble, not grandmothers. Mackintosh rushed to get the judge on the bench, but the damage had been done. Many prospective jurors looked as though they also had a tear or two in their eyes.

The third day of jury selection was a day of legal squabbling, with both sides trying to plant ideas in jurors' minds—the defense that Creffield was a brute, and the prosecution that Creffield had already been punished for his crimes by serving a term in the penitentiary.

Morris, in the form of a long "question," recited an abbreviated account of Creffield's deeds. In one "question" Morris managed to get in, among other things, how George and Esther, "brother and sister were devoted to each other before Creffield's advent," how Donna deserted her husband and three small children so "that she might follow the fanatical pervert," how Esther's "apparent mental derangement" was "a result of her association with the blighting cult," and how Creffield maintained a camp on the coast where women had "suffered countless privations and hardships." Morris asked whether these events and circumstances, as an explanation for the defendant's mental attitude toward Creffield, would create any prejudice against him in the prospective juror's mind.

The prosecution objected to the "question" on the grounds that it wasn't a question, but a speech. Judge Frater said the juror could answer the "question"—if he could remember what it was.

Morris's "question," as he had hoped it would, had an obvious effect on the prospective jurors. "As the nauseating story of Holy Rollerism was unfolded several talesman grew deeply interested in their own feet," the *Oregonian* said. "Others sniffed covertly, and one or two made no effort to control their emotions as the wretched picture of the wrongs young Mitchell's family had suffered was painted to their minds in broad, unmistakable English."

It also had an effect on George, who displayed the first real agitation he had shown since the proceedings began. At the mention of his sisters, he lost his passive, stoical air. He bowed his head, and his eyes too became riveted on his shoes. He didn't look up until some minutes after Morris was done speaking, and then he seemed restless and ill at ease, shifting his position frequently and drumming nervously on the table in front of him.

Shipley, in another lengthy "question," called Creffield " a brute" and "a reptile." Miller objected to the epithets applied to the deceased.

"Objection sustained."

Shipley immediately asked practically the same question— but this time omitted the words *brute* and *reptile*.

The day's proceedings then reached a climax, the *Daily Times* said, "when Morris declared that he was there to defend his client and was going to do it, regardless of the ideas of the prosecution or the court. Mr. Mackintosh grew sarcastic, Mr. Miller expounded the law and Mr. Shipley punched the air full of holes with his yellow pencil."

Judge Frater excused the prospective jurors and summoned the four attorneys to a conference like a group of schoolboys who had behaved badly in class. He instructed them to limit the examination of the prospective jurors to "to a more usual line of questioning and thus avoid the constant fire of objections, arguments and more or less personal remarks between the opposing sides."

Judge Frater's reprimand changed little. As the prospective jurors filed back into the box, Morris was overheard to say he would fight until "Hell freezes over."

Mackintosh replied: "Let the fireworks go on," and they did.

The attorneys fought and bickered over every new phase of the case and then would tell the prospective jurors that their "heated words are merely professional necessities" and that they were "personally just as good friends as ever." As the day

THE MORNING OREGONIAN, WEDNESDAY, JULY 4, 1906.

JURY WHICH IS TRYING GEORGE MITCHELL AT SEATTLE FOR KILLING EDWIN CREFFIELD. THE SMALL PORTRAIT IS THAT OF THE ACCUSED

Morning Oregonian

George Mitchell and the jury

wore on, George sat in his chair, pushing his chin ever further into the palm of his hand.

By the afternoon of the third day of jury selection, not only the regular monthly venire of ninety prospective jurors, but also the special venire of sixty prospective jurors called specifically for this case had been exhausted. That evening the sheriff served notices to thirty men whose names had been drawn just hours earlier, telling the surprised men they had to be in court the next morning.

The fourth day of jury selection proved to be "tedious for everyone concerned," the *Telegram* said. "A penny firecracker would have awakened half the courtroom with a start. Two of the men in the jury box shamelessly slumbered during a good portion of the day. Prosecuting Attorney Mackintosh spent his periods of leisure in the seclusion of the bailiff's easy chair and occasionally jumped up with a start. John F. Miller was much interested in the building operations going on outside, which juror Dore, from an advantageous point near the window seemed to be superintending."

At 4:30 that afternoon, after all hope of securing a jury that day had been abandoned—the defense was still entitled to four more peremptory challenges and the state to two—Morris and Shipley reviewed their notes one last time. "May it please the court," Morris said, "the defense accepts the jury as it now stands."

"We have no further challenges to make," Assistant Prosecutor Miller then said to a startled courtroom.

"The whole courtroom," the *Oregonian* said, "spectators, lawyers, witnesses, Judge and prisoner gave one great sigh of relief."

The jury—two ranchers, a farmer, a restaurant keeper, a paperhanger, a foreman at the water department, a post office worker, a clerk, a grocer, a cement contractor, a cook, and a saloon keeper—was at once sworn in and sent to the jury-room.

Mackintosh said that he could complete his side of the case by the next evening . . . unless delayed by protracted cross-examination. Morris assured him that, in his "professional opinion," the cross-examination of the state's witnesses would probably be the shortest on record in a murder trial.

***

Behold, God will not cast away a perfect man, neither will he help the evil doers.—Job 8:20

CHAPTER EIGHTEEN

THE TRIAL

MURDER TRIAL THE SENSATION
OF THE HOUR IN SEATTLE
Headline, Portland *Morning Oregonian*, June 29, 1906

The crowd that gathered before court convened on Friday was probably the largest ever seen in a Seattle court-house. At least fifty women were among those in the packed courtroom, and scores stood outside in the corridors, patiently hoping they might get a chance to go in.

John F. Miller made the prosecution's opening statement, "a brief review of the evidence of the shooting," the *Daily Times* said, "made in as nearly a dispassionate manner as Mr. Miller's virile personality would allow." From Miller's statement it was clear the prosecution was going to depend on a strict interpre-tation of the law to win a conviction. Shoot an unarmed man in the back and you are guilty of murder. Period.

Doctor Emil Bories, the first doctor on the murder scene, and County Coroner Frank M. Carroll, were called to testify about their autopsy findings. The autopsy showed that there were powder marks on the back of Creffield's neck, that the bullet entered at the base of the skull, snapped the spinal cord at the

Seattle Daily Times
Maud Hurt, Chief D. F. Willard and Sergeant Charles Tennant

second vertebra at the base of the brain—its most vulnerable point—and after breaking the jawbone, lodged near the right side of the neck. The wound had caused instant death by cutting off the action of the respiratory organs.

The defense hoped the jury noted that Creffield's death couldn't have been quicker or more painless. Creffield may have thought of himself as being the second Christ, but at least his executioner had shown more compassion than the first Christ's—none of this nailing a man on a cross and then letting him hang for hours with a crown of thorns on his head.

Doctor Bories also noted that "Creffield had a fine brain" and that "all his organs were well developed and in good condition."

On cross-examination, the defense asked about the Widow Creffield's behavior. Doctor Bories said that when he first arrived she was lying across Creffield's "lifeless form, stroking the hair and muttering, 'Joshua, Joshua. They can't kill Joshua.'"

"I misunderstood the woman," Doctor Bories said. "Thinking she said it was all a 'josh' I said to her: 'Madam, this is no josh; this man is dead.'"

A small victory for the defense—getting in testimony about "Joshua" before the prosecution had a chance to object. The defense was looking for any chance to bring into evidence Creffield's brand of religious fanaticism. Too bad the doctor hadn't seen the Widow Creffield rolling about the ground ripping off her clothing while praying and referring to Creffield as the Second

Seattle Post-Intelligencer
George Mitchell

Savior. If he'd been able to testify to seeing that, then the defense would have really been off to a fine start.

Doctor Bories went on to say that by the time Creffield's body was ready to be taken to the Bonny-Watson Funeral Company, the Widow Creffield hadn't just become unusually cool and collected, she also showed so little emotion that he said: "I could hardly believe that she was the wife of the man who lay dead."

A series of eye-witnesses to the shooting were called. J. Tuchten, a jeweler, testified that he was on the other side of the street when he heard a shot and saw Creffield fall. He also said that he was "particularly impressed by the calm demeanor of the man who did the shooting," that the man "stood near the body, smoking a cigar, and showed no signs of emotion."

Point for the prosecution. Young Mitchell—outside of having just killed someone on a public street—was acting like a sane man in control of himself.

While Tuchten was still on the stand, Miller, in as dramatic a tone as he could muster, bellowed: "Call Mrs. Creffield." She was being brought in to be identified as the woman beside Creffield at the time of the shooting. The defense said there was no need to do this, that they would not contest that the Widow Creffield was that woman. But the prosecution summoned her anyhow—a little drama to keep everyone awake during their side's cold presentation of facts.

The Widow Creffield walked in wearing mourning attire and with widow's weeds in her jet black hair.

Mourning attire? Widow's weeds? Had she finally accepted that her husband was dead?

Possibly. When visiting Creffield's grave with her father, her father had asked: "Why is he there, Maud, if he is divine?"

"Oh, it isn't Joshua any more," she sighed. "It is only Edmund."

While this was psychologically a move in the right direction for her, it didn't help the defense any. So much for their hope—slim as it was—that she might snap and would suddenly start ranting before the jury that Creffield wasn't dead, that He would rise from the grave to confound His enemies.

The Widow Creffield followed the bailiffs through the crowd and stopped halfway up the center aisle. George was the only one in the room who didn't turn his head or crane his neck to see her. His eyes, as they had been all day, were fixed upon the jury. Her eyes were fixed upon the judge.

Morris's and Shipley's eyes, like those of almost everyone else's in the room, were fixed upon the Widow Creffield. But Morris and Shipley weren't watching her out of curiosity. They were afraid she might have a gun. They always feared that she or another of Creffield's flock might try to shoot George or either of them.

Many of Creffield's flock, including many of those who had been at the camp on the coast, were now in Seattle. After George Hodges, the timber cruiser who had stumbled upon the starving group at Cummins Creek, contacted O. V. Hurt, O. V. contacted William McMillan and Milton Beem. When Hodges had asked other homesteaders to help the women, he was repeatedly turned down. He might as well have been trying to get help for plague-infected rats. But William and Milton respected O. V. too much to turn down his personal plea to rescue his family.

It took some doing, but William eventually persuaded the group to leave their camp despite Creffield's orders to stay put until his return. William took them to Waldport and put them on a boat to Tidewater. From there Milton drove them by wagon to the Hurts' home. It poured during much of the three days it took to get the group safely to Corvallis. Milton, who despite being protected by a slicker and gum boots got thoroughly soaked, said that he never heard a single complaint from the thinly clad women. He also heard no mention of Creffield. Instead, they wrapped themselves in blankets and spoke frequently about the "enjoyable" time they had in camp.

Some of the group were still at the Hurts' home, but others were now in Seattle. Because of this, at all times during the trial either Morris or Shipley stood against a wall so that he could see everyone in the courtroom.

Miller now pointed at the Widow Creffield, and asked Tuchten if she was the woman with Creffield when he was gunned down.

"I don't think so," Tuchten answered.

The prosecution was getting drama—but not the sort it had wished for. The Widow Creffield in court that day was much different from the woman Tuchten had seen in May, so different that he didn't recognize her. She was no longer "comely looking" as she had once been, but was now a "little woman, with ashy-gray complexion"—or so said the *Seattle Post-Intelligencer*.

And more than her appearance was different. Her whole manner was different. "Whatever it was in her—religious fervor, fanatic belief in her husband or a sense of martyrdom—" the *Daily Times* said, "gave her an expression and a bearing different from any ordinary woman. Her appearance was startling. It sent a thrill which was almost a shiver through the men inside the rail who turned in their chairs to meet that blazing look in her eyes." No, this was not the drama the prosecution had hoped for.

"Step closer, Mrs. Creffield," Miller instructed.

She walked to the rail and stood directly behind George. She said nothing, her eyes still fixed upon the judge.

John F. Miller, King County
Assistant Prosecuting Attorney

"Is this the woman?" Miller asked again.

"I don't think so," Tuchten said. "I'm not sure."

John A. Whalley, an insurance man whose office was in the Colman Building, testified that he heard the shot and ran to the window. He said he saw a woman striking at a man who was backing away from her. "She was striking wildly," he said, "and Mitchell was warding off the blows."

Whalley said he ran to the scene and when he arrived the woman was bending over the body. "She kept repeating to Mitchell in the intervals, 'He didn't hurt you,' or something to that effect," Whalley said.

On cross-examination, the defense asked how the woman addressed the body, hoping Whalley would remember her calling Creffield "Joshua."

"Objection. Irrelevant."

"Objection sustained."

Doctor W. C. Capps, a dentist in the Washington Block, and Peter Wooley, a bootblack who had a stand at the foot of Cherry Street, told substantially the same story. "Wooley," the *Daily Times* reported, "proceeded to fill the courtroom so full of explosive English of the Italian variety that the bailiff had to open a window. He was utterly unable to answer 'yes' or 'no' to any question and each query brought out an excited review of his idea of the whole affair."

Police Captain John Sullivan, H. P. Ford, Chief D. F. Willard, Sergeant Charles Tennant, and Patrolman Ernest LeCount all testified that after the defendant's arrest he had been "cool and collected and showed no evidences of agitation," so cool and collected that one of the first things he did after arriving at the jail was ask that a telegram be sent to O. V. Hurt: "I've got my man. I am in jail here. George."

LeCount said that when he asked the defendant why he had killed Creffield, the defendant replied: "I have only done my duty"— Creffield was "the leader of the Holy Rollers, a cult that was driving women out of their minds and robbing them of their chastity."

Seattle Daily Times

Kenneth Mackintosh. King County Prosecuting Attorney

Louis B. Sefrit, a reporter for the *Daily Times*, testified about a conversation he had with the defendant shortly after the shooting. The defendant readily admitted he'd killed Creffield, and had done so because the man had "ruined" his two sisters. Morris, on cross-examination, asked Sefrit how he'd answered the defendant when the defendant asked him what he would have done under similar circumstances.

"Objection."

"Objection sustained."

The damage had been done, though, for it is likely that every man in the jury box was now asking himself the same question: *What would I have done under similar circumstances?*

When the Widow Creffield testified, she looked to be physically weak and emotionally flat. "No ordinary widow ever acted as she acted on the witness stand," the *Oregonian* said of her. She acted as though she were a disinterested party in the case. She didn't act hostile, or angry, or sad. She acted as though she were recounting the details of a murder of a complete stranger, not of a man she was married to—and certainly not of a man she viewed as the Second Savior.

In a voice barely above a whisper she told how on the morning of May 7, standing next to Creffield, she was startled by a loud explosion in front of Quick's Drugstore.

"What was the first thing you did then?" Miller asked.

"The first thing I did was to turn around, and I saw George Mitchell."

Miller pointed to the defendant and asked whether he was the man who had fired the gun. She looked at George intently for a moment.

"Yes, that is the man."

"What did you say to Mitchell after the shooting?"

"'Why did you shoot? He never did you any harm.'"

"Did the defendant make reply to this?"

"Yes."

"What did he say?"

Suddenly the Widow Creffield looked dizzy. Miller rose and poured her a glass of water. After she had drained the glass, Miller asked her what the defendant did next.

She said he had calmly put his revolver in his hip pocket. Fearing he might fire again, she rushed up to him, she said, and seized him by the hands. He drew his hands free and seized her by the wrists. After a moment he released her and she dropped down beside the dead man.

Miller asked her to demonstrate how she had grabbed the defendant and how he had pushed her away from him. As she rose, she practically fainted, sinking to her knees and falling into Miller's arms. Miller helped her back to the witness stand, and said he had no more questions.

"The woman was trembling on the verge of a breakdown," the *Daily Times* said, "and the jury as well as the spectators, were on edge lest she tumble from her chair."

The defense had fantasized about the Widow Creffield doing some tumbling during her testimony—but not tumbling of this sort. Morris was now going to have to be very lenient with her during his cross-examination, lest the jury's sympathies shift from young Mitchell to her.

Morris was also going to be very limited in what he could question her about, having to confine himself to topics related to her examination by the state.

Morris began by asking her when she had married the man who was killed.

"April 3rd, 1906," she said.

Morris then asked whether she had been married to him before.

"Objection."

"Objection sustained."

Morris asked whether anything had happened that made her suspect any danger to Creffield from the defendant.

"Not in Seattle," she replied.

A small break for the defense. "Just previous to coming to Seattle," Morris asked. "What about that?"

Miller was on his feet. "Now, if the court please," he began, but was interrupted by laughter throughout the room. "If I were the judge of this court," Miller was overheard saying, "I would clear all that rabble out of the courtroom." Especially the grandmothers, no doubt.

Morris asked the Widow Creffield what she had said over the body of the dead man.

"Objection. Immaterial."

"Objection sustained."

Morris asked the Widow Creffield to spell her husband's name.

"C-R-E-F-E-L-D."

Morris then asked whether there were any other names her husband had been known by. He wasn't really interested in the variations in the spelling of Edmund Creffield's name—E-d-m-u-n-d, E-d-w-i-n, E-d-m-o-n-d, or F-r-a-n-z E., C-r-e-f-f-i-e-l-d, C-r-e-f-e-l-d, C-r-e-f-i-e-l-d, or C-a-r-e-f-i-e-l-d. No, he was hoping she would say "Joshua." It would have been an added bonus if she would say "Joshua, the Holy Prophet, an apostle, the same as those mentioned in the Bible"; but for now he would be happy if she would just say "Joshua."

It didn't matter, because before the Widow Creffield could answer, there was the inevitable: "Objection!"

"Objection overruled."

Overruled? Finally, one of Miller's objections was overruled. Seizing the opportunity, Morris bluntly asked: "Was your husband ever known by the name of 'Joshua'?"

Miller was irate. "Counsel ought to know better than to act that way!"

"I'm not so smart as you are," Morris replied.

"You wouldn't ask such a question as that if you were" was Miller's quick retort. He asked the court to instruct counsel to stop asking questions that counsel knew would be objected to, and then withdrawing them. Such questions were posed, Miller said, for the sole purpose of planting ideas in the juror's minds. Judge Frater agreed, and ruled that such questioning wasn't proper cross-examination and excused the Widow Creffield from the stand.

The prosecution of George Mitchell had been brief—six hours—and to the point. Mackintosh and Miller established that the killing was deliberate, that it was executed calmly and deliberately, and that, throughout, young Mitchell maintained the attitude of a "sane" man in control of himself.

"The prosecution has aimed at calmness and coldness in its presentation of facts and its examination of witnesses," the *Daily Times* said. "It has aimed to throw an air of finality and of matter-of-factness about its every move. It has sought to impress the jury with the simplicity of the case and thereby with the fact that nothing can mitigate its array of frigid facts indicating meditated murder. The very appearing of anything tinging upon emotion has been ruthlessly crushed by Mr. Miller, and in this effort he has been ably seconded by Judge Frater."

Just as the prosecution attempted to curb any natural tendency to emotion on the part of the jury, the defense would aim to encourage it. Seattle could hardly wait to hear all the lurid details.

***

REVELATIONS EXPECTED
Headline, *Seattle Post-Intelligencer*, July 1, 1906

CHAPTER NINETEEN

AN INHERITED STREAK OF INSANITY

CREFFIELD'S GHOST CONTROLS HIS FLOCK
Headline, Seattle Sunday Times, July 1, 1906

S ilas M. Shipley spent the entire Monday morning session making his opening statement. "We are not before you for the purpose of pettifogging, or attempt to befog the real issue before you," he said—promptly going on to say the defense's position was that while they would not deny that the defendant had "fired the ball from his revolver which severed the bond connecting the soul of Creffield with his body and sent him to his grave in the cemetery," the defendant hadn't been "in the full possession of his senses" when he did so.

In other words: Young Mitchell admits he killed Creffield— but we contend that he was crazy at the time.

The defense, Shipley said, would show that "a certain sequence of events" led to the defendant becoming mentally unbalanced.

In other words: We will tell the sordid details of the Holy Roller orgies.

This was what the spectators—the rabble—had been waiting for. They hung on Shipley's every word as he told the story of Creffield, beginning with his days in the Salvation Army and ending with his death in Seattle. Shipley said this story would be corroborated by witnesses the defense planned to call. But he knew it was likely that some—if not all—of the story he outlined might never be corroborated, that the prosecution would make objections *ad nauseam* during witnesses' testimony. So, since his opening statement might be the defense's only chance to get these scandalous doings before the jury, he crammed as many details as possible into it.

"It was not pleasant," the *Daily Times* said, "this awful revelation of baseness indulged in by those who had become dead to all sense of moral and physical decency." It was obviously not pleasant for young Mitchell who, throughout Shipley's recital, intently watched the faces of the jurors while nervously interlacing his knotted fingers and biting his lips until they were white.

"We will then show evidence bearing upon the early life of this young man," Shipley said, "tracing him from birth to manhood." Shipley spoke of the defendant's father, Charles Mitchell, "a man of strong peculiarities and eccentricities, a man who could see no good in things only as they were seen through his glasses." Shipley said that this was "a strong family characteristic and that it was handed down from father to children."

In other words: We plan to suggest that almost the whole Mitchell brood is crazy.

Shipley spoke of the defendant's own religious beliefs in spiritualism, how he believed the spirits, particularly his mother's, were telling him "he was the only man living who possessed the power to rid the world of this man who had brought ruin and disgrace, not only upon the people Mitchell loved best, but upon others whom he knew and of whom he was fond."

In other words: Maybe young Mitchell really was crazy when he pulled the trigger. Don't you think someone is crazy if he believed the spirit of his dead mother told him to kill someone?

Shipley concluded his statement by telling how, after Donna Starr deserted her family to join Creffield, young Mitchell went to her home and took "the motherless babies on his lap, one of seven months, one of three and another of five years," and cried over them. Shipley said that young Mitchell told the motherless babies that the spirit of his own mother had told him where

Seattle Post-Intelligencer
George and Perry Mitchell and Silas M. Shipley

their mother had gone, that "he would bring mamma back to them."

In other words: We can't come out and say what the "real issue" before you, the jury, is—that Creffield was a fiend who deserved to die—so we must befog the issue a bit.

"His manner was calm and unimpassioned," the *Oregonian* said of Shipley during his opening statement. "Such a recital seemed to need no emphasis."

Perry, described by the *Oregonian* as resembling young Mitchell closely, "except that he is tanned and ruddy," was called to testify about the streak of insanity that ran through his family. Of the six Mitchell children, only Perry and one other brother, David in western Washington, were not considered to be religious fanatics. Perry testified about his sister,

Esther, being committed for treatment of "mental weakness" to the Boy's and Girls' Aid Society—the children's version of the loony bin. Perry told how when Esther was in the Aid Society she refused to recognize him and George as her brothers—that they were her brothers in name only, she said. Perry said this preyed so on George's mind that George was unable to eat or sleep. Perry said that he told George "if he didn't quit worrying, he would soon be as 'nutty' as the 'Holy Rollers.'"

Perry said he thought George finally did go nutty when he claimed he'd been talking with the spirits and "God had commanded him to deliver up the spirit of Creffield." Perry said that in April, George, penniless and still weak from the measles, said "he was going to find Creffield, even if he had to walk from place to place in order to get him."

"I am God's agent," George had said to Perry. "I am chosen by God to hunt Creffield down and I am going to do it."

How much crazier sounding can you get?

Perry also testified that his father, Charles Mitchell, was a "religious and political crank" with a "quick temper." He said his father frequently changed religious affiliations, and couldn't hold a civil conversation with someone who didn't have the same beliefs as himself.

On cross-examination, Perry was asked whether he had made an effort to talk his nutty brother out of the idea of killing Creffield? "No," he answered.

What else could he have said? *Of course I didn't try to talk George out of it. I wanted Creffield dead just as much as he did?*

Charles Mitchell, the religious and political crank, was in Seattle during the trial, but was not in the courtroom. He had visited his son George briefly in jail one morning during jury selection. "It was a clasp of hands," the *Daily Times* reported, "a mutual assurance of pleasure at the reunion, inquiries as to health, and that was about all." There was nothing dramatic in the meeting, their first in almost seven years. After five minutes George had to go, but his father assured him he would see him in court later that day.

Charles, described by the *Telegram* as a "smooth-shaven man of fifty-seven years, slightly stooped, browned by toil, and with hairs scattered with the gray of long years and recent sorrow," had come from Illinois to Washington to attend a most bizarre family reunion. Among the attendees were George, a son who was currently on trial for murder; Perry, a son who believed in the right of personal assassination; Esther, a daughter who was thought bright but deranged; and Donna, a daughter who was an admitted adulterer. It wasn't a family a father could easily be proud of.

Charles didn't like the tack Morris and Shipley were taking to defend George. "When my son's attorney wrote me for money with which to acquit him by proving him to be insane, I emphatically replied that I would give no money for that purpose," he said. "I believed that my son, George, thought that he had committed a justifiable act when he killed Creffield, but I was unwilling to have him perjure himself even to save his own life. I love truth and righteousness."

After his visit with George, Charles Mitchell went to see Esther, and never did return to court that day—or the next day, or the next.

Esther had come to Seattle before the start of the trial to help the prosecution convict George.

> *I hope my brother will have time to repent his sins before they hang him* [she said when she first walked into a Seattle police station]. . . .
>
> *My brother had no right to kill Creffield. If he says that Creffield did me any harm, he lies, and he knows it. Creffield always treated me properly as he did all of his other followers. They sent him to the pen simply to break up the religious camp we had. He was not given a fair trial. The people at Corvallis did not like us and they thought if they sent him to the pen we would all desert him.*
>
> *They committed perjury to send him to the pen. Every one in Corvallis knew it was a put-up job. When we did not desert him and leave Corvallis, the people there began trying to send us to the insane asylum. I am sane and always was. So are the rest. They sent me to a home*

*in Portland because they said I was crazy but too young
to go to the asylum.*

*I know Joshua will arise. I shall certainly testify
against my brother. He never helped me.*

I am sane and I know Joshua will arise said practically in
the same breath? Not exactly the type of credible witness the
prosecution was looking for.

And Esther's willingness to help hang her brother?

> *This may be in accord with legal law known only by
> professionals, but the great code of blood relationship,
> known to everyone, contains no such precept. A queer
> psychological problem is this girl, scarcely out of her
> teens. A girl who looks like a rational woman and who
> talks like one on every subject except her brother and
> Creffield. The hideous influence that held her in thrall
> during Creffield's life is just as strong now that her self-
> exalted ruler is in the grave.*
>
> *Every sentiment that the human heart holds dear
> has been blotted out of her being by this pitiable fanati-
> cism. Sisterly love has been swept aside by emotional-
> ism of the crudest and most depraved sort. Honor, self
> respect, everything that life holds, she willingly and
> gladly sacrifices and calls the whole world to witness
> the sacrifice.*
>
> The *Star*

In the end, Esther, described by the *Daily Times* as "slight,
frail, girlish—far from being a woman such as one would imagine to be one of the principal figures in such a case," was called
to testify not by the prosecution, but by the defense. Instead of
asking her about her supposed mental weakness, however,
Morris asked her about her older brother, Fred. Had anything
happened to him in Portland three and a half years earlier?

After a moment's hesitation she said: "Nothing accidental."

That was one way of putting it.

Shipley had mentioned Fred Mitchell during his opening
statement, saying he had "always shown traces of a mental

condition which witnesses described as 'being off,' and not right in the head." Such talk escalated in January of 1903 when friends of his began commenting among themselves how strangely he was acting of late— even stranger than usual—how he was rambling on now almost non-stop about God—the family obsession. Then, for no apparent reason, he resigned from his position as a motorman for City & Suburban. The next morning, the chambermaid at the Merchants' Hotel in Portland where Fred was staying, found him lying in a pool of blood, moaning: "I want to die."

Los Angeles Times
Esther Mitchell

Three or four hours before he had shot himself in the head with a revolver. The ball went through his scalp and lodged itself under the skin. Fred then fired a shot under his left breast. That ball went under his heart and through his chest.

Asked why he had attempted suicide, Fred spat out: "None of your business. Attend to your own affairs. I've troubles of my own." He was taken to the Good Samaritan Hospital, where it was assumed he would die.

But he didn't die. In fact, he was alive and well and somewhere in Seattle during the trial. It was known that he routinely met with Esther and other Brides of Christ, but he was intentionally avoiding speaking to George or his attorneys.

Donna Starr was also in Seattle. She initially came with the idea of helping her brother. After she got back from the camp on the coast she told her husband, Burgess, that she had seen the error of her ways and that she and he should go to Seattle to see if they could be of some assistance.

This renewal of sisterly love didn't sit well with Esther . . . or apparently God. "Tell her for me," Esther said to her brother

Perry, "that last night I had a visitation from God and He is very angry with her for coming here. . . . I told her she was wrong to think of coming here and I did all I could to keep her away. And now I don't want to see her or have anything to do with her until she has made her peace with the Almighty and obtained forgiveness for violating His wishes."

Soon thereafter, Donna apparently did make her peace with the Almighty and her faith in Creffield was renewed.

> *The newspapers kept lying about Creffield. . . .*
>
> *They've all lied about Creffield. Only one side of the story has been told. Creffield and his friends kept silent under all the infamy and charges heaped upon him. He was too good and great a man even to answer his accusers. . . .*
>
> *They just hounded him to death. George Mitchell and his friends had it all fixed up to kill Creffield. He knew it and he made no attempt to escape them. Oh how they lied and lied about him! He never did the things they said he did, and he was vilified because people didn't know him, didn't understand him. . . .*
>
> *There is no brotherly or sisterly feeling between us [George Mitchell and myself] any more. I say he should be punished just like any other man. There was no justification for the cold-blooded crime which he committed. He had no wrongs to avenge. My sister and I were fully responsible for our own acts, and it was none of George Mitchell's business what we did. . . .*
>
> *Why should he escape punishment? It was the premeditated and cold-blooded murder of a good and a harmless man. The murderer's lawyers worked day and night to fix up lies for the witnesses to swear to.*
>
> Donna Star

Even though Donna now took the position that God was angry with George Mitchell—henceforth she would always refer to him as "George Mitchell," not "George" or "my brother"—the defense still called her to the witness stand. They decided they would just limit the questions they asked her. But Donna had

Seattle Daily Times
Donna Starr

other ideas and didn't appear in court at the appointed hour. Consequently, Judge Frater issued a bench warrant charging her with contempt of court, and detailed a deputy sheriff to give her an "escort."

When she was escorted in, she had two of her children with her. One of them, upon spying her Uncle George, ran straight to him. George took her up on his knee, where the little girl sat with her tiny arms about his neck and her golden-haired head snuggled against his shoulder. It was a touching scene, made more so because Donna didn't even so much as glance at George Mitchell.

Donna, described by the *Daily Times* as "peculiar looking," gave her testimony in a hesitant and reluctant manner. Morris first asked her to identify two letters. One letter was familiar to all by now, the letter she wrote the night she left for Creffield's camp on the coast, the letter that told Burgess: "I cannot wait until daylight because the babies would cry to go with me. I have taken about $3.50 of your money, but I guess I have been worth that much to you. It is not enough to pay my fare, and I will have to walk to the place I am going."

The second letter came as something of a surprise. It was one Donna had written to her brother-in-law Clarence Starr and his wife Hattie. In it Donna asked for their forgiveness for the wrongs she had committed against them, said she now realized she had been wrong, but she had been under another's power.

"Don't tear that, Mrs. Starr," Morris exclaimed as he saw Donna take the letter in both hands, and start to fold it. "I want it."

SALVATIONISTS TO WED.

Phoebe Mitchell.

Elaborate preparations are being made for the Hallelujah wedding of two of the most prominent Salvation Army workers in Portland, tomorrow evening, August 5. The contracting parties will be Sergeant-Major Phoebe Mitchell and Treasurer Peter Vanderkelen, formerly of Belgium, both members of Portland Corps, No. 1, 26 Davis street, where the marriage will take place. The ceremony will be performed by Brigadier Mrs. Stillwell, of Los Angeles, Cal., the pioneer officer of the Salvation Army, who opened the work in Oregon and Washington 18 years ago.

Peter Vanderkelen.

Evening Telegram
Phoebe Mitchell and
Peter Vander Kelen

Then came a question that seemed to baffle Donna—and many of the spectators: "What, if any, relationship exists between yourself and this defendant?" After a long pause, he repeated the question. "What, if any, relationship exists between yourself and this defendant?"

"I don't understand," Donna said. "He's my brother."

Of course he was, but that was exactly the point Morris was trying to get at, that she was related to George, and like so many in the family she had an inherited streak of insanity. Just look at her, the defense was subtly saying, she is clearly off, and not right in the head . . . just like her brother George.

George had one sister who didn't come to Seattle for the trial, Phoebe Vander Kelen. Shipley, though, had alluded to her during his opening statement: "We will show further by the evidence that the sisters [Phoebe and Esther] went to Portland and eventually took up the work of the Salvation Army, following in the footsteps of the father, and the inherited tendency manifested itself in all of the children."

Morris had wanted to call Phoebe to the stand, but George wouldn't hear of it. She was the one sister of his who—outside of signing the papers committing Esther to the Boy's and Girl's Aid Society—had had nothing to do with the Creffield affair. George wanted her kept out of it.

Phoebe, thirty-one, was a sergeant-major in the Salvation Army, and except for field officers, held the highest position in Portland's corps. The day after Creffield's arraignment, August

5, 1904, she married another Salvation Army officer, Peter Vander Kelen.

"It was a picturesque crowd that jammed the chapel to the doors," the *Oregonian* had said of Phoebe's wedding. "It was composed of people in all walks of life. Some of those in attendance had dropped in from the streets out of curiosity, the odor of the saloon still about them; others were people whose names are household words in Portland. There were saints and sinners, priests and profligates."

Brigadier General Stillwell, the pioneer officer of the Salvation Army in Oregon and Washington, came up from Los Angeles to officiate at the wedding. She read the marriage vow of the Salvation Army, an unusual marriage vow that was in a book of Army laws and regulations:

> *We do solemnly swear that we seek this union not alone for our own happiness, though we hope that through it it may be advanced, but because we believe we will be better fitted to carry on the work of the Salvation Army. We will in no way let this union come between us and the work of the Salvation Army. We will each of us not object to anything the other may desire to do to further the work of God through the Salvation Army.*

After the ceremony Phoebe addressed the audience, declaring that she recognized the importance of the step she had just taken, and intended always to live up to the vow of the Army, to never let her marriage come between her and the Army's work.

And she was considered George's most normal sister.

Esther and Donna's time on the witness stand "proved to be a disappointment for neither went further than to acknowledge her relationship to the defendant and to tell of the fact that another brother, Fred, has attempted to shoot himself in Portland," the *Daily Times* commented.

In other words: They had proved to be a disappointment to spectators who had hoped to hear about scandal, not family relations.

Seattle wouldn't have to wait long, though, before their more prurient interests were addressed.

───※───

If while fighting for our Savior on the battlefield below,
we find ourselves surrounded by a strong and mighty foe;
Let us follow our Commander, He will safely bring us through,
He will never, never leave us, What he promised He will do.
Go on, go on, don't murmur or complain,
Shout glory hallelujah! While we reap the golden grain;
Go on go on, onward ever on;
Each day "the way" grows brighter, Soon our heav'nly home we'll gain.

From the Reverend Knapp's
Bible Songs of Salvation and Victory

CHAPTER TWENTY

TESTIMONY

**DRAMATIC TESTIMONY OF RUINED HOME,
DEBAUCHED WIFE AND DEBASED SISTERS**
Headline, *Seattle Star*, July 3, 1906

Not surprisingly, the courtroom was overflowing with spectators when O. V. Hurt was called to testify on Tuesday. The temperature outside was in the mid-nineties, making it almost unbearable inside. Judge Frater announced that, thereafter, only those who could find seats would be allowed in. As long as the heat wave continued, people would no longer be allowed to stand in the rear aisle or to sit on the window sills.

O. V., described by the *Oregonian* as "stockily built, intelligent and kindly of appearance," began his testimony: "I met the defendant, Mr. Mitchell, in Portland, the last week in March. I told him Creffield was out of prison and described to him the effects of his power over the womenfolk."

O. V.'s testimony, and the testimony of many others, was liberally sprinkled with phrases like "I told George Mitchell" or "when I talked the matter over with George Mitchell, I told him" or "all this I told George Mitchell." On the stand O. V. was supposedly repeating a conversation he had had with young

Mitchell, a conversation in which he supposedly told young Mitchell Creffield's story from beginning to end.

This testimony could not be dismissed as hearsay because it was not offered as proof of Creffield's actions but as proof of young Mitchell's state of mind when he killed Creffield.

Can we, the defense counsel help it if the jury after hearing this testimony, might reach a verdict that Creffield was a fiend who deserved to die?

Tears filled O. V.'s eyes most of the while he was on the stand, especially when he spoke of his wife Sarah being committed to the insane asylum. Several times he paused and fought for self-control, and at other times he leaned far out of the witness chair, looked straight into the jury box, and grew almost hysterical as he recounted the wrongs done him. Bit by bit, the causes of the ruination of his family were exposed. His story was one of grief and shame, of how Creffield brought devastation, division, and insanity to a heretofore happy family of which love had been the keystone.

"That man [Creffield], gentlemen of the jury, ruined my life," O. V. said as he concluded his testimony. "He ruined my home and my family. I told Mitchell the man ruined his sisters."

"If Creffield was guilty of one half of that which Hurt charges against him," the *Star* said, "it would be hard to find a jury anywhere on earth that would convict his slayer of murder in the first degree."

Throughout O. V.'s testimony prosecutors Mackintosh and Miller repeatedly objected to questions or asked that statements be stricken from the record. O. V. had implied in his testimony that when he told young Mitchell Creffield's story, it came as news to him, as if perhaps George had spent the last few years hiding in a hole under a house—things like that had been known to happen in Oregon.

These objections were based on the fact that it was highly improbable that stories—true or not—of the doings of Creffield came as news to anyone in Oregon in March of 1906—especially to the defendant, and that it was highly improbable that this one conversation resulted in young Mitchell having an epiphany.

Oh, so that's why so many of my friends were committed to the insane asylum in 1904, and that's why Esther is now running around saying she's going to be mother of the next Christ. I must go and kill this brute who has debauched my sisters!

Seattle Daily Times
O.V. Hurt

Although Judge Frater sustained most of the objections, the prosecution wasn't helped. The jury looked agitated that Mackintosh and Miller were indirectly implying that O. V. Hurt—an "intelligent and kindly" man who had suffered so many wrongs—was not being completely truthful. Not to mention that the repeated interruptions were hindering the flow of the telling of this revolting but riveting story.

After O. V.'s testimony, upon seeing O. V. talking to George, Mackintosh said privately: "Any man could be proud of a friend like old man Hurt. He's one of the finest old men I ever met." Mackintosh and Miller meant no disrespect to O. V. when making their objections. They were just doing their duty.

"It did not matter to him [Mackintosh] whether the reward be the political oblivion of the dog catcher's wagon or the honor of a seat upon the bench of the superior court which he was addressing," the *Daily Times* said. "He performed his duty as he saw it with the law of the land behind him and a conviction that he was doing his full duty in his heart."

Despite the heat, few spectators left the courtroom during the lunch recess. They didn't want to miss anything, as Donna Starr's husband, Burgess, was scheduled to testify in the afternoon. During the recess Burgess, described by the *Telegram* as "a man of robust stature and intelligent appearance," sobbed with his head between his hands, declaring that "he would give

Seattle Daily Times
Burgess Starr

his soul up to damnation a thousand times if he might thereby restore his family to the happy state in which it was before Creffield's advent."

Burgess's testimony began: "Two or three years ago I first mentioned to George Mitchell that Esther, his sister, was attending the meetings of Creffield, and I told him that I did not think it was an appropriate place for her to go." He covered many of the same points O. V. had covered, and like O. V., he wept on the stand. He was continually drying his cheek with a handkerchief, especially when he testified that Donna, his wife, was "the most fanatical of all Creffield's followers." When Burgess spoke of Donna's going to the coast to join Creffield, and abandoning his children—George's nieces and nephew—George, for the first time since the trial started, laid his head on his arms and cried.

"I had a talk with George Mitchell when he was in the hospital, early in April this year," Burgess concluded with. "He seemed 'off' at that time, and told me he was going to kill Creffield."

On cross-examination, Miller asked "Does it seem commonplace to hear a man talk about killing another?"

"No."

"Why then didn't you tell the officers of the law if you believed Mitchell to be insane and dangerous?"

"I did not believe George would do what he said he would," Burgess replied. "George told me there would be no trouble, as he was commanded by God to remove Creffield."

What else could he have said? *Right after O. V. Hurt informed me that George had succeeded in killing Creffield, I looked at my own revolver, and cried: "Oh, if he had only been seen in Portland!"*

Both Lewis Hartley and Edwin Baldwin, described by the *Post Intelligencer* as "two men in the prime of their lives, perhaps beyond it—men of an age when carefully considered judgment is supposed to have conquered the rash impulses of youth," testified that they had been ready to kill Creffield on sight. Lewis testified to telling young Mitchell about following Cora and Sophie, his wife and daughter, to the coast.

"My object, gentlemen, to be frank with you, was to kill Creffield," he said. "Having no gun with me, I went to a second-hand store and bought a cheap weapon. By mistake or trickery, I don't know which, the dealer sold me a center-fire revolver and rim-fire cartridges. When the party took a boat to cross the bay to South Beach I drew a bead on Creffield. Had my cartridges been all right that would have ended the matter. The gun snapped and Creffield got away . . . . Later, when I met Mitchell, also hunting for Creffield to kill him, I told him how I had missed the Roller. He did not seem surprised nor displeased. . . . He said the reason I had failed was because God had left it for him to kill Creffield. He seemed utterly out of his mind."

Poor Mackintosh and Miller. What sort of cross-examination could undo the damage of such testimony?

A dignified man admits on the stand, under oath, with no prompting, no trying to hide behind the Fifth Amendment, that he not only wanted to kill Creffield, but that he tried to kill Creffield. His only regret, he says, is that he failed to kill Creffield!

Edwin Baldwin testified to seeing young Mitchell at the Albany railroad station in May when both of them were looking for Creffield. He testified that at that time he told young Mitchell about his daughter Una and what Creffield had done to her, how he, her own father, "would remove her from the earth, rather than permit her to ever again get under his control." He testified that he begged young Mitchell for the privilege of killing Creffield.

Edwin said that, in his opinion, young Mitchell was "crazy" at the time, as he would talk only on one subject—that of the harm done his sisters and the necessity of losing no time in fulfilling his destiny of killing Creffield. "I tried to show Mitchell," Edwin said, "how much better it was that I, in my old age, with but, at best, only a few more years to live, should find Creffield, and remove him from the earth, than that he should persist in his determination."

"Testimony of this kind," the *Oregonian* said, "coming from men of reserved and conservative manner, had a profound effect upon the jury."

Prosecutor Miller, on cross-examination, sought to discredit Edwin's testimony by asking him why, if he seriously thought the defendant was insane, he didn't try to disarm him. Some in the courtroom looked at Miller with incredulity.

A man says that he'd rather remove his daughter from the earth than permit her to ever again get under Creffield's control, and now the prosecution is asking him why he didn't disarm the defendant if he thought he was insane? Has everyone gone insane—defendant, witnesses—even the assistant prosecuting attorney for King County?

"Sir, you ought to be able to get fine clothes without grafting in this case and trying to punish this innocent boy," one of the rabble, an elderly Baptist church worker, said to Miller afterwards. "Your efforts at this trial will never do you any good, and you will live to be sorry for what you are trying to do." Miller, dressed in an immaculate blue suit, tan vest, highly polished shoes, and a straw hat of the very latest style, raised his hat and stood for a moment waiting for a further attack from the woman. When none came, Miller replaced his hat, and bade her good day.

The woman who had chastised Miller was only one of George's many female admirers. Like Creffield, he was getting quite a following—although his was viewed as being a lot healthier.

Better to be entranced by a murderer than someone claiming to be the second Christ.

"The interest of women in the case is becoming marked," the *Oregonian* noted. "This afternoon there were more women than men in the courtroom, and all listened eagerly to the revolting testimony adduced. . . . While the testimony seems to be the principal attraction, Mitchell is also a drawing card, and there is a continual craning of necks for a better view of him."

And not all of his female admirers were old. Speculation on the identity of one beautiful young woman dressed in a white suit who at every noon recess presented George with a large bouquet of roses provided the attorneys and the other officers of the court a welcome diversion. No one knew who she was, but, naturally, it was assumed she was "a young women of high character and standing."

Evening Telegram

Lewis Hartley

This had the makings of a wholesome romance—far different from the perverted affairs Creffield had had.

It became customary for the deputy sheriff who escorted George to and from the jail to allow him a few minutes conversation with the mystery woman, and George always wore on his lapel one of the roses she had given him. During the day he would frequently turn to see if she was there. And she always was. And she always responded by smiling at him.

James Berry, described by the *Telegram* as "a well-to-do business man," and one-time fiancée of Maud Hurt, now become the Widow Creffield, testified that he "told Mitchell" about how he himself had been a supporter of Creffield's. That was until "he told me that he needed money to build a tabernacle," James testified. "He told me that I must sell all my valuables, including my automobile, and give the money to him . . . . Then Creffield and I had a falling out, as I would not do the things he said."

After that, James said, Creffield loudly threatened that God would "smite" him.

What tame testimony this was after stories about a man having sexual relations with children in front of their mothers and then having sexual relations with mothers in front of their children. A well-to-do businessman being asked to give up an automobile—even a new $690 Oldsmobile—was hardly the same sort of villainy. But it did show what an all-around scoundrel Creffield was.

Lynn County deputy sheriffs John Catlin, described by the *Daily Times* as "a little man well along in years . . . a veritable Dogberry . . . also garrulous," and George Van Dran, described only as "an Albany hotel-keeper," also testified to seeing young Mitchell at the train station. Both said they believed he was "crazy." They said they urged him to eat, but he had said he couldn't until he'd accomplished his mission.

John spoke of "turrible heavy rains in southern Oregon," of late trains, and of many other incidents that fixed in his mind the day the defendant was in Albany.

On cross-examination, Miller asked John why, if he believed the defendant was crazy and intent on killing a man, he hadn't detained him, or at least searched him. "That certainly should have impressed you as being your duty as an officer of the law," Miller said.

"Young man," Catlin snapped, "I, with my twenty-five years as an officer, believe that I know what is my duty. In that time a man has many experiences, and I have learned that it does not do to arrest or search every man who acts kind of crazy."

Even judge Frater couldn't help chuckling at this.

Doctor F. W. Brooks, said by the *Daily Times* to be "one of the most prominent physicians in Portland," and Harriet Hager, a nurse at Portland's Good Samaritan Hospital, gave testimony similar to one another's. Both testified that they had known young Mitchell for a number of years, that "he was a man of good reputation," that they had attended him when he had the measles in April, that he was extremely weak mentally and physically when left the hospital, and that he "had left the san-

itarium long before he should have." They both testified that
while young Mitchell was suffering from a fever he claimed his
mother's spirit had revealed to him that he had to "bring this
unholy influence of Creffield to a close."

And like everyone else who heard George threaten Creffield,
they said they did nothing to stop him.

What could they have been expected say? *The spirits, as we
testified, didn't reveal to young Mitchell "the manner" in which
he was to accomplish this mission. How could we have known he
was going to gun the man down?*

Mary Graham and William Gardner (no newspapers gave
descriptions of them), matron and superintendent of the Boys'
and Girls' Aid Society, both testified that, in their opinion,
"Esther Mitchell was crazy." Gardner came to Seattle a few
days before expected, and for some reason Judge Frater allowed
him to sit at the defense's table with young Mitchell and his
attorneys. Usually all witnesses waited outside the courtroom
until they were called to testify.

Mary Graham testified that "Esther was incorrigible in her
Holy Roller practices, insisting upon rolling on the floor and
praying until late in the night." Graham also said she was
afraid Esther "might be seized with a hallucination that God
had commanded her to kill some of the children or keepers."

Gardner testified that young Mitchell came to him to ask
that special care be taken of his sister, as Creffield was planning to abduct her from the Aid Society. Gardner then said that
when he asked young Mitchell whether he wanted to see
Esther, Mitchell became excited, and cried: "No, I cannot stand
to see her! I never want to see her while she is in that condition!"

On cross-examination, Miller asked: "Mr. Gardner, you
remember my visit to you at Portland some weeks ago, do you
not?"

"Yes."

"Am I mistaken in my impression that you distinctly told me
at that time that you had never seen George Mitchell?"

After a moment Gardner replied: "Yes, you are in error in
that respect."

The mayor and two other men from Newberg, George's child-hood hometown, were called to testify to the streak of insanity that ran through the Mitchell family. All of them were well acquainted with Charles Mitchell, young Mitchell's father. Morris asked each of them similar questions, essentially about any "oddities or eccentricities" they might have noticed about the elder Mitchell. Miller objected to the testimony. It was one thing, he said, to show a family history of insanity, another to show a family history of "eccentricities." The objections were sustained. The only testimony the men succeed in getting before the jury was that "the defendant's reputation in Newberg was good." But, of course, everybody by now already suspected that.

Seven of George's friends—including Anna Hager and Louis Sandell, brother of Mollie Hurt—were called to testify about young Mitchell's insane behavior shortly before the murder. They all testified that George had always been a man of "good character" until shortly after he left the hospital. Then his actions were so peculiar that, as Louis Sandell said, "Mitchell was as crazy as a loon."

On cross-examination of Anna Hager, Miller asked whether she herself wasn't a spiritualist.

Yes, she was.

So it was not her opinion that the belief in spirits constituted "mental unsoundness"?

"No." It was her opinion that the problem George had was that "the spirits with whom he conversed with were not the proper kind of spirits."

Not the proper kind of spirits? Miller asked no further questions.

As none of George's friends could be classified as insanity experts, most of their testimony about his mental unsoundness—his looniness—was found to be inadmissible and was ordered stricken from the record.

And so the defense called an insanity expert—or as a head-line in the *Post Intelligencer* reported, "MITCHELL INSANE EXPERT TESTIFIES." Actually, five "experts" testified: Doctor

Donald A. Nicholson, "an expert in nervous diseases"; Doctor W. I. Miles, "one of the foremost medical men in the city"; Doctor Arthur C. Crookall, onetime superintendent of the Minnesota State Asylum for the Insane and now a "Seattle medical expert"; Doctor John Wotherspoon, "an insanity expert"; and Doctor Wright, yet another.

Shipley asked the doctors hypothetical questions about an imaginary man behaving as George Mitchell had behaved. What sort of diagnosis would they make of such a man?

"I would say such a man was possessed with a delusion," Doctor Nicholson said, "and had lost control of himself; that as a result of this delusion he was insane. The fact that he had expressed this desire for such a long period, in opposition to the arguments of others, would show he had a delusion. The belief in the direction of God for one man to kill another is pretty generally agreed among authorities not to be the working of a normal mind."

Doctor Nicholson also stated that the danger such an imaginary man believed his sisters were in, especially in light of their past connection with the Holy Rollers, might tend to make him insane.

Shipley then asked questions about the probable mental condition of other members of such an imaginary man's family. Doctor Nicholson stated that he would expect to find similar mental conditions, or "dispositions," although not necessarily similar actions, in them.

On cross-examination of Doctor Miles, Miller said: "The founder of the Mormon church claimed that he had received a revelation from God, and that he had been directed by this divine inspiration." (Joseph Smith, founder of the Mormon church, said that he had had a vision that Jesus Christ told him not to join an established church because all churches were wrong, and later Moroni, an angel, told him that the story of the first North Americans was engraved on a buried plate. Smith claimed to have found the plate and in 1830 published his translation, the *Book of Mormon.*)

"Was that an insane delusion?" Miller asked Doctor Miles.

"If he actually believed it," Doctor Miles answered, "it was."

Miller said that there were some people who believed that

prayers are answered, and ills are cured by prayer. "Do you regard such beliefs as insane delusions?"

"If adhered to beyond the point of reason, it is," Doctor Mills said, adding that "those holding such opinions were entitled to their beliefs, and so long as they did not carry them to the point of absurdity, the 'divine' healers could not be classed as demented."

Miller, formed his own hypothetical situation. "A certain sect believes the Christ has not yet appeared, while another insists that he came in Jesus. . . . Pick the insane delusion."

"There was none," Miles held.

Afterwards another elderly woman cornered Miller as he left the court. "Are you not ashamed of yourself in trying so hard to indict that boy who did a brother's duty in trying to defend his sister against a reptile?" she wailed.

When John Manning, Multnomah County's district attorney in Portland, stepped up to George Mitchell and warmly shook his hand in Judge Frater's courtroom, many realized it was an unusual sight. A public prosecutor didn't appear in the interest of a man accused of cold-blooded murder every day. Manning's action produced a murmur of satisfaction and approval among young Mitchell's friends in the courtroom—meaning all of the spectators—all of the rabble.

> *If George Mitchell had killed Creffield in Multnomah County I would never have issued an indictment against him* [Manning had said beforehand]. *In fact, even if I had been willing to prepare an indictment there could have been found no complaining witness in that part of the country who would have attached his or her name to the complaint.*
>
> *There is no possibility that Mitchell or any other man who would have had the nerve to put Creffield out of the way would have ever had to suffer any penalty for an act that would only have been considered in the light of a public benefit. No court in the state of Oregon would ever have convicted Creffield's slayer of any criminal act in removing such a beast from the face of the earth.*

"The appearance of Mr. Manning on the stand," the *Oregonian* commented, "was the signal for opening hostilities." And indeed it was. After stating his name and occupation, Morris asked Manning to tell the jury what he knew of Creffield's power over George's sister, Donna Starr.

"Objection," Miller said, practically before Morris finished asking the question. "The material is irrelevant, immaterial and incompetent."

"Sustained!" Judge Frater said, and dismissed Manning from the stand.

M. P. Burnett, Sheriff of Benton County, was then called and after the usual preliminaries was asked a question similar to that asked Manning. Not surprisingly, Miller objected. Judge Frater then expressed annoyance at Morris's persistence in asking questions that he had already ruled against. What followed was one of the liveliest legal skirmishes in a trial full of lively legal skirmishes, a skirmish that ended with Morris stating that he would "insist upon entering every scintilla of evidence," that the defense intended "to overcome every obstacle put in their way by the state—even if it takes all summer!"

And who knows—if Judge Emory hadn't been murdered the next day, the trial might have gone on all summer.

And when they shall have finished their testimony, the beast that ascendeth out of the bottomless pit shall make war against them.—Revelation 11:7

CHAPTER TWENTY-ONE

TWO OTHER MURDERS

MURDER KEPT FROM MITCHELL JURORS
Headline, Portland *Evening Telegram*, July 9 1906

That Saturday Judge George Meade Emory was sitting with his wife on their front porch when Chester Thompson rushed up and demanded to see Charlotte Whittlesey. Chester was trying to renew his courtship with the young woman but had been thwarted by her parents and her uncle, the judge. "She's not here," Judge Emory said. Chester, bareheaded—it's already been established by the *Albany Democrat* that sane people don't go bareheaded—pulled out a revolver and fired three times. The right kind of cartridges in the gun, Judge Emory fell dead before his astounded wife.

"I was in the tank when young Thompson was brought in," George said. "I did not realize the danger to me in the killing of Judge Emory until the attorneys spoke of it . . . . But that seemed so different from my case that I did not think much of it."

The cases may have seemed different to George—a love affair gone wrong, versus saving the virtue of a family; but Morris worried that if the jury heard about the Emory shooting, they would just see the cases' similarities—another young man who would probably plead temporary insanity after brazenly shooting someone.

Compounding matters, there was yet another murder that people all over Seattle were talking about. On the first day of George's trial, stories about his case shared the nation's front pages with stories about young Harry Thaw's murdering Stanford White in cold blood.

What is happening to today's youth? people were wondering.

On June 25 much of New York's high society was packed into Madison Square Garden for the opening of a new musical, *Mamzelle Champagne*. The show was so dull that people left early or milled about chatting with friends in the roof garden. Suddenly Harry Thaw, in front of dozens of witnesses, pulled out a pistol and shot Stanford White three times. White lay dead in a pool of blood, his face blackened and unrecognizable from powder burns.

"Good God, Harry!" Harry's wife, Evelyn, cried. "What have you done?"

"All right, dearie," he calmly said. "I have probably saved your life."

As screaming women fought their way to the exit, the manager tried to restore order by jumping up on a table and shouting: "Go on playing! Bring on the chorus!"

"He deserved it," Harry said to the arresting officer. "I can prove it. He ruined my wife ['life,' some thought he said]."

At the time Harry's mother, Mrs. William Thaw, was in England visiting her daughter, the Countess of Yarmouth. When she heard about the shooting, she announced that she was prepared to pay a million dollars to save her son's life—no need to post signs around town requesting donations to assist young Thaw. To represent Harry, Mrs. Thaw hired "the Napoleon of the Western Bar," Delphin Michael Delmas, born in France and now an attorney from San Francisco. Described to be a man "short in stature but mighty in voice," he had a record of nineteen acquittals in nineteen murder cases.

Stanford White, the victim, fifty-two, a big man with red hair and a big moustache, was at the time America's most distinguished architect. One of his most famous creations was the

Evelyn Nesbit   Harry Thaw

building he died in, Madison Square Garden. Although married,
he spent much of his time in the company of young women,
including Harry Thaw's wife, Evelyn Nesbit. And he didn't just
keep her company. White, Harry said, had been seducing her
since she was a child.

"He seemed very kind and fatherly," Evelyn said of White.
"He always treated me just like a father except in the way he
took advantage of me. Outside of this one awful part of his life
he was very nice, very kind. . . . Outside of that one terrible
thing Stanford White was a very grand man."

*Outside of that one terrible thing Stanford White was a very
grand man? Was Evelyn insane? Then again, was it any odder
than Esther Mitchell thinking her seducer, Edmund Creffield,
was the Second Savior?*

Like Esther Mitchell, Evelyn Nesbit first met her paramour
when she was a teenager. It was in 1901 when she was sixteen
and in the chorus of the musical *Florodora*. She was a beauty
with an oval face, copper curls, hazel eyes, a voluptuous mouth,
and a splendid figure, one of the girls that Gibson men in gray
cutaways and top hats asked: "Tell me, pretty maiden, Are there

any more at home like you?" To which the girls demurely replied: "There are a few, kind sir, but simple girls, and proper too."

White befriended not only Evelyn, but her mother too. When Evelyn's mother went to visit friends in Pittsburgh, White offered to care for Evelyn. "You may leave her with me in perfect safety," he assured her mother. But as soon as White was alone with Evelyn in his house, he seduced her after giving her champagne.

During Harry Thaw's trial Evelyn testified that she had "told Harry" about this seduction. As in George Mitchell's trial, having a witness testify to telling the defendant a story was the only way of getting the murder victim's foul deeds before the jury. It was not hearsay because it was not offered as evidence of White's seductions, but as evidence of Harry's state of mind when he killed White.

> *He* [White] *came to me and told me to finish my champagne* [Evelyn said], *which I did, and I don't know whether it was a minute after or two minutes after, but a pounding began in my ears, then the whole room seemed to go around . . . .*
>
> *Then I woke up, all my clothes were pulled off of me, and I was in bed. I sat up in the bed, and started to scream. Mr. White was there nude. . . . There were mirrors all around the bed. There were mirrors on the side of the wall and on top. Then I screamed, and he came over and asked me to please keep quiet, that I must not make so much noise. He said, "It is all over, it is all over." Then I screamed, "Oh, no!" . . .*
>
> *He said that everything was all right. . . He said everybody did those things; that all people were doing those things, that that is all people were for, all they lived for . . . . And then I looked at him and said, Does everybody you know do these things? And he said, "Yes." And the first thing I could think of was the Florodora sextette. I asked him if the sextette did these things. He sat down and started to laugh, and laughed and laughed and laughed.*

Evelyn testified that after she had "told Harry" this story, it preyed on his mind constantly until, in an insane "brainstorm," he decided to kill White.

"No jury on earth will send me to the chair, no matter what I have done or what I have been, for killing the man who defamed my wife," Harry said. "That is the unwritten law made by men themselves, and upon its virtue I will stake my life."

Harry Thaw, thirty-four, hoped to be viewed as a hero, as George Mitchell was. On the surface, their cases seemed similar. Both of them had killed men who had committed reprehensible acts—Harry a man who had done "those things" with most of the *Florodora* sextette, and George a man who had done "those things" with most of Corvallis's Salvation Army garrison.

But Harry Thaw was never viewed as a hero, for he was almost as vile as his victim. Harry, son of William Thaw, a *nouveau riche* Pittsburgh railroad and coke magnate, had been in one notorious escapade after another before this. His studies at Harvard focused almost solely on the finer points of poker, and he had once lost $40,000 in a single game. On another occasion he threw a party in Paris at which his guests were the city's leading whores.

When his father died, Harry was given an allowance of $200 a month until such time as he showed himself responsible enough to handle his $5 million share of a $40 million estate. His doting mother, however, enabled him to resume the playboy life he had enjoyed by upping his allowance to $80,000 a year.

Before their marriage, Harry traveled with Evelyn through Europe. After their travels, Evelyn went to a celebrated shady lawyer, Abe Hummel, and swore out an affidavit about Harry mistreating her in a castle he rented in Austria:

> *The said Thaw said he wished to tell me something, and asked me to step into my bedroom. I entered the room, when the said Thaw, without any provocation, grasped me by the throat and tore the bathrobe from my body, leaving me entirely nude except for my slippers. I saw by his face that the said Thaw was in a terrific, excited condition, and I was terrorized. His eyes were glaring and he had in his right hand a cowhide whip.*

He seized hold of me and threw me on the bed. I was powerless and attempted to scream, but the said Thaw placed his fingers in my mouth and tried to choke me. He then without any provocation, and without the slightest reason, began to inflict on me several severe and violent blows with the cowhide whip. So brutally did he assault me that my skin was cut and bruised. I besought him to desist, but he refused. I was so exhausted that I shouted and cried. He stopped every minute or so to rest, and then renewed his attack upon me, which he continued for about seven minutes.

He acted like a demented man. I was absolutely in fear of my life . . . .

It was nearly three weeks before I was sufficiently recovered to be able to get out of my bed and walk. . . .

One day my maid was in my room taking things out of the drawers and packing them away. I found a little silver box, oblong in shape, and about two and a half inches long, containing a hypodermic syringe and some other small utensils. . . . I realized then for the first time, that the said Thaw was addicted to the cocaine habit . . . .

During this entire period, while I was in this condition of non-resistance the said Thaw entered my bed and, without any consent, repeatedly wronged me. I reproved the said Thaw for his conduct, but he compelled me to submit thereto, threatening to beat and kill me if I did not do so.

Evelyn Nesbit affidavit

Evelyn Nesbit may have looked like an innocent—much like Esther Mitchell—a young girl who was taken advantage of by unscrupulous men, but Evelyn wasn't a complete innocent. After having the affidavit drawn, Evelyn, at the suggestion of Stanford White, coerced Harry into marrying her by threatening to show the document to the authorities and have him charged him with "corrupting a minor."

Why did she want to marry "the said Thaw," a man she knew was a paranoid sadist? For one of the oldest reasons: greed. She wanted wealth and a position in society. "This is a case where a woman lay like a tigress between two men, egging them on," New York's district attorney, William Travers Jerome said.

If George's jury now found out that a third young man in as many months had publicly murdered someone, it would be very hard for them in good conscience to acquit George.

"A desperate effort may be made tomorrow by the prosecution to get some inkling of the murder of Judge George Emory before the jury," the *Oregonian* commented. "Some chance remark, some slight intimation or else a bald reference to the tragedy may be given. It is a subterfuge and a trick, and one likely to result in punishment for contempt of court, but the attorneys representing the state may attempt to influence the jury by letting the arbiters of Mitchell's fate know that another man has been shot down in Seattle by a youth who will plead insanity."

The prosecution promised they would make no such attempt, and Judge Frater did his best to prevent the jurors from hearing about the latest murder from other sources. He went so far as to instruct the bailiffs to take the jurors to and from their meals by a new route so they wouldn't see the courthouse flag flying at half-mast.

Morris stated that in order to hasten matters and make it possible to adjourn court on the day of Emory's funeral, the defense would waive the right to put a number of witnesses on the stand.

That settled, the trial proceeded—until the cholera epidemic broke out among the jurors.

Save yourselves from this untoward generation.—Acts 2:40

CHAPTER TWENTY-TWO

THE VERDICT

**GOD BLESS YOU, GEORGE,
WE'RE PRAYING FOR YOU.**
Headline, *Seattle Star*, July 2, 1906

It turned out it wasn't a full-blown cholera epidemic, just one very ill juror, H. E. Start. Doctor John B. Loughary was called in to examine him. Ironically, the defense had at one time considered calling Doctor Loughary—a "brain specialist" and former assistant superintendent of the asylum at Steilacoom—as a witness, but thought he might hurt their case and not help it. For a time then, the prosecution thought about calling him as a rebuttal witness. Now the doctor was being called in to make a diagnosis on Start.

"Cholera morbus," he said, an illness "characterized by profuse vomiting and purging." It can be fatal, so Doctor Loughary said it would hardly be advisable for Start to take his seat in the jury box. If Start couldn't finish the trial, however, a mistrial would have to be declared.

After the attorneys and the judge discussed the matter, it was decided to leave the matter with the juror and abide by his decision. Start said that he would try to carry out his duties.

"May it please the court, your honor," Morris then said, "we

offer to submit our case without argument. We realize that
every one concerned in this trial has been placed to considerable
inconvenience and are anxious to bring proceedings to a speedy
close. We are willing to let the case go to the jury on the instructions of the court."

*Why couldn't George Mitchell have chanced upon Creffield in
Canada?*

While appearing to have put the jury's interests—especially
poor Start's—before his client's, Morris's real objective was to
prevent Prosecutor Miller from making his closing summation.
Miller was an eloquent and persuasive speaker who had been
known to win cases on the power of his closing arguments
alone. There was talk circulating among members of the King
County bar—many of whom on this day had joined the rabble
and were also spectators in the courtroom—that Miller had prepared an argument that was so convincing that at least one or
two jurors would surely vote to convict George Mitchell of first-
degree murder, and even the most biased jurors would find him
guilty of second-degree murder.

"On behalf of the state," Miller said, almost sputtering, "may
it please the court, we would gladly accede to the suggestion of
counsel were it not for the fact that we deem it our duty to proceed as is customary. It is not for personal reasons that I oppose
the suggestions of counsel, but because of the fact that I feel we
would not be doing our duty by the state if we agreed to waive
the right to which we are entitled under the law."

Judge Frater, also caught off guard by the defense's tactic—
he hadn't even finished preparing his instructions to the jury—
said he agreed with Miller and told the prosecution to proceed
with their closing arguments. Mackintosh gave his summation
first, saving Miller for after the defense gave theirs.

Mackintosh's closing argument was short, as he was leaving
the most dramatic and critical parts of their case for Miller to
cover. Prefacing his argument with the customary "May it
please the court and gentlemen of the jury," Mackintosh dwelt
for a few moments on the tediousness of the trial and on the
supposed desire of all concerned to have it over as soon as possible. He stated that the defendant had seen Creffield when the
latter was a block and a half away from the scene of the shoot-

Seattle Daily Times

Silas M. Shipley and Will H. Morris

ing, had waited until his intended victim had passed, then approached him from behind—and "fired the cowardly shot."

The question before the jury, Mackintosh stated, was whether or not the facts of the killing constituted a deliberate and premeditated murder. "There are three defenses in a case of a killing of one man by another. One of these is that of self defense, another is where the murderer makes his escape and then tries to prove an alibi, and the third is, as in this case, where the man is caught in the act and then sets up the plea of insanity; all other defenses having been eliminated by the nature of the crime and the conditions surrounding it."

Mackintosh spoke of the difficult situation the prosecution had been put in because of the peculiar nature of the evidence admitted to establish the insanity claim. "There was no way in which the statements of the various witnesses as to the doings of the Holy Rollers could be refuted," he said. "Even had these statements been false, they had, according to the testimony of the witnesses been made to the defendant, and consequently the effect on his mind is a matter of legal consideration."

Furthermore, he said much of the testimony appeared to have been "prepared beforehand, and with a view of securing the acquittal of the defendant." Mackintosh also cautioned the jury not to pay too much attention to "expert evidence prompted by the pocketbook."

And of Donna Starr, "the only sister of the defendant who had been seduced by Creffield," Mackintosh said, she "was of an age where she was capable of reasoning for herself, and . . . the fact that she had given away to the teachings and desires of the dead man was no reason why the defendant should come to Seattle and commit murder."

Mackintosh quoted the decision of Judge Orange Jacobs in the case of William McAllister vs. Washington Territory: "The world has had quite enough of that kind of insanity which commences just as the sight of the slayer ranging along the barrel of a pistol marks a vital spot on the body of the victim, and ends as soon as the bullet has sped on its fatal mission."

Mackintosh urged the jury to remember the statement each of them had made under oath—that "in arriving at a verdict the character of the victim of Mitchell would not be taken into consideration," and that they would not allow sympathy to influence them.

Once Mackintosh had finished, Morris stood up and announced that the defense would waive its right to argument.

My God, why couldn't George Mitchell have chanced upon Creffield in Canada?

Morris's legal maneuver was brilliant. By waiving his right to argument, Miller would be precluded from making his final argument. Of course, Morris didn't say that, declaring instead that he was doing this because the jurors were worn out, one was seriously ill, and the issue was "clear to the court and jury."

Judge Frater was also taken off guard, but he concluded that in such an important case he would rule that the state should be allowed to make its final argument. Besides, he still hadn't had an opportunity to finish preparing his instructions to the jury. Morris then said the defense was ready with a long argument. Shipley was prepared to give a speech several hours long, and he himself proposed, if necessary, to read testimony from the trial at length.

Miller conceded defeat. He knew the jury would blame him—not the defense reading testimony at length—for any more delays. He said he would be willing to forgo giving his closing argument as long as the court explained to the jury that the waiver was by "mutual consent."

And so, after a brief recess, Judge Frater gave his instructions to the jury:

> *One who takes human life cannot be said to be actuated by malice aforethought or to have deliberately intended to take human life, or to have "a wicked, depraved and malignant heart" or a heart "regardless of social duty and fatally bent on mischief," unless he at the time had sufficient mind to comprehend the criminality or right and wrong of his act, and sufficient power of will to choose the right and avoid the wrong . . . .*
>
> *The court instructs you that the nature, character and degree of insanity or loss of reason which exonerates a person from criminal responsibility is not easily explained or understood . . . .*
>
> *You are the sole and exclusive judges of the facts and the degree of credit to be given to the testimony of the different witnesses who have testified before you. In weighing their evidence you have a right to consider their demeanor upon the witness stand, their manner of testifying, their apparent candor and fairness or lack of it, the interest which they have in the result of the trial of the case, if any, their bias or prejudice for or against the defendant, if any is shown, the opportunities they have for knowing the facts with reference to which they have testified and from all the facts and circumstances it is*

*your duty to give proper weight to the testimony of each
and every witness who has testified before you.*

Judge Frater instructed the jurors that they could return one
of three verdicts—murder in the first degree, murder in the second degree, or not guilty. The verdict of manslaughter was not
an option. At 3:14 p.m. George Mitchell's fate was in the hands
of the jury. None of the spectators, not even the ones who were
members of the King County Bar, left the courtroom. Most
believed that the jury would return the verdict in a few minutes.

"Right here I wish to state that if an acquittal is obtained,"
District Attorney John Manning said, "one of the greatest facts
in praise of the attorneys for the defense is the credit of winning
against the masterly fight put up by Mr. Mackintosh and Mr.
Miller to secure a conviction."

Mackintosh and Miller may have put up a masterly fight, but
at that moment they felt that it had all been for naught. All the
objections, all the wrangling and bickering about the introduction of this or that bit of evidence—it had all been a waste of
time and energy. They felt that the jurors, even if they didn't
believe George Mitchell was insane, were going to "perjure"
themselves in order to free him. "It's a strong word," the *Star*
said, "but it fits."

"Had the defense rested when the old man from Corvallis [O.
V. Hurt] finished telling the jury of the debasing practices of the
Holy Rollers," a member of the prosecuting attorney's office
said, "the case would have been decided by the jury without
leaving the box. We have been beaten for a week."

At 4:40 p.m., after less than an hour and a half of delibera-
tion, the jury had reached a verdict. Clerks and courthouse visitors rushed from all surrounding offices to listen to the
announcement.

Judge Frater appeared nervous as he mounted the bench. He
admonished the spectators that, no matter the outcome of the
case, he would not tolerate any demonstration. George bit his
lower lip till it seemed he would bruise it, and he breathed so
heavily that the heaving of his chest was apparent to those in
the furthermost corner of the crowded courtroom.

The verdict was handed to Judge Frater and he handed it to the clerk, Dell Case. Case read it in a clear, strong voice that everyone in the crowded room could hear.

"Not guilty."

Despite Judge Frater's warning that he would not tolerate any demonstration, those that weren't in the front row directly under his eyes—even some members of the King County Bar—applauded and cheered.

For a moment afterwards George sat in his chair motionless and stared straight ahead of him. Then he reached out and grasped the hand of Will H. Morris, his senior counsel.

Bailiff Gallagher pounded his gavel in a vain attempt to bring order to the court. Yelling, so he could be heard over the noise, Judge Frater ordered George be "remanded into the custody of the sheriff."

"What is that, your honor?" shouted Morris. "This man is innocent, and I want him to be free! If you are going to give him into the custody of the sheriff I want to begin habeas corpus immediately."

Judge Frater acknowledged his error, saying he was merely trying to get the crowd under control and out of the courtroom by the instruction, and that, yes, yes, the sheriff should let George go and the jurors were excused from further duty.

As the twelve jurors passed George, he shook each by the hand and thanked him. "From the introduction of the first testimony," one of the jurors said, "there was never any question as to what the verdict would be."

As George elbowed his way into the corridors of the courthouse, women rushed after him. They followed him down three flights of stairs to the jail doors where he headed to gather his belongings. Women peeped through the bars as the jailers and the prisoners greeted him with shouts and cheers. He shook hands with all of them.

"Goodbye, boys," he said to Deputy Sheriff Larson and Sheriff Smith. "You've been mighty good to me, and I want to thank you for it."

"Mitchell was a very unusual prisoner," Sheriff Lou Smith said. "He was quiet and kind, and in the short time he was here we had come to like him very much. In fact, there have been few here whom we cared for so much as that boy."

"It was hard enough to spend two months in jail," George said, "but they have been kind to me here and they have made it just as pleasant as possible. So far as one can enjoy confinement, I have found pleasure in it, but of course, no one really enjoys being locked up."

As George left the courthouse and walked downtown with Perry and his attorneys, people all along the way yelled congratulations. Extra editions of the afternoon papers announcing his acquittal reached the business district before he did.

Perry could hardly contain his, joy—smiling, laughing, and constantly patting George on the back. "George and I are going to stay in Seattle for a few days," Perry told Morris and Shipley. "He has not seen anything of the city as yet, you know."

George had other ideas, though. "I want to get away from it all here," he said. "Just as soon as possible, I want to get back to Portland. I expect to be there tomorrow night." And then for some reason he added: "But something may prevent it."

The verdict buries Rollerism forever [O. V. Hurt said]. *It went to the grave with Creffield. It is past history, and I thank God and the Seattle jury for it. And to Will H. Morris and Silas M. Shipley, whose untiring efforts on entirely inadequate compensation* [\$650] *have done so much to secure the verdict of acquittal, immense credit is due. Finally, the Oregonian and other Portland papers, and the Seattle papers, whose influence was exerted from the first on the side of right and justice, have aided materially in helping to stamp out this guilty cult from the Northwest. God bless the newspapers of the country.*

In conclusion, I desire to add that it is a solemn thing to take a human life. Few are the times that such an act is justifiable. But it is also a solemn thing to enter a household and take the light and happiness out of it, or to enter a mind and take its sanity away. If George Mitchell did the one, it was because someone else did the other, not once, but many times. I hope all the past

Rollerism is buried, and that this is to be my last public or private utterance on the hated subject.

It wasn't his last utterance on the subject, though, for the real madness began soon thereafter.

Go, and sin no more.—John 8:11

THE MADNESS

CHAPTER TWENTY-THREE

SEEKING RECONCILIATION

MADNESS
Headline, *Corvallis Gazette*, July 16, 1906

The day after George's acquittal, Charles Mitchell called on Police Matron Kelly and asked where his daughter Esther was. He wanted to take her home with him to Illinois. He agreed with Shipley, who had told him "that so long as she stays here surrounded by scenes and people which will always revive and continue the outrageous beliefs taught by Creffield there is no chance of her ever being herself."

Charles had already begged Esther to go home with him, but she had said she wanted to stay with the Widow Creffield. The widow, who always called Esther "dearie" or "darling," was equally devoted to the young woman. It would be hard to separate the two.

Shipley said, be that as it may, if Esther refused to leave the Widow Creffield—a woman who he thought was probably insane and a woman whom Esther was obviously wholly under the influence of—Charles should hire some men to put her on a train . . . by force if necessary. Shipley had spoken to Assistant Prosecuting Attorney John F. Miller about this, and Miller had said he would not interfere if such a plan was carried out.

When Esther had called on Miller after the trial, he too had tried to persuade her to go back home with her father. "I do not ever care to see any of my people again," she said, "for they have not treated me right. George lied about us and we will have no more to do with him." But Miller wasn't proposing she go home with George, but with her father. She said that her father's home "held no pleasure" for her and that she "had never been able to get on" with him or her stepmother. What about one of her other brothers? None of them had paid any attention to her, she said—except maybe Fred, but he "was addicted to the use of liquor." Still, Miller thought she would be better off in Illinois with her father than in Seattle with the Widow Creffield.

Matron Kelly, though, didn't think the women were that off. "During the time the two women were under my care they were quiet and lady-like," she said. She told Charles that Esther and the Widow Creffield had rented a room at the Pretoria Rooming House at the corner of Sixth Avenue and Pike Street and planned to find work in Seattle. When Charles went to visit them, he brought along Fred. George had very much wanted to see his sister, too, because he wanted to seek a reconciliation with her. But he thought it best if he were not present at this particular meeting.

Esther was cordial with her father and brother Fred, but she said that she had no intention of going back to Illinois—and that since she was now eighteen she could do as she pleased. She then softened her tone, adding: "I do not hate George. I did not wish to have him hanged, but I do believe that he ought to have received some punishment for the killing of Creffield."

Maybe Esther isn't crazy the way people say she is, Charles thought. Maybe she really can care for herself.

Besides, he didn't have the money to take her back with him anyway. He asked her at least to come to the train station to see him off that evening. He was going to go to Dayton, Washington, to visit his son David, and then he intended to return to Illinois—alone. He would leave her in Seattle and pray for the best.

George and Perry had planned to leave Seattle that day, too, but Louis Sandell had asked them to spend the night as his guests in southeast Seattle. They accepted his invitation, as it

Morning Oregonian

Union Depot in Seattle

could be a time to begin rebuilding friendships. A small group of Holy Rollers, including Frank and Mollie Hurt, were also staying at Sandell's.

Esther did go to the train station to see her father off, but when she saw George was there too, she promptly left. She didn't even take the time to say goodbye to her father.

The next day when Fred arrived at the train station to see George and Perry off, he told them that he'd visited Esther again and tried one last time to convince her to say "goodbye" to George. She adamantly said "No." Just in case she changed her mind, Fred told her that her brothers were taking the 4:30 p.m. train for Portland from the Union Depot. So Perry was pleasantly surprised when he saw her standing behind a pillar at the station. She was scanning the faces in the crowd, presumably looking for him and her other brothers.

Esther

Fred

Perry

George

Diagram showing how Esther Mitchell killed her brother

Evening Telegram
The shooting at Union Depot

"Why, Esther," Perry said, putting his arm around her and kissing her.

"I just came down to see you off," she said. She was dressed for the occasion. A jaunty new sailor hat sat squarely on her head, and a white satin ribbon was tied in a neat four-in-hand on her throat, the ends of which streamed down over a white shirtwaist. Her dark skirt was a bit short, barely coming down to the tops of her shoes. Draped over her arm was a coat.

Perry waved to George, whom Esther had not seen yet. George, not knowing whether his sister intended to speak to him, turned and faced the ticket agent's office. Esther hung back until Fred pleaded, "Won't you say goodbye to George before he goes away?" Reluctantly she walked up to George and took his hand. "Goodbye," she said softly.

The four of them chatted for a few minutes. George, as always, said little. He was glad that Esther had forgiven him enough to come to the station. He knew that she hated him for what he had done, but he hoped that, in time, she would see that he had acted only out of love.

At about 4:20 the station master announced "Traaa-in for Tacoma . . . Centralia . . . Chehalis . . . Kelso . . . Vancouver . . . Portland . . . and all waaay points." As the brothers rose, Esther offered to accompany them to the platform. They walked down the south corridor of the main waiting room, Perry and George in front, and Fred and Esther in the rear. Fred offered to carry Esther's coat. That wasn't necessary, she said. Fred insisted. It really was too warm for a coat, he said.

As Fred took the coat from her arm, Esther took a revolver that had been concealed beneath it, and pressed it close to George's left ear. The revolver's report reverberated through the vast waiting room, and George Mitchell fell dead at his sister's feet.

⟡

"I have no regrets!" for the past is all clear,
With its labor of love for my Savior so dear;
On his errands so sweet I have sped with delight,
All my pleasures by day and my song in the night:
"I have no regrets!" bless the Lamb that was slain!
"If I could I would do it all over again."
From the Reverend Knapp's
Bible Songs of Salvation and Victory

CHAPTER TWENTY-FOUR

No Remorse

Eye for eye, tooth for tooth, hand for hand,
foot for foot.—Exodus 21:24

"Oh, Esther, how could you do it?" Perry cried, dropping
to his knees beside George, his hero. "Esther, Esther.
How could you? How could you?" Fred grabbed
Esther and she sank into his lap. Bystanders rushed to the
scene, including, by a curious coincidence, Officer Huth, the
policeman who had arrested George after he shot Creffield.

"I am George Mitchell's sister and I shot him," Esther said.
Like George, she submitted to arrest without protest.

George's body lay in the center of the main waiting room
until Deputy Coroner Shirley Wiltsie arrived and ordered it be
taken to the Bonney-Watson Funeral Company, the same establishment that Creffield's body had been taken to. While waiting
for a patrol wagon to arrive, Esther, with hardly a quiver of an
eyelash, watched her brother's face turn black and a pool of
blood form around his head.

Within twenty minutes of the fatal shot, the *Daily Times* had
an extra edition on the streets. By evening's end, they had put
out seven extra editions. The story of George's murder received
bigger headlines than his acquittal—literally. The headline,

Seattle Daily Times
Headlines screamed the news.

"AVENGE DEATH OF CREFFIELD," covered two-thirds of a page, the word *avenge* alone covering one-third of a page. It wasn't often that a woman who had been chosen to be the mother of the next Christ committed fratricide in a crowded train depot.

"It is almost too terrible to believe; however, I can't say that I am s u r p r i s e d , " Prosecuting Attorney Kenneth Mackintosh said upon hearing of the murder. "Nothing in that case would surprise me."

Police Chief Charles W. Wappenstein declared that he had had enough of the Holy Rollers and that no more of them would be tolerated in Seattle. "I wish," he said, "these Oregon people would kill each other on their own side of the river [the Columbia River]."

Assistant Prosecutor Miller was pale when he arrived at the Bonney-Watson Funeral Company. "I can't believe it," he said, looking at George laid out on a slab. "I can't believe it."

The limbs had stiffened before the body could be straightened out, and George's head was turned to one side. A reporter lifted the head so that Miller could get a better look at the face.

"That's the boy," Miller said. "That's the boy. My God, what is this country coming to!"

The reporter asked about the case, but Miller ignored him.

"Let me out of here," he said, leaving for the police station. "I don't want to stay here."

At the station Perry was so distraught that he could hardly tell officers his version of the events. "When I saw her at the depot she came toward me as though she was glad," he said. "She greeted George without saying anything, but in a manner that indicated that she was ready to be reconciled." Perry sat sobbing and holding his head. His shirt was stained with blood from a nosebleed, and tears ran down his cheeks leaving grimy streaks. "I do not care to talk over this thing any more," he whimpered. "How can we ever get over this?"

Fred, who was much cooler and calmer, nervously twirled George's cap in his hands.

> *This is all I have to remember my dead brother by* [he said].

> *No one had the slightest intimation that Esther would ever attempt to harm George, although we looked for some such attempt from Mrs. Creffield.*

> *Esther is not to blame. Don't treat her too hard, for she did not know what she was doing. I believe the act was done at the instigation of Mrs. Creffield, who has her completely in her power as "Joshua" held his victims. I can't believe that my sister was in her right mind and committed this awful crime. Her mind has been broken down by the influence which Creffield held over her and this, followed by the killing of him, and the constant companionship of Mrs. Creffield since she came to Seattle, must have caused the loss of her reason.*

Esther was composed as she was escorted through the crowd that had gathered at the police station. Almost as soon as she entered Police Chief Wappenstein's private office, she looked straight at him and with absolutely no signs of remorse said: "I killed him because he killed Joshua. We were commanded to do it."

"It is the eyes that attract most attention," the *Post Intelligencer* said of her. "She has a way of fixing them on her questioner, with a piercing gaze that makes it at once apparent that here is a woman who with the right kind of stimulus, is capable of almost any act, no matter how it may appear to the world at large."

"My brother ruined me when he told the newspapers the lie that Creffield had seduced me," Esther said. "He knew it was a lie. He never was my friend. When I was a mere child he would not do anything for me."

Erased from her memory was how she and George *had* doted on one another after their mother had died and their father had abandoned them, how George *had* cared for her then as best as a boy of eleven could, how George *had* always shared his meager earnings with her, stopping only after the money he sent her "was steadily finding its way into Creffield's pockets."

Now Esther was saying of George: "I am glad he is dead."

> *I am ready to pay the penalty for what I did. George had to be punished for killing Joshua. . . .*
>
> *He was a holy man. My brother was of the world and was defiled. It was right that he should be punished for what he did, and the law set him free. . . .*
>
> *I did right, but I know the law does not think that I did right. I might as well hang. My brother George ruined my reputation. When a girl's reputation is gone she has nothing to live for. I never could get away from the stories he told after he shot Creffield. Creffield never did me any wrong and my brother had no right to say he did. . . .*
>
> *Mrs. Creffield had been out once or twice looking for George, and if she had got the chance she would have done it. . . .*
>
> *Mrs. Creffield and I had talked over the matter of killing George. The one that had the best chance was to do it. . . . I thought that I would have a better chance to do it than Mrs. Creffield, as my brother George wanted to see me, and I believed that he would think nothing about me going to the depot. . . .*
>
> *I took the gun yesterday and my brother Fred walked with me down to the depot when my father went away. They wanted me to see George, and I didn't want to, because I couldn't get the gun unwrapped. I had the gun wrapped up and concealed, and I refused to see George.*
> [The Widow Creffield had told her to not put it directly

next to her bosom, to wrap it so that her perspiration wouldn't rust it.]

When I went home I took the gun and placed it under the mattress. Then I took it out about noon today and kept it with me. My brother Fred was up to my room today and said that Perry and George were going to Portland at four o'clock. I went to the depot and saw Perry get his ticket, and I followed him.

At last I saw George, and I shook hands with him and I was walking to the door with him. He and Perry were walking in front and Fred and I were walking behind.

At that time I had the gun in my coat, having removed it from my bosom where I had it concealed.

Fred offered to carry my coat, and I told him "all right."

Then I was walking to the door and George was in front of me.

It was just the chance I wanted and I shot him. . . .

I fired once, and tried to fire another [shot], but there was such a loud noise made by the crowd that I don't know whether I fired again or not.

I shot him in the head, and I knew if I hit where I intended it was sure death.

I intended to follow him to Portland if I did not shoot him here.

When the police matron searched Esther, she found only a few cents upon her and no train ticket. Esther had planned, if it was necessary, to have her brother buy her a ticket to Portland, where she would kill him. She had given the rest of her money to the Widow Creffield. If Esther failed to kill George and was arrested—or killed herself—the widow was to try her hand at slaying George.

The police didn't have to search long for the Widow Creffield who had said she "would walk to Walla Walla to see George Mitchell hung." She telephoned the chief to tell him that she was at a grocery store on North Broadway. She had been visit-

TAKEN YESTERDAY MORNING IN HER PRISON CELL AT SEATTLE BY
WEBSTER & STEVENS, PHOTOGRAPHERS.

Morning Oregonian
Esther Mitchell, in a Seattle jail

ing the cemetery, she said, and when she left it she heard that Esther had accomplished her mission. She said she presumed that she too was wanted. When Detective George Brown arrived at the store, he found her patiently waiting for him.

Back at the station, she readily admitted to conspiring with Esther to kill George. As always, as she spoke, the features of hers commanding the most attention were her large, expressive, dark eyes.

I had as much right to cause his death [she said] *as he had to kill my husband . . . .*

As soon as George Mitchell shot my husband, I made up my mind to kill him. . . . Every once in a while I spoke to her [Esther] *about killing George. Sometimes, my courage was weak, and then the papers came out and praised him so. I got courage again and made up my mind to do it. . . .*

During the trial of George Mitchell I became aware that public sympathy was with him and the verdict of the jury came as no surprise to me. During the trial I was unable to sleep nights and would often pace the floor in the middle of the night, thinking of the deed and that the murderer would evade punishment. . . .

When I heard the jury said "not guilty" I went up to Esther's room and told her I would kill him. . . . I told Esther from what was said—what I heard—they [the Mitchell brothers] *suspected me and I didn't think I would get a chance to kill him. She said she would do it then. . . .*

At first I wasn't willing to let her, but afterward I became willing. . . . I told her I would be glad if she would, and that I was determined he had to die. . . .

It cost me much more to let Esther do the deed than if I did it for myself, for I didn't know whether she would accomplish it as satisfactorily as I would. . . .

When Esther left me, she left with the understanding that if she got a chance at the depot she would kill him. . . . I told her I would be greatly relieved when I heard that she had killed him. . . .

Well, I feel a great deal more relieved, not because Mitchell was killed, but because my husband's death was avenged.

Police Chief Wappenstein asked whether she would speak to reporters: "No, I do not wish to see them," she said. "Now is the time for them to go and mourn over the man they have been praising for killing my husband."

As soon as Mackintosh heard that Esther had killed George, he sent two "insanity experts" to the jail: Doctors Alex H. McLeish and John B. Loughary, former superintendent and assistant superintendent of the asylum at Steilacoom. Doctor Loughary was the "brain specialist" that Morris and Shipley had thought about calling as a witness during George's trial, but didn't call. There were two possible outcomes of his and McLeish's examinations: if they declared the women were insane, the state would send them to an asylum; if they declared the women sane, the state would try them for first-degree murder. Under no circumstances would Mackintosh release these murderers as he had George Mitchell.

The Widow Creffield said there was no need to waste time with these examinations, as she was not planning to plead insanity. "I expected to be punished at the time, and expect to now," she said. "I will not admit that I am crazy, for I am not . . . . I don't care what comes now."

Esther said she too would never plead insanity.

Such a course [she said] *would be the height of folly.*

And besides I don't think that a jury will look upon my act as justifiable because of the manner in which I committed the deed. . . . I will not enter a plea of insanity because I think that would be false and I am not insane in the least, as anyone who has the slightest acquaintance with me can testify. . . .

Before shooting my brother I gave all the possible results the fullest consideration. I knew that I would be arrested, and that the excuse I had for doing what I did would not be considered by the court. . . .

I knew what I was doing—I committed the deed intentionally. That is all there is to it. . . .

Asked whether she knew the punishment for her crime, she said: "What, for murder in the first-degree? It is hanging isn't it? I suppose that is what they will do with me." Reminded that it was a plea of insanity that kept her brother from the gallows, Esther replied: "Yes, he was set free, but he didn't enjoy his liberty long, did he?"

After his initial examination, Doctor Loughary said he would need to meet with the women every day for two or three weeks before submitting his final findings, but for now he said they were rational on all subjects except one—Creffield.

⚜

"And ye shall be hated of all men for my name's sake: but he that endureth to the end shall be saved."—Matthew 10: 22.

Chapter Twenty-Five

"What can papa do for you?"

God sent His mighty pow'r To this poor, sinful heart,
To keep me ev'ry hour, And needful grace impart;
And since His spirit came To take supreme control,
The love-enkindled flame Is burning in my soul.
'Tis burning in my soul, 'Tis burning in my soul;
The fire of heav'nly love Is burning in my soul.
The Holy Spirit it came, all glory to His name!
The fire of heav'nly love is burning in my soul.

From the Reverend Knapp's
Bible Songs of Salvation and Victory

By the time Esther emerged from the police station, several hundred people had gathered, and the authorities feared mob violence. Patrolmen were stationed at various points outside the building to keep the rabble in check if it went out of control. Matron Kelly held Esther's arm as she faced the crowd, but the young woman's steps were firm, and it was clear that she did not want the assistance.

Esther was put in Lou Smith's custody, the sheriff who had said of her brother, George: "There have been few here whom we cared for so much as that boy." He took her to the county jail in a private carriage, and at her request, drew the blinds to shield her from curious onlookers. At the jail she was locked alone in a cell off the jailers' office.

"Not once during the night did she murmur," the *Star* reported all knowingly. "For her there were no horror dreams, no blood-stained phantoms of a murdered brother to trouble her girlish sleep; no vision of the gallows disturbed her slumbers. No young woman in Seattle went to sleep with a lighter heart than did Esther Mitchell last night."

The Widow Creffield arrived at the jail sometime after Esther and was locked in the women's tank. She spent the night "surrounded by the off-scouring of

Morning Oregonian
Attorney Will H. Morris

the red light district," and "the oaths that fell from the lips of other women prisoners, and the sight of a burly negress sitting on a table smoking cigarettes, disgusted her."

The next morning the jailers said that the two women "rose bright and refreshed, dressed with care, going over every little detail of their toilets with the care of women planning a social day."

To the jail officials these two women are a revelation. Crime is an old story to these officers of the law, but never in all their experience have they had to do with prisoners who are as indifferent to what the future may have in store for them as are Esther Mitchell and Maud Creffield.

These men of the law have seen confirmed criminals haunted by the thought of what they have done; have seen thugs and murderers pace their cells at night and grow haggard and old with worry and fear and scheme as to how liberty can be obtained; but never before have they seen anyone in their charge display as great an indifference as do these two women, one a girl in her teens with the blood of a brother upon her hands and the belief that she will be hanged possessing her, and the other, a shade less guilty in the eyes of the law, but holding to her heart the satisfaction that she is avenged for a husband's death and fully cognizant of the likelihood that prison walls will be the horizon of her world so long as she may live.

The *Daily Times*

"I am in hopes of hearing from my father," Esther said. When Perry and Fred had telegraphed him the news, they assumed he would return immediately from David's. Charles had only been in Dayton for a couple of days, but he was already viewed as a curiosity there because of his marked religious fervor—his Salvation Army uniform making him all the more conspicuous. He did cancel an appointment he had to preach at the United Brethren Church, but he refused to return to Seattle.

She will have to abide by the consequences of her crime [Charles said]. *I cannot help her, but I glory in her determination not to plead insanity, agreeing with her that she had better die upon the scaffold with truth upon her lips. I am an honest and upright Christian and do not justify falsehood under any circumstances, however great the provocation. . . .*

She is no more crazy than I am. I have been called crazy, but I hope that the species of insanity with which I am afflicted is incurable. If religious enthusiasm is to be regarded as insanity, then God grant that I shall continue insane.

My daughter was above the average girl in intelligence and nothing but the powers of a strong hypnotist could have induced her to do what she did. . . .

I believe that until some more powerful hypnotist

*than Creffield shall take action in the matter, the vic-
tims will continue to be the fanatics that they have been
for some time.*

Esther's brothers weren't about to help her either.

If she [Esther] *wants a lawyer to defend her she will
have to find one herself* [Perry said]. *I owe her nothing,
she killed George and she should take the consequences.
She preferred Mrs. Creffield to us and now she should
pay the penalty. . . .*

*It's pretty hard. She is our sister. We know that, and
that's what makes it so hard, but after all we've done
and tried to do, she killed George, and I don't see how
we can do anything to save her. . . .*

I do not care what happens to her. . . .

I do not believe that I ever want to see the girl again.

"I will not be defended at my trial," Esther said. "I have no
money and have no friends to whom I could go for it if I would,
and I would not. . . . I understand that when anyone has no
money the court gives them a lawyer, but I don't see what is the
use so far as I am concerned."

"Esther shot and killed George in depot this afternoon,"
Louis Sandell wired O. V. Hurt who was already back in
Corvallis.

"My God," O. V. said. "What could the girl have been thinking of to do such a terrible thing?"

He promptly sent his daughter Maud a telegram, the messages's seven words speaking volumes about his character:
"What can Papa do for you, dear?"

He was still the Widow Creffield's papa and she was still his
dear. His love was unconditional. No matter what she did—plot
the cold-blooded murder of a dear friend, shame the family
name, spurn his love and say he was defiled—he would always
be her papa and she would always be his dear.

He had sacrificed practically everything he had to help pay
for George's defense, so now he had little left to pay a lawyer for

his own dear. No lawyer with a good reputation wanted to handle the women's cases, but many who had small practices were willing to take it on for the publicity it would give them.

"Have arranged defense for you and Esther," O. V. said to his daughter in a second telegram. "Will write. Father and Mother." And he did write.

> *My Own Dear Girl,*
>
> *I hardly know how to commence to write to you this morning. I expected to see you before this, but the attorney said I could do nothing by going. I wired you yesterday that we had secured help for you, and this is all we can do now until your trial. Then we will be with you. Only God knows my feelings.*
>
> *Oh, Maud, my heart is broken about this, and after all I love you more than I ever did. You're my daughter, and nothing, as I told you at the depot, could drive me away from you. But I cannot realize that my sweet Maud would have ever allowed herself to do such a rash act. My God! My God! help us at this time.*
>
> *I know they will not hang my girl, but I am afraid of the penitentiary. Don't talk too much, Maud; don't talk to anyone but your lawyer. I will send him to you. I can't write more at this time. Write to me, dear, and tell me all.*
>
> *Your Loving Father*

Although pleased that her parents still obviously cared for her, the Widow Creffield said she hardly thought it worthwhile for them to waste money on her. When her attorney arrived at the jail she asked how he could defend her? Was he not really disgusted with her.

"No," Will H. Morris, said. He wasn't really disgusted with her, he said, but had "come to extend his sympathy."

O. V. wasn't about to put his dear's fate in the hands of any one but the best. So, he mortgaged his house and hired the law firm of Morris, Southard, and Shipley.

For where your treasure is, there will your heart be also.—Matthew 6:21

CHAPTER TWENTY-SIX

"HUMAN LIFE IS TOO CHEAP
IN THIS COMMUNITY"

MRS. CREFFIELD LOADED DOWN WITH
WEAPONS TO KILL GEO. MITCHELL
Headline, Portland *Evening Telegram*, July 13, 1906

"I am greatly upset by the shock, but there is nothing else, in view of the circumstances, that I can do but offer assistance to my deluded daughter," O. V. Hurt said when asking Morris and Shipley to defend the Widow Creffield. "My little home here will only bring about $500 on a mortgage, but I am willing to sacrifice it for my daughter's sake. If the two women are tried together, I am willing to back both of them."

Morris and Shipley were at a loss. It would be inappropriate for them to defend women charged with the murder of a former client, but they had too high a regard for O. V. simply to say "No." They told him that they would help secure good counsel for the women.

And until then?

Yes. They would do what they could for his dear.

I feel it my duty as a father to assist her all I can [O. V. said in a statement to reporters]. *While I deplore the act as much as anyone living and am not upholding the deed, I do not think she was mentally responsible, con-*

sidering the strain she has been under. I have said so all along and I feel sure of it. I consider Esther Mitchell in the same unbalanced mental state. . . .

I have fought with all my power for the destruction of Rollerism. I went to all honorable ends that a man can go to in the defense of George Mitchell, and I would do it all over again. More deeply, perhaps, than any other human being do I feel and know what George Mitchell's removal of Creffield meant for families affected by Creffield's doctrine, and it was by that token that I felt a freed slave's gratitude for the verdict of the Seattle jury and the restoration of George Mitchell to his liberty.

But all this does not mean that because Maud Hurt Creffield and Esther Mitchell plotted and accomplished the death of George Mitchell, I, the father of one of these, shall turn my back on her, and though knowing better than do all others how she is duped, deluded, hopelessly irrational, join in general cry for her destruction. In every case, no matter how mean, the law contemplates a defense. In the present moment, if Maud Creffield's father does not stretch out his arms, who will? To those who impugn me let me say, if Esther Mitchell had once said to Mrs. Creffield, "Don't kill George Mitchell. He is my brother," George Mitchell would have been alive this day. In saying this I desire to shift no blame from one of these unfortunate creatures to the other, but merely to keep all the facts in view when the deplorable subject is under discussion. . . .

All I ask is a fair trial and no favors. Let the evidence on both sides be heard, and let the verdict be on the evidence and the law. I ask no more.

After making this statement, O. V. received an anonymous letter threatening that if he continued to aid his daughter, he would be "fixed."

Police Chief Wappenstein was thunderstruck when he learned that the Widow Creffield had three revolvers—

although she never had more than one in her possession at any time. Did they have another conspirator who gave them a gun? If not, where did the money come from to buy a gun? Weren't she and Esther penniless?

"When Mrs. Creffield was turned over to me by the police she had a revolver," Matron Kelly said, giving the chief the gun. "This was the one that she took from her room immediately after the killing of her husband by George Mitchell. When she came to my house, I asked her for the revolver and she gave it to me."

The second revolver was given to the Widow Creffield by someone during the time she was under the matron's care.

> *I found her with the weapon in her possession* [the matron said]. *Taking it from her I demanded to know what she intended to do with it. She merely smiled and refused to answer. . . .*
>
> *After the women were discharged by the court and released from custody, they wished to secure the return of the revolvers. To this I would not assent. Esther told me they wished to pawn the revolvers and get some money. I told her that if she wanted money I would lend it to them. She smiled again and said she was not entirely broke. All she wanted was the guns.*
>
> *"If you don't give them to me I'll only have to go down and buy another," said she. But I refused. . . .*
>
> *Tuesday night she* [Mrs. Creffield] *returned to my house to get some clothes she had left there. She asked me to give her the two revolvers I had. I again refused, and she said, "Why you might as well give them to me. I have money enough to buy another one." I thought nothing of the remark at the time. . . .*
>
> *Neither of the girls cared to discuss the killing of Creffield during the time they were in my charge, but Maud stated to me once that there would be more shooting. I replied that there had already been too much, but she answered that there was more to come. . . .*
>
> *I never saw any sign of insanity in either of them, and I have had a great deal of experience with insane*

people. The only thing which made me doubt Mrs. Creffeld's sanity at times was the strange light in her eyes.

The only thing which made her doubt Mrs. Creffield's sanity at times was the strange light in her eyes? Talk of more shootings didn't strike her as being a sign of someone who was a bit off? She thought nothing of the remark that Esther had enough money to buy another gun? Had the matron also gone mad?

"The police matron was guilty of gross carelessness," Chief Wappenstein said. Had he known these details, he said, he would have had the women watched after they were released from police custody.

So who had given the women the second and third gun? "Frank Hurt," Fred Mitchell said, demanding that the Widow Creffield's brother be arrested immediately. "I know that there is a colony of these people who have ruined my sister, and Frank Hurt has been providing them with money," he said.

The Widow Creffield said Frank was unaware that she and Esther were planning to kill George, that in fact he was probably very upset when he heard about the deed. He wasn't high on the list of suspects, as he—unlike others from Creffield's flock—had never said anything against George. He took after his father in that respect—not publicly denouncing those he opposed.

What about Donna Starr, Esther's sister? "George Mitchell is no better than any other criminal who commits murder," she said after George's acquittal, "and he should have been punished just like any other man. The trial was a farce, the verdict a travesty of justice."

Burgess suspected his wife may have been in on the plan. During their stay in Seattle, Donna had talked to Esther daily, sometimes calling her as many as eight times a day. One day her phone bill was thirty-five cents! Furthermore, before Burgess and Donna left Seattle, Esther had asked Donna for money.

"About how much?" Donna asked.

"Oh, not a great deal," Esther replied. "Just enough to tide me over for a few days, and then I'll not need any."

And then there was Donna's reaction upon hearing about George's murder. Burgess learned of it first, hearing of it while waiting for George and Perry's train in Portland. Despite the fact that Donna had told him that under no circumstances was he to bring George home with him, he worried that the news might still upset her.

He saw to it that she didn't see any copies of the special edition papers. After supper he said as gently as possible: "Can you stand to hear some terrible news?"

"I think I can, what is it?" she replied.

"Esther killed George this afternoon."

Seattle Daily Times

Judge Archibald Frater

Her lips tightened and a strange look crossed her face. It was an expression a sister would be expected to have after hearing her brother had just died. But it passed in a flash. Donna smiled and began playing with her little girls. "I am not sorry that Esther did it," she said. "I am glad. Esther did the right thing. It was only a just retribution. . . . She did the right thing."

When Donna's joy over her brother's death was reported, she too began receiving threats. "If you do not desist I, or if I cannot, some other member of the club, will mete out to you what your sister dealt her brother. G. C. G.," one letter said. Donna took the letter to District Attorney John Manning. He had no sympathy for her or any of the other Holy Rollers. He took no action, and G. C. G.'s identity was never learned.

The Widow Creffield and Esther had told no one of their

plans, least of all Donna. "We did not talk to anybody about it," the Widow Creffield said. "Mrs. Burgess Starr, a sister of Esther and George, was the one person above all others that we tried to keep in ignorance. Esther knew that she could not keep a secret and she kept warning me not to let her know anything about our plans. No one but Esther and I knew what we were going to do."

In fact, when Donna told Esther she was going to leave Burgess so that she could live with her and the Widow Creffield, Esther urged her not to. "Stay with your husband," Esther had said. "He is good to you, and as long as he is you will have nothing to regret."

Police learned that the murder weapon hadn't been given to the women, but that the Widow Creffield had bought it at Spangenberg's Cutlery Store.

Previously I had thought of Mrs. Creffield as some ill-dressed and eccentric individual [Herman Spangenberg, said when explaining that he hadn't recognized his now infamous customer]. *When she was in our store Mrs. Creffield was dressed very neatly, talked in an ordinary tone of voice, and there was not the slightest thing about her actions or manner which would lead anyone to believe that she was other than perfectly sane. . . .*

The woman said she wanted a revolver to keep around the house. She said she wanted to pay about $10 for the weapon. I told her that there was none at that price. The cheapest we had was $6 and the next lowest was $14. She examined the $6 weapon I showed her for a few minutes and bought it. She also bought a box of cartridges for 60 cents. . . .

Had there been the slightest doubt about her actions we would not have sold her the gun. . . . The woman selected the gun, had it wrapped and paid for it, leaving the store quietly and as if bent upon the most natural business in the world.

So where did the women get the money to buy a gun? The court. Neither had received compensation for the two months they were detained while waiting for George's case to come to trial, but they both received witness-fees for testifying at it.

There was an immediate call for gun control. The *Post Intelligencer* published an editorial headlined: "TOO EASY TO GET PISTOLS."

> *Seattle has been shamefully disgraced before the eyes of the country by three murders within a very few weeks of each other. Each murder was committed with a pistol.*
>
> *It is a difficult matter to regulate, it is true, but it should not be impossible to make it more difficult than it now is for anyone to purchase deadly weapons. A person determined to commit murder doubtless will find the means of accomplishing the crime, but if it is made difficult for such persons to procure revolvers that class of crime should become less.*
>
> *One thing needed is a mandatory ordinance with heavy penalty, providing that no dealer in firearms shall sell any weapon to any person without ascertaining that person's name and address, which shall at once be reported to the chief of police; and that all persons purchasing firearms shall also procure a license from the city to have them in their possession. No person desiring to make proper use of firearms can take serious exception to some such precautionary provision. It is practically impossible to procure deadly poisons at a druggist's without a reputable physician's prescription, or other authorization, and a pistol is as deadly as any poison. The form and prescription of such an ordinance may be left to the city's law officers, but a new ordinance is needed at once.*

There was also much discussion about how wrong George's acquittal had been and how wrong the public had been to support him so enthusiastically.

Human life is too cheap in this community. It is not only held too cheap by those who recklessly murder others on our streets and in the victim's own house, but by the public in general.

The demonstration made by the spectators in this courtroom when George Mitchell was acquitted was a disgrace to any law abiding community.

When a jury of twelve men returned a verdict of not guilty in a case where it was clearly proved that the defendant was guilty of a cold blooded murder under the laws, the spectators applauded their act.

They made a hero of a man guilty of murder in the eyes of the law and demonstrated their approval when a jury failed to do their duty and freed a murderer.

Judge Archibald Frater

The long editorials in George's defense were quickly forgotten by the editors, and superseded by ones denouncing George's release. For instance, the *Daily Times* had once said: "It may not be technically correct to take the life of such a scoundrel—but if there were more men like George Mitchell there would be fewer human beasts and still fewer broken, ruined women in insane asylums and on the streets." Now the *Daily Times* said:

Before the common eye Mitchell was justified in what he did—but he was not justified by either the moral or statutory law. . . . If Mitchell were insane enough to carry murder in his heart for two and a half years before consummating the deed he wasn't sane enough to be allowed to go at large after his acquittal—but should have been arrested promptly, and sent to Steilacoom, where the State incarcerated the insane.

The *Daily Times* also questioned the competence of the jurors, noting that "under our laws no man could serve upon the jury that tried Mitchell who knew anything about the story—which practically relegated the whole subject to a lot of men who at least do not read the daily newspapers."

"Juries are too lenient and the law is too loose," Deputy

Coroner Shirley F. Wiltsie said. "I am amazed at the number of autopsies upon murdered persons which I am called to perform. This thing of allowing men and women to kill in Seattle should be stopped some way."

Wiltsie and County Coroner Frank M. Carroll—who had supervised Creffield's autopsy—supervised George Mitchell's autopsy, while "brain specialist" John B. Loughary handled the knife. Of most interest to the physicians was not the cause of death—the carotid artery had been severed, and death was due to hemorrhaging—but the appearance of George's brain. Was

City of Seattle Archives
John F. Miller

it like the brains of others declared to be insane?

As soon as the brain was removed from the skull, the physicians crowded around it. The bullet that killed George had plowed through his skull and lodged in his right jaw bone, but didn't damage his brain. Esther's bullet had entered George's head at about the same spot as George's bullet had entered Creffield's head. This was no coincidence. Esther declared that she aimed at that spot on the head because, from Creffield's murder, she knew this meant certain death for the victim.

Every convolution, fold, dimple, and bump on George's brain was studied. "[After] a close and exhausting scrutiny," the *Star* reported, "it was the unanimous opinion of the experts in attendance that Mitchell's brain, instead of indicating anything abnormal, gave every indication that the boy in life had been gifted with more than average intelligence."

George Mitchell's death certificate listed "the cause of death" as "murder," with a "gunshot wound through head" cited as a "contributory factor." The death certificate for "Franz E. Crefield" simply listed "the cause of death" as "external violence."

The physicians declared that George Mitchell was as sane as

any ordinary man when he shot Creffield. Assistant Prosecutor John Miller said: "The discovery that Mitchell had a normal brain has merely confirmed the contention of this office that he was sane when he committed the murder." Furthermore, Miller said, the state would use the autopsy findings against Esther should her attorneys, like her brother's attorneys, declare that insanity ran in the Mitchell family.

Before this bit of evidence could be used in a murder trial, though, it was reported that Esther Mitchell had committed suicide. "It's a good thing," Manning said when he heard the news. "Mrs. Creffield ought also to commit suicide."

We share our mutual woes,
Our mutual burdens bear;
And often for each other flows
The sympathizing tear.
From the Reverend Knapp's
Bible Songs of Salvation and Victory

CHAPTER TWENTY-SEVEN

GRIEF

Ev'ry deed you have committed will appear before the throne,
All your inner, hidden secrets then shall certainly be known;
All the courts of heav'n assembled, what a gathering that
will be!
If you are not saved and ready, what a dreadful day for thee.
From the Reverend Knapp's
Bible Songs of Salvation and Victory

The report of Esther's suicide proved to be the reporting of a rumor. But at about that same time the Widow Creffield actually did report something almost as astonishing—she was having doubts about her husband's teachings. Not only that, she was also willing to speak to reporters about this.

> *After all this trouble I am firmly convinced that our belief along certain lines was not right . . . I am not the woman that I was when in company with Mr. Creffield, for I have become more or less sensitive to the fact that there were some funny teachings in our religion. . . .*
> *I have changed my belief since the time my dead husband was leading us in Oregon. We had both changed and we believed differently at the time of his death than*

*before. There are several things regarding our belief
which has changed. I might say that we eliminated all
the things the public generally condemned and had
reorganized our creed. . . .*

*It would not be right for me to say what features of
our practices were eliminated after the reunion in
Seattle this spring. When we were doing what we did in
Oregon we thought it right, and this being the case, and
having changed when we found further light and
viewed our practices as wrong, it is not for the public to
know what the inner workings of our religion was. . . .*

[And of her future?]

*I am willing to go to the penitentiary for life. I am as
happy here as I have been since my husband died. He's
dead and it does not make much difference what they do
with me or where they send me. I am tired of living any
more. . . .*

[And finally]

*There is one thing the reporters don't ask me about.
Everybody seems to think that I am a hardened criminal without the least bit of feeling and sympathy. I don't
shed tears the way other people do, but my heart is
almost breaking.*

*Won't you please tell the people that no woman ever
felt for her bereaved old parents more than I do. Tell
them that I would gladly give my life if I could return
them half the comfort that has been stolen from them.*

Soon after this, the jailers said they noticed a great change
in the Widow Creffield. She was no longer an automaton and
was now capable of expressing emotions. Her spell of fanaticism
seemed to have vanished. The Widow Creffield was once again
Maud.

Four days after the shooting, Perry and Fred Mitchell left for
Oregon with George's body—leaving from the same depot where
George had been killed, taking the same route he had planned
to take. From the moment that George's body arrived at the
Bonney-Watson Funeral Company, people came to view it. Most

Oregon Daily Journal
George Mitchell lies in state in Newberg, Oregon.

walked quietly by, stood for a moment and then left. Many of
the women brought flowers picked from their own gardens. A
profusion of sweet peas, nasturtiums, and other old-fashioned
varieties filled the funeral parlor. Little of the morbid curiosity
that people had exhibited when streaming past Creffield's body
was evident. Nearly everyone displayed genuine grief, and
many broke into tears.

One of the first mourners was the mysterious young woman
in the white suit who had brought George roses every day during his trial. Looking for some time into his still face, she laid a
bouquet on his chest and wept quietly. Afterwards, she disappeared in the passing crowd.

George's brothers had worried that he might be laid to rest
in a pauper's grave. "I think George ought to be buried beside
his mother," Perry said two days after the murder. "There's a lot
there and there's room enough for us all in it, and I think that's
where we all ought to be when our time comes."

Within a day of this announcement, $130.30 had been donat-
ed by readers of the *Star* for funeral expenses. The Bonney-
Watson Funeral Company's bill was $126, but they wrote off
$76. The remaining money was used for transporting the body
from Seattle to Portland, the funeral at the Friends' Church

cemetery in Newberg, and the purchase of a monument for the grave.

After the funeral, Perry went to Corvallis to see O. V. Hurt. He told O. V. that what made this so painful for all concerned was that both George and Esther had been family favorites. Perry said he expected he would be called to be a witness at Esther's trial, but that he no longer wanted her to be convicted. He said that right after the shooting he felt bitter towards her, but that now he had no such feelings. Now, he said, he would only be on the witness stand against his will, and, as far as he and Fred could, they would help her.

Upon hearing this, Esther shed the first tears she was seen to shed since her arrest. "I am glad of it," she said. "Fred and Perry were always good friends of mine. I always liked them. I knew that they would help me as much as they could . . . I am glad my brothers think well of me still, but I do not want their help."

Esther too would now speak to reporters.

"I have to do something to pass away the time," she said while polishing her shoes all the while.

"Do you look forward to the future?"

"No, I don't. I live from day to day and let the future take care of itself."

"Are you ever troubled by the memory of the shooting?"

"Not a bit, but I don't care to discuss that subject."

"Are you still a believer in Holy Rollerism?"

"Holy Rollerism? What is that? I don't know anything about it. The doctrine of Mr. Creffield? Is that what it is called? You apparently know more about it than I do. I have my faith, yes, but that also is something I do not care to talk about."

"Do you believe that Creffield was a holy man and was sent by God?"

"I never said I did."

She then made a request: "If you are from the *Post Intelligencer*, will you please deny the report in the evening papers that I mentioned the name of 'Joshua' to their reporter?"

And finally: "The evening papers said that I killed my brother because I was commanded by God to do so," she said, looking

George Mitchell's tombstone includes a tribute.

up and smiling. "That is wrong. I did it because he ruined my character. I am willing to hang. I killed my brother."

In August, before Esther's case went to court, she became sick with typhoid fever. As it was thought she might die, and would therefore soon have to atone for her sins on earth, some thought she might ask for forgiveness for killing George. She didn't.

> *Esther Mitchell is now lying on her cot in a little cell at the county jail tossing in the delirium of typhoid fever . . . .*
>
> *Not for one instant, so far as her jailers have been able to determine, has this girl suffered the slightest compunction for her crime, and now in her delirium she maintains the same serene indifference to her rash act and its possible results to herself. Not once during the almost incessant ravings of her fever-tortured brain had*

she mentioned the brother she killed, nor the man Creffield whose life this brother took to protect the virtue of the sister who repaid his kindness by murdering him close upon the heels of an acquittal by a jury. . . .

Now, however, she is beyond any restraint which she might have exercised while in her right mind, but the events of a month ago have evidently left no impression. During her almost incoherent mutterings this girl has talked of her childhood and of other things so trivial as to cause wonder that they ever made any impression upon her, but of the thing which one would believe must have seared her memory beyond the power of an instant's forgetting, she makes not a mention.

The Sunday Times

The deputy sheriffs permitted Maud to tend Esther. Up to this point the two had been separated from each other in the jail—Esther was kept in the cell off the jailer's office, while Maud was housed with the other women prisoners.

"So far I have felt no bad effects of prison life," Maud said. "The others here sleep and smoke all day, and are moving about all night preparing midnight dinners and so on. I have not become accustomed to sleeping in the day as yet. Nor to smoking either." But then she added: "The other women prisoners were very kind to me, and I try to be as kind as I can to them."

Now she was a dutiful nurse to Esther. "The woman who has played such an important part in the shaping of the girl's life does not leave her companion's bedside even for sleep," the *Daily Times* reported. "The night jailers declare that late at night upon their rounds they find her sitting by the girl's bedside, ready to minister to her needs."

<hr>

MAY NEVER FACE JURY OR JUDGE IN THIS WORLD
Headline, *Seattle Sunday Times*, August 12, 1906

CHAPTER TWENTY-EIGHT

INSANITY?

DID ONLY WHAT THE SPIRITS COMMANDED
Headline, *Seattle Star,* September 18, 1906

Esther recovered, but again something delayed her being brought to trial. Frank Hurt now swore to a complaint alleging that she and his sister Maud were now insane, were insane when George Mitchell was killed, and had been insane for a number of years before that. Judge Frater immediately appointed an "insanity commission composed of experts on alienism." It was something he had wanted to do practically from the time the two women were arrested.

I have no official knowledge of what the defense is to be in this case, but my understanding is that it will be insanity [he had said soon after the murder]. *There was considerable evidence introduced in the trial of George Mitchell to show that Mrs. Creffield had been confined in an insane asylum and that Esther Mitchell had become insane and was confined in the Boys' and Girls' Aid Society in Portland. Taking this evidence into consideration I think that it would be advisable if an insanity commission was appointed to report to this court whether or not these women were sane or insane when George Mitchell was killed. If the commission should report that they were insane I should send them both to the insane asylum and thus save the county and the tax-payers the expense of a trial.*

Mackintosh was aghast. "The reports of Doctors Loughary and McLeish [the two doctors who had been examining the women since the day of George Mitchell's murder] convinced me there was nothing in the mental condition of the women to warrant calling a commission," Mackintosh said.

He admitted that Judge Frater had the power to call an insanity commission, but he held that that should not preclude his right to demand a criminal trial. "You can say for me, that these women will be put on trial for murder in the first degree," he declared. "The desire to save the county expense is far from being a sufficient reason for turning the women loose without any attempt to convict them." Such an act, he believed, would be equivalent to announcing to the world that King County would rather save a little money—an anticipated $5,000—than prosecute people who commit murder within its boundaries.

This time around, the newspapers supported the prosecutors. "Seattle is not dodging her responsibility," the *Daily Times* said. "These people came from Oregon, it is true. But they committed a crime in Seattle—and violated the laws of this State. Washington is not only ready, but anxious to stand the necessary expenses of the trial for the simple reason that Seattle and the state of Washington do not propose to permit this to be a dumping ground for the criminal elements of other states. . . . Let's stop this 'cheap talk' about insanity and about saving a few dollars in court expenses. It's law and order we want, and we cannot have these without a strict enforcement of the penalty for their violation."

John F. Miller submitted an affidavit stating that questions about the women's sanity should be thrashed out before a jury when the women were put on trial for murder, not by an insanity commission. Judge Frater refused to consider Miller's affidavit. No matter how many affidavits the prosecutor's office submitted, he said, he was still going to hold sanity hearings.

Seattle Daily Times

An editorial cartoon addresses the insanity issue.

The prosecuting attorneys had requested that all the proceedings be conducted in open court. This request was denied, and many examinations were held behind closed doors without the attorneys or the judge present. The three physicians were also the only ones allowed to ask questions of the witnesses.

Even before testimony began, Mackintosh said he knew the commission's report would state that the women were insane, that he was being "jobbed." "Judge Frater came to me shortly after these two women had been arrested and suggested that a commission be appointed to inquire into their sanity," Mackintosh said. "I told him that in my opinion such a step would be useless, for I believed that it would be impossible to find a reputable physician who would find the women insane. To this Judge Frater declared that he would find a commission that would find the women insane."

Before the commission was appointed, a number of doctors claimed that they had been called upon by someone who told them that Judge Frater was putting together a commission *guaranteed* to declare the women insane. The man asked them, the doctors said, if they were appointed to such a commission, could they be counted on to declare the women insane? Frater denied ever sending anyone out asking such questions. That would constitute fraud, he said.

John B. Loughary was one of the doctors who claimed to have been approached in such a manner, and although not appointed to the commission he—having been one of the doctors who had been examining the women since the murder—was allowed to testify before it. But he said that when he did appear before it, he was "absolutely prevented" from testifying that he thought the women sane. The commission also refused to let Doctor Alex H. McLeish testify before it, even though he was the other doctor who had examined the women regularly.

There wasn't "one reputable physician of ability in it," Mackintosh said of the insanity commission that was supposed to be "composed of experts on alienism." Doctor Kenneth Turner, who headed it, was Frater's family physician. Although currently a member of the King County Medical Association, Turner's first application for membership two years earlier had been denied because of his "ethical standing in the profession." The other two doctors on the commission were R. M. Ames and J. H. Snively. Snively had finished medical school just a year earlier and had never before tried to determine anyone's sanity.

When Perry and Fred entered the courtroom before giving their testimony, Esther sprang from her chair, threw her arms about their necks and kissed them affectionately. "I don't want any of you to do anything for me," she then said solemnly. "I don't care whether they hang me or not, and I don't want the impression to go to the world that I am insane. I did a good deed, and I want the world to know it." She went back to her seat, leaving Perry in tears.

John F. Miller testified about conversations he had had with the two women. He said both had "always been reticent about their creed," although "they seemed to believe in a life after death." He said he himself didn't believe "in the immoral procedures alleged to have been indulged in by the followers of

Creffield," but allowed that "if such practices were carried on they were certainly unusual and irrational."

Of Miller's statement about the "alleged practices" of the Holy Rollers, O. V. Hurt said that the practices were even more "vicious and immoral" than what he had been able to bring himself to testify to. In his testimony before the insanity commission he himself emphasized that when his daughter Maud had been released from the Oregon Insane Asylum, she was released into his custody as a paroled patient who had not been cured of her insanity, and that she was still a paroled patient. He said his daughter had been somewhat insane for years, and that there had been several cases of insanity in his family. Finally, he said, Creffield had convinced his flock that he was going to be martyred and that one of his flock would be called to avenge his death.

Maud's mother had wanted to be there, too, as Will H. Morris thought her testimony would be useful. She was in such frail condition, however, that it was thought that if she were to go to Seattle, it would be necessary to take her on a stretcher.

Frank Hurt, who had remained quiet during George's trial, was evasive when he now testified. He claimed that although he had been a member of Creffield's church until the time of Creffield's murder, he knew little of its inner workings. He said that while he was a member he had believed in the practices of the church, but he now denounced them. Even though he was the one who had sworn to a complaint that resulted in this hearing, he would not state whether he thought the women insane.

Fred Mitchell, who had avoided having anything to do with George during his trial, now testified that, in his opinion, there was no question that Esther had been mentally unbalanced for some time. He was not pleased when the commission questioned him about his personal life and habits. He said that the physicians were "exercising a great deal of curiosity" on irrelevant subjects.

Perry Mitchell, James Berry, Superintendent William Gardner, and Matron Mary J. Graham, gave practically the same testimony now before the insanity commission as they had in George's trial.

Many of the police officers who had had dealings with the two women testified, including Jailers Smith and Larson who said that they believed the women were sane, although they "both acted unlike any other prisoners they had ever had to deal with."

Will H. Morris testified that shortly after he first met the two women, he came to believe that both were insane. He said that during the trial he was wary of all of Creffield's flock. As a precaution against the possibility that one of them might shoot George in the courtroom, he swore many of them in as witnesses even though he had no intention of calling them. After they were sworn in, they were then only allowed in the courtroom while they were testifying. Morris said he was so thoroughly convinced of Esther's and Maud's mental instability that, after George's acquittal, he warned the authorities that the two women should be closely watched because he feared they might kill George.

"I believe these women have such a weak mentality," Morris said, "that it will be impossible to convict them before a jury of twelve men and do not think the county should be put to the expense of trying it. I do not think they will ever become normal and think the place for them is an asylum."

Before Maud began her own testimony, she said she felt faint and needed to eat something. When she did testify, she said that even before she met Creffield, she had been deeply religious, was active in the Methodist Church as a child, and joined the Salvation Army when she was a teenager. After meeting Creffield, she came to believe that "the Army was teaching the Bible in a narrow manner." She was so impressed with Creffield's teachings, she said, that she left the army and joined him in "The Church" and married him in 1904.

On the morning of Creffield's murder, he told her "that his blood would soon flow at the hands of the enemy." She claimed that at the time she had no reason to believe someone would want to kill him, but if he thought this was so, "it must have been a demonstration of the supernatural powers which conveyed the idea to his mind." He also stated, she said, "that his death would be avenged"—but he did not state by whom.

She said that after her husband was killed, she was so disturbed that she could not receive a message from God. Entering into a state of prayer, she pleaded with God to tell her what to do. She said she eventually had communications with her husband through the spirits, and acted according to the instructions given her by those spirits in conspiring to kill George.

> *When I became composed it was witnesseth through my spirit that it was the will of God that I should kill George Mitchell. I feared that my desire and not the will of God was speaking to me, so I again entered into a state of prayer. Again God's word came to me that I should kill George Mitchell. There could be no mistake that it was God's will.*
>
> *My husband's spirit also spoke to me telling me that it was his wish as well as that of God that I should avenge his death. I knew that if I were to fulfill the word of God that I would be subjected to the penalty of man's law. But then I never considered the laws of men when the will of God has been made known to me.*

She was asked why, if she had been commanded by God to kill George Mitchell, she let Esther Mitchell do the slaying.

> *Until two days before the killing I intended to do it, knowing it was God's will that I should do so. At that time Esther came to me and said that God had made known to her that it was His will that she should kill her brother, George. Both of us had been in a state of prayer. I did not believe her. I was certain that it was God's will that I should do the killing. However, both of us again entered into a state of prayer and it was witnesseth to me that Esther was correct and that it was God's will that she should do the killing. . . .*
>
> *Esther told me that God had made it known to her that the reason she had been spared was to do the killing. She said that she had never suffered the persecutions that the others of the flock had suffered for the*

sake of the religion, and that God had made it known to
her that the time had arrived for her to do her part.

Doctor Turner pointed out that in her confession after her
arrest she had stated that she had been motivated by revenge,
not religious convictions. He handed her a stenographic report
of her confession, but Maud refused to read it. "I know what is
there," she said. She said that, before the murder, she and
Esther had agreed upon the statement they should give police.
Their reason for this was that they believed the public would
laugh at their religious motive and "mock and scoff at it."

Since her incarceration, she said, God had made it known to
her that, regardless of the consequences, she should make the
public aware of the true motives behind their act. "I know my
Heavenly Father approves of the act, and I know that if I had
not obeyed the command to aid in the killing of Mitchell I would
have suffered during the rest of my life," she said. "If I had it to
do over again I would do just as I did. If God told me to kill others, I would do so."

Why didn't she kill Morris and Shipley?

"I would have killed them if the spirits had told me to."

Did George's death make her happy?

"I am satisfied. I am certain that I have fulfilled God's will. I
was not happy. I am never happy. I care nothing for happiness
on earth. I simply wish to do God's will."

Was she willing to hang for murdering George?

"I am anxious to pay the penalty of the law. I would be glad
to give up my life for taking George Mitchell's life. I have fulfilled the purpose for which God placed me in this world and I
care not what happens to me." If her life were taken, she said,
she would still work for Creffield's church in spirit.

When Esther testified, she declared that "God had ordained
Creffield for the restoration of the world," and that, when her
brother George had killed the man ordained for this mission, "it
was God's will that he should be killed."

I wanted to see my brother punished for shooting Mr.
Creffield. I realized he was my brother and admit the

*feeling was unusual under ordinary circumstances, but
he did a great wrong and should have been punished.
When I was told by God it was my duty to kill him, I
was glad. It was not hard to do for I was given strength.
At first I felt burdened, before I did it, but I soon realized it was God's will and He would care for me. If I had
not done it, I would have suffered. I had never shot a
pistol before, but was not afraid. . . .*

*Under the same circumstances I would do the deed
again, and if I was told by God to kill someone else, I
would do it without hesitation. I would kill myself if
God told me to and have thought many times of doing
so. Since killing my brother, I have not had this desire.
. . .*

*When I killed George, Mrs. Creffield and I planned
every movement beforehand, but we did not consider
any way to escape afterwards. We did not want to get
away. . . .*

*I made the statement I made in police headquarters,
knowing it was false, in the hope that I would be
lynched. I was tired of living, and knew that if I was
killed, I would get some rest anyway. I am willing to die
for the religion. I have never suffered as much as the
others, and I want to.*

*I am not insane. I knew what I was doing, and I do
not want to be sent to any asylum. I am perfectly willing
to hang. Many times I have thought of killing myself,
but I know that God had saved me for a great work. I
did not know what the great work was until I received
the divine message that it was the killing of my brother.
I am satisfied and glad I did it.*

When, on Wednesday, September 19, the insanity commission informed Judge Frater that it had finished its examinations, he ordered them to turn in their report the next morning.
He told them that they didn't need a transcript of the proceedings while they deliberated. If any of the attorneys wanted a
copy of the transcript, he said, they could get a copy from the

court reporter when he finished his transcription—which would be in eight to ten days.

In making their report, the physicians relied heavily on the book *Berkeley on Mental Diseases*. Of particular interest to them was a passage on paranoia:

> *Women are more frequently affected than men. In youth the patients are more noticeably deficient; they are apt to run after fancies or are terrified by night visions. Often they undertake long fasting, attend revival meetings, become excitable and uncontrollable . . . .*
>
> *To attend churches and listen to exhortations is to them the elixir of life. No reasoning can undermine their foundations, and although opposition and ridicule may for the moment make the patients doubt the correctness of their conceptions, certainty returns after an hour of reflection. These persons support their illogical misconceptions by diligent reading of the Bible, misapplying passages to their individual aims. . . .*
>
> *The slightest opposition calls forth the powers of wrath and the opposer is denounced as the child of the devil. . . .*
>
> *Patients of this class are, as a rule, found unbearable and soon find their way behind the walls of an institution. There the delusions continue and the loss of liberty is regarded as a consequence of their holiness and the institution as a place of martyrdom. . . .*
>
> *Comparatively few of these patients are really dangerous as long as they are unopposed, though occasionally one receives the command of God to destroy the life of some sinful individual. . . . The medical treatment of this form of paranoia is, so far as any hope of cure is concerned, without avail.*

The next morning, the physicians reported to Judge Frater:

> *As a result of its labors, the commission is unanimously of the opinion that the subjects of this investigation were at the time of the commission of the crime*

charged against them, and are now, suffering from a form of insanity commonly classified as paranoia.

Further, that because of this disease, they were at the time of the commission of the crime, possessed of such a deranged mentality as to make them unable to distinguish between right and wrong, and therefore irresponsible criminally.

Further, that these individuals belong to a class of lunatics dangerous to be at large, who persistently follow their morbid inclinations, regardless of law or ethics, and should be placed under restraint in an institution for the proper treatment of such cases.

Judge Frater was now free to send the women to the asylum at Steilacoom. Or, because of a loophole in the law, he could order them to be shipped to their side of the Columbia River— thus saving King County even more money. Chapter 138 chapter of the Statutes of Washington, 1905, said that people who were found to be insane but were not residents of Washington could legally be transported back to their home states. It was possible that both women would be free within days.

O. V. Hurt was overjoyed. When he told Maud about the findings of the insanity commission, she didn't seem to care. All she said was: "I am glad for your sake."

<hr />

MAY GO SCOTT FREE
Headline, *Corvallis Times,* September 25, 1906

CHAPTER TWENTY-NINE

POISON?

Our souls cry out, hallelujah! And our faith enrap-
tured sings,
While we throw to the breeze the standard Of the
mighty King of kings.
On the vict'ry side, on the vict'ry side, In the ranks of
our Loud are we;
On the vict'ry side we will boldly stand, Til the glory
land we see.

From the Reverend Knapp's
Bible Songs of Salvation and Victory

Judge Frater said that unless restrained by the State Supreme Court, he intended to have Esther and Maud sent to Oregon—and there they were likely to be set free. Even though the two had been found to be lunatics by an insanity commission in Washington, the women couldn't legally be admitted to the asylum in Oregon until an insanity commission there also declared them to be lunatics. So, if Sheriff Smith took them to their side of the Columbia River, he would have to release them, and they would be free to go wherever they wanted.

When Oregon's Governor Chamberlain found out about this,

he let it be known that Oregon didn't want them back. "If it is true that the judge has made such an unusual order," he said, "he has committed a judicial outrage that ought to subject him to impeachment."

"If we wanted to be that small," said Multnomah County Judge Webster, "the boundary line between Oregon and Washington is not very far distant, and we could very easily dump all our crazy people upon them and save ourselves a whole lot of botheration and care."

The Supreme Court did issue an order restraining Judge Frater from "deporting" the women until it reviewed the case. Before a final decision came down, O. V. Hurt received a telegram from the jail that said he should come at once, for Maud's sake. The telegram didn't say what was wrong—but it didn't matter. O. V.'s dear needed her papa, so he and Sarah left immediately for Seattle.

When they arrived at the jail, Maud was rail thin and appeared to be on the verge of a nervous breakdown. They tried to bolster her spirits, telling her her case was far from over, and that there was still a good chance she would be home with them soon. This being the first that Sarah had been out for some time, O. V. thought it best that they stay only a few days. But O. V. assured Maud that he would return. Soon. And, as always he loved her very, very much.

At 11 P.M. on November 17, just five days after her parents left, Maud let out a piercing scream. She and Esther had spent much of that evening playing cards with the other prisoners. Around ten, Maud took a cold foot bath, and after that she and Esther went to their cell.

"Both of the women appeared to be in unusually good spirits at the time and called a cheery good night to me as I left them," said Deputy Sheriff Phil Kearney.

Annie Rooney, an inmate, passed their cell a short time later and saw the two women with their arms about each other. They exchanged good nights with Annie, and that was the last heard from either of them. Until Maud's scream.

When the jailers, Joe Hill and A. McKinnon, reached the cell, Maud was moaning loudly. Her face was contorted and she was having convulsions and muscle spasms, all the while clutching her left side near her heart. They laid her on the cot and rubbed her hands and ankles, trying to restore circulation. Doctor Shirley F. Wiltsie was called, but by the time he arrived, Maud Creffield was dead.

Esther kissed Maud repeatedly, hiding both their heads under a sheet. "She was all right when we went to bed," Esther sobbed. "She was in my arms when she first felt pain. She fainted, screamed and fainted. . . . Send a message to Mr. Hurt, please. Let me stay with the body."

When the dead-wagon arrived, Esther's eyes never left the body, watching the undertakers lay it in a basket, cover it with a sheet, and carry it to the waiting wagon. Like the bodies of Edmund Creffield and George Mitchell, Maud's body was taken to the Bonney-Watson Funeral Company.

Doctor Ames, who had been on the insanity commission, was now worried about Esther. "I believe that Esther Mitchell will commit suicide within a short time," he said. "The attachment between her and Mrs. Creffield was such a close one that I believe the woman, with her weak and unsound mentality, will grasp the first opportunity that offers itself of taking her own life. . . . The attachment existing between those two women was, I believe, without parallel."

Police Matron Kelly stayed with Esther all the next day—in part to keep her company, and in part to keep her from killing herself. "I am all alone now." Esther said. She also said that before her death, Maud had told her things she couldn't bring herself to tell her parents. What were those things? Esther said that she too, under no circumstances, would ever tell anyone.

When Matron Kelly finally left for the evening, the other eighteen women inmates made sure one of them was with Esther at all times. They were also grieving, for they too had grown to love Maud.

And, of course, O. V. Hurt's grief was immeasurable.

She seemed despondent and depressed, due, I think, to the delay in the settlement of her deportation case before the supreme court. We all had expected it settled long before now, and it is certain that it would have

been decided within a few days. I do not think, however,
she entertained any thought of suicide, although she did
ask her mother that if anything did happen to her that
she be buried beside Creffield.

I think she died from grief and a broken heart. When
Creffield was killed Maud felt that all her life had been
taken from her and she thought so until her death. She
told us repeatedly she had nothing more to live for.
Maud failed in health considerably while confined in
jail.

"The death of the Creffield woman will save the county several thousand dollars," the *Daily Times* coldly said, "as it would have cost considerable to have tried her case if the supreme court overrules the findings of the insanity commission." The county didn't get off completely, as it still had to pay for an autopsy performed on Maud's body by doctors Carroll, Wiltsie, Powers, Crookall, and Snyder.

After Maud's death, Sheriff Smith had searched her and Esther's cell looking for poison. The last person, outside of the prisoners and jailers, to see Maud was her cousin, Attie Bray—now Attie Levins. Attie had recently married Sampson Levins, one of Creffield's last male followers. Had Attie perhaps brought Maud poison?

"I saw Mrs. Creffield, but certainly I did not bring her any poison," Attie said indignantly. "Maud Creffield did not want poison. We had talked several times of suicide and Mrs. Creffield always said that self-destruction was cowardly. But for the fact that it was cowardly and that God had forbidden her to commit suicide, Mrs. Creffield frequently said she would like to kill herself, for she had no desire to live. But she always told me that it was her duty to live and meet whatever punishment was given her, and declared she was going to do it."

"We were very intimate and knew each other's innermost secrets," Esther said, also claiming Maud would never have taken poison. "If she had been intending to commit suicide I would have been told of it and would have gone out of this world with her. Only one thing could have induced her to have done such a thing and that would be a command from above. Had such a command come she would have communicated it to me for she told me everything, and more especially she would have told me of any such message as that. It was our wish that we should die together if we passed from this world. She would not have left me of her own will without a word about her plan. Another thing that makes it impossible that she committed suicide is, that she looked forward to the time when she would be sent to Oregon. She did not care for her own sake what became of her, but her father and mother were so anxious to have her near them, and they have suffered so much for her sake that she was anxious to have this come about."

Still, every item in the women's cell was carefully examined. And, afterwards, the sheriff said: "There is nothing to indicate that suicide had been committed. There is no trace of poison anywhere."

Doctor Wiltsie thought that Maud's symptoms were more like those of someone with heart disease than someone who had taken poison. Also, Jailer vanMeer had said that Maud had had many fainting spells that she blamed on heart trouble. But just to be sure, Doctor Carroll ordered an autopsy be done.

Heart problems were promptly ruled out. Doctor Carroll reported that Maud's heart seemed to be in particularly good condition. Her lungs, liver, kidneys, and bowels also looked to be in a normal and healthy condition. Her urine was tested and it was found that she had been suffering from uraemia. Uraemia can kill rather suddenly.

An initial examination of the stomach contents indicated no poison, but the presence of a poison couldn't be ruled out until the stomach was chemically analyzed. The organ was placed in a bottle and turned over to C. Osseward, a chemist.

Osseward cut up the stomach's contents, subjected them to a treatment of alcohol and tartaric acid at a temperature of seventy degrees, cooled and then squeezed the mixture through a series of filtration systems, evaporated what was left at a temperature of not over forty degrees until it was half of its former bulk, refiltered the mass to eliminate the fatty matter and the albuminous substances as far as possible, did some more filtering, more treatments of alcohol, and more evaporating, added ether to extract as much of the coloring matter as possible, and added a weak solution of sodium-hydrate until it showed a distinct alkaline reaction to turmeric paper.

"Some alkaloid was present in my solution," Osseward said after he'd done all this. "The question was which one." His next procedure was a simple one—he tasted the solution. It was bitter, leading him to believe the alkaloid he was dealing with was strychnine. To confirm his suspicions, he applied five different color tests, the most sensitive of which—the sulphuric-permanganate test—could show as little as .000001 of a grain of strychnine. "There is at least a grain in the solution," he reported to Doctor Carroll.

"I believe that Mrs. Creffield took the strychnine in the crystallized form and in that case a grain would have been sufficient to cause her death," Doctor Carroll said. "One eighth of a grain is considered the maximum dose and is administered in so large a quantity only in extreme heart failure."

Doctor Carroll said that Maud's last moments could now be explained. The irritant in the stomach was responsible for congestion at the base of the brain and brought on convulsions, convulsions violent enough to cause Maud to bite through her tongue—a common occurrence in strychnine poisoning. Although a very sure way of killing oneself, death by strychnine is also very painful.

"The finding of the poison in the stomach proves conclusively that Mrs. Creffield did not die of natural causes," Doctor Carroll said. Maud had, in his expert opinion, committed suicide.

O. V. Hurt purchased two adjoining lots in the Lake View Cemetery. The last favor Papa could do for his dear was to fulfill her wish that she be buried with Creffield. Even if he had wanted to take Maud's body back to Oregon, it wouldn't have been allowed on a train. The autopsy had been so extensive that it was impossible to keep embalming fluid in it.

After the autopsy, no visitors—outside of family and friends—were allowed to view the body. Maud's family wasn't about to have another spectacle like the one that had followed Creffield's death, where hundreds thronged to the funeral parlor for no purpose other than satisfying morbid curiosities.

Creffield was exhumed—his body finally rising from the grave six months after his death—and laid beside Maud. In a final loving act that had to have pained him, O. V. ordered a tombstone be made for his dear that says, "Maud, Wife of Edmund Crefeld."

"The mistakes she made were innocent ones," O. V. said.

Esther was permitted to attend Maud's service at the Bonney-Watson Chapel. The funeral was private and, besides Esther, those

Morning Oregonian

Maud, wife of Edmund Creffield

attending were O. V., Mae, Frank, and Mollie Hurt, Morris, Shipley, Police Matron Kelly, and William A. Holzheimer. Holzheimer was an attorney Morris had arranged for to represent Maud at all future proceedings. Esther stepped in front of the casket and, bowing over the glass enclosure, looked woefully at Maud's gray face and wept loudly. When she was returned to the county jail, as had been her way since the death, she took to her bed and was near tears for days. She would never overcome the loss of her close friend.

In January of 1907 the Supreme Court upheld insanity commission's findings pronouncing Esther and Maud insane. But the court also declared that Esther couldn't be deported to Oregon.

By now Esther—pale and fragile, with no light or sparkle in her eyes—was easily the most pitiful looking inmate in the women's ward of the jail. Most of her days were spent sitting in the far corner of her cell looking through the window at Mount

Rainier. Sometimes she would gaze blankly at the others talking and playing cards and could be seen hastily brushing away a tear as it ran down her cheek. Gloomy, dejected and morose, she said she didn't join in because she wanted to be away from the noise.

"I don't care where I go," she said when asked whether she would rather go to an asylum or stay in jail. "I would as soon be in an insane asylum as here." When Police Matron Kelly came to take her to the asylum in Steilacoom, Esther had a grief-stricken look as she left her cell, the cell where Maud died. She said goodbye to the other women on the ward, women whom she had little in common with and hadn't become intimate with, but women who had always sympathized with her. They congratulated her on the outcome of her case.

Esther bade a cordial farewell to jailers Fred Hill and Emil Larson and asked them to tell the night jailers goodbye for her. She had been a model prisoner, and her jailers, as had been the case with her brother George, had nothing but kind words to say about her.

The week that Esther was taken to the asylum, Mildred Crawford fell upon the damp floor of a Portland mission and began rolling and praying. Services were being conducted by Martin L. Ryan, the one Creffield was tarrying with in 1902 when God first revealed to him that he was "God's Elect." For hours on end Mildred rolled, sang, rolled, prayed, rolled and rolled and rolled through spittle and dirt in a packed foul-smelling hole-in-the-wall called the St. John's Gospel Mission.

This was done for the purpose of sanctification, to clean the "torturing devils" out of her body. While Mildred rolled, "the grown-up Negroes and whites of both sexes were allowed to negotiate cataleptic stunts," the *Evening Telegram* reported, "stand on their heads, swim frog-fashion on the filthy floor and scare away the multitude of devils with which the whole howling mob seems to be obsessed."

"She was called by the Lord, to become the leader of the Pentecostal faith," her mother Florence said. "The Lord has called her to preach, and last night spoke in the language of tongues, in Chinese, Japanese and Spanish, and she interpreted all. We have been scourged and reviled and spat upon by the devil and his followers, but we would just as soon be in jail as outside. We have got to speak the word when God puts it in our mouths."

One of the things Mildred was reported to have said was: "The Lord is coming soon. He will take his bride." Thereafter Mildred was known as the "Bride of the Lord."

Mildred Crawford was nine at the time.

But her's is another story.

***

PADDED-CELL RELIGION IN TWO FORMS IS RAMPANT IN PORTLAND

Headline, Portland *Evening Telegram*, December 31, 1906

CHAPTER THIRTY

FINAL CHAPTER

Every place that the sole of your foot shall tread upon, that have I given it unto you, as I said unto Moses.—Joshua 1:3

S hortly after Esther was committed to the asylum, O. V. and Sarah Hurt moved to Waldport, where they bought a nine-room house with a beautiful garden on the Alsea Bay. After Maud's death, Sarah's health continued to deteriorate, and O. V. hoped that moving to the coast would help her—which it did.

Soon thereafter, with his wife Hattie, Clarence Starr, one of Sarah's brothers, also moved to Waldport. When Sarah, Clarence, Hattie, Hattie's brother Edwin Baldwin, and Edwin's wife Victoria were children, their families were neighbors on the Alsea Bay. In fact, Victoria's parents, David and Orlena Ruble, are considered to be the founders of Waldport. In 1884, David, having no transit, used the stars as his guide when he laid out the town's streets on a sand spit that had once been an Indian burial ground. Graves could be found everywhere, and it wasn't uncommon for people to overturn rocks with their feet and discover that the rocks were actually human skulls.

O. V. also bought the Hosfords' homestead, across the Yachats River from where Creffield had hoped to establish his new Eden. The town of Yachats is laid out on this land. Eventually, almost everyone connected with the Holy Rollers moved either there or to Waldport, eight miles to the north.

O. V.'s daughter Mae—his "little girl"—married a man named Frank Johnson. They bought a hotel in Yachats that had been owned by John Silvers, "a big fellow with big ideas," who sold part of Yachats, although he didn't own an inch. He salted a gold mine in town, but when the gold ran out, so did he—leaving almost as fast as Creffield had. Frank Johnson died in 1950 at the age of seventy-one, and Mae Hurt-Johnson died in 1980 at the age of ninety-four.

When the road to Cape Perpetua was being built in 1912, Mae and Frank's hotel was filled to capacity with twenty-eight boarders, and many slept in cabins behind it. Burgess Starr, who eventually divorced Donna, did the cooking for the road crew. Burgess died in 1936 at the age of sixty-five. "Providence did not always light his pathway as he most desired," his obituary said, "yet he had a happy faculty of seeing the bright side in everything and had a good word for all."

Frank Hurt died in 1920 at the age of thirty-seven while laying a line of traps on a stream with Frank Johnson. The two were a short distance apart when Johnson heard a single shot from Hurt's direction. He assumed Hurt had killed an animal he'd found in a trap. When Johnson came back and couldn't find his brother-in-law, he walked down the stream and found him dead, a bullet through his head. The Coroner ruled that "Hurt came to his death from the accidental discharge of his gun."

Ten years later, in 1930 Mollie Sandell Hurt married James Berry. When James had returned to Corvallis in 1906 after testifying before Esther and Maud's sanity hearing, he walked into his wife Clara's room and found her trying to kill herself by swallowing carbolic acid. The two soon thereafter divorced. James insisted on taking custody of their son, Kenneth; then, instead of taking care of the boy himself, gave him to O. V. and Sarah Hurt to raise.

James then wed a woman by the name of Tensie Johnson. That marriage didn't last long, and in 1916 he married Donna Starr, and the two of them ran a store in Yachats. Their marriage wasn't happy either. James drank heavily and, when drunk, was abusive. One of the worst nights was Christmas Eve of 1917. "He came home drinking, the town is ten miles from our place," Donna said. "He had some meat smoking in the smoke house; he left the little boys to keep up the fire; they burnt the meat and he blamed me for it, cursing and swearing and beat me."

James hit her in the head several times. He then knocked over the chair she was sitting in, breaking the chair and severely bruising her. "It was because I had let the meat burn, I didn't know anything about it," Donna said.

On another occasion he tried to choke her. "I ran in between them to separate them," said Rachel, Donna's oldest daughter. "He started to choke her and beat her up; I talked to him a long time; then he went in the store and got another drink and came back, and kept that up all night."

"I was unnerved," Donna said. "I wasn't like myself. I nearly had a nervous prostration several times, nervous breakdown . . . . With tears in my eyes, I begged and begged, it was the same thing over." The two divorced in 1919. Donna died in 1947 at the age of sixty-seven.

A year after his divorce from Donna, James married a Christian Scientist, Alice Kent. It was another disastrous marriage. He drank more heavily than ever, remaining drunk for days at a time, and frequently threatened to kill both himself and Alice. In 1925 he had a glandular operation "for the purpose of rejuvenating him sexually and renewing his youth sexually." Afterwards, his sexual appetite was insatiable. When it was more than Alice could take, he told her that he could "only live with a woman just so long" and for her to get out and go. At the time he was also seeing a married woman. "If he has incurred debts and failed to pay his taxes," Alice said when filing for divorce in 1927, "it is because he has wasted his money upon other women and upon intoxicating liquor."

James Berry was still married to Mollie when he died in 1943 at the age of sixty-five. Mollie died in 1959 at the age seventy-eight. She is buried next to Frank Hurt, and her headstone says, "Mollie, wife of Frank Hurt."

One of Mollie and Frank Hurt's children, Virginia Esther, married James Berry's son Kenneth. Virginia Esther died of influenza in 1931 at nineteen. Kenneth Berry, whose father had been the first man to have an automobile in Corvallis, died at the age of twenty-six in an automobile accident nine months after his wife's death.

Ruth, Frank and Molly Hurt's baby who was one of those rescued from Creffield's coastal camp, died in 1999 at the age of ninety-three.

Lewis and Cora Hartley eventually reconciled, and after losing a fortune in mining claims in the Bohemia District, they too moved to Yachats. Lewis died in 1937 at eighty-three, and Cora died in 1945 at eighty-six.

Warren Hartley and his wife, Aileen, moved to Newport, fourteen miles north of Waldport. Warren was a funeral director there and was terribly busy when influenza swept through the country after World War I. His only son, Vernon LaMar— Cora Hartley's grandson whom she had "damned everlastingly" in 1906—was one of the many local victims, dying in 1919 at the age of fourteen. In 1933, at the age of fifty, Aileen, a Christian Scientist, died after a long illness. Warren died in 1959 at the age of seventy-six.

In 1910 Sophie Hartley became the Yachats postmistress and ran a store. In 1913 in the Hurts' home, she married George Mitchell's brother, Perry. Perry became a mail carrier. He died in 1961 at seventy-six, and Sophie died in 1970 at eighty-seven. They are buried in the Yachats Cemetery, not in the Mitchell family plot in Newberg. In 1906, when Perry was trying to raise money to take George Mitchell's body back to Oregon, he said: "George ought to be buried beside his mother. There's a lot there and there's room enough for us all in it, and I think that's where we all ought to be when our time comes." George was the last Mitchell buried there.

Phoebe Mitchell-Vander Kelen and her husband Peter had one child, whom they named Charles, presumably after Phoebe's father, Charles Mitchell. Phoebe died in 1909 when, during an epileptic seizure, she dislocated one of her cervical vertebrae. She was thirty-three. Peter Vander Kelen left the Salvation Army, remarried, and became a city street cleaner in Portland. He died of tuberculosis in 1918 at the age of thirty-nine.

Charles Mitchell moved to Yachats and lived there with his son, David. Charles died in 1926 at seventy-eight and David died in 1962 at eighty-nine.

Olive Sandell, Mollie Hurt's sister, married Art Carpenter, the mail carrier who once got his feet out of his stirrups just before his horse plunged to its death in going around the Devil's Churn at Cape Perpetua. Olive and Art homesteaded almost in Cape Perpetua's shadow and less than three miles from where she and others had camped at Cummins Creek in 1906. Both died at the age of seventy-nine—Art in 1946 and Olive in 1956. It is rumored that Olive's ghost, a friendly one, still resides in the house she and Art lived in.

Sampson Levins and Attie Levins (née Bray) homesteaded up the Yachats River until they died: Sampson in 1957 at eighty-nine, and Attie in 1967 at eighty-six. When Attie's sister, Rosa, got married in 1907 to Rufus Stonefield, Rufus's uncle, George P. Stonefield, had to help them elope. The couple had to marry in secret because Rosa's father, Ira Bray, kept a tight rein on Rosa after Attie fell under Creffield's spell. Attie's mother, Georgianah Bray (née Starr) didn't fare well after Attie's involvement with Creffield. She died of unknown causes in in 1909 at the age of forty-nine. Her grave, even to this day, is well tended and overlooks the ocean near where she homesteaded. Ira's grave, on the other hand, in a cemetery near Attie and Sampson's homestead is so overgrown that no one knows—or even cares—exactly where it is.

Edwin Baldwin, who in 1906 said, "I tried to show Mitchell how much better it was that I, in my old age, with but, at best, only a few more years to live, should find Creffield, and remove him from the earth, than that he should persist in his determination," died in 1947 at his daughter Una's home in Corvallis. He was eighty-nine. His wife Victoria died in 1941 and Una died in 1959.

O. V. Hurt went on to be county commissioner, was appointed Collector of Customs for the Port of Yaquina, and bought into a mercantile, forming the firm of Walker, Lebow & Hurt. He died in 1943 at the age of eighty-five, and his wife, Sarah, died in 1946 at the age of eighty-five. They are buried in the Yachats Cemetery located on the site where they lived when they were

first married. Buried near them are many of their friends and
family members into whose lives Creffield had also brought
upheaval.

> *Vic Hurt has gone to his Valhalla and with his pass-*
> *ing he leaves a county and hundreds of friends to mourn*
> *him, a county that he served so well in public life for*
> *many years, and friends that he made by his honesty,*
> *kindness and personal charm. In his earlier years he*
> *served his country in a federal capacity as Indian Agent*
> *at Siletz. He was of the old school, he was a pioneer of*
> *the Oregon Country. The type of man that helped in the*
> *building of America. His word was his bond, a promise*
> *made was a promise kept. He was keen of mind until the*
> *end, interested in world and local events—and always*
> *concerned about the welfare and health of his friends—*
> *and now as we are saddened by his demise, we are*
> *cheered by the memory of the man, the recollection of his*
> *worthwhile career, his deeds and friendship. Already in*
> *our hearts there stands a monument to him etched with*
> *the words— "Vic Hurt, a true American in every sense of*
> *the word."*
>
> O. V. Hurt's obituary in Waldport's
> *Lincoln County Times*

James Berry's marriage to Donna Starr wasn't his third marriage, but his fourth. His third marriage had been to Esther
Mitchell. Esther's physical health and disposition improved
rapidly while she was in the asylum at Steilacoom. For a long
while she never brought up George, but if someone else mentioned him, she insisted that she had done the right thing in
killing him. She always considered that her relations with
Creffield had been quite proper and failed to understand why
they should have been objected to by her family.

By 1909, though, A. P. Calhoun, superintendent of the asylum said: "The girl has recovered. For some time she has
appeared rational, and we could find no symptoms of any danger of the return of her affliction." With the approval of the cur-

rent King County Prosecuting Attorney and Judge Frater, Calhoun granted Esther parole.

At the time, John F. Miller was mayor of Seattle, and he later went on to serve as a congressman. Kenneth Mackintosh's career also wasn't irreparably harmed by the Mitchell/Creffield trials. He eventually was appointed to the Washington State Supreme Court and was made Chief Justice in 1927. Judge Frater continued to serve as a King County Superior Court justice until his death in 1925. His son, John A. Frater, was then elected to the position.

Morning Oregonian

Esther Mitchell

One of the stipulations of Esther's parole was that O. V. Hurt, who was appointed her guardian, should return her to the asylum if she showed any signs of insanity.

Frank and Mollie Hurt picked her up in Seattle to take her back to the coast. On the way, they stopped in Portland. Esther went to the offices of the *Morning Oregonian* and asked Amanda Otto, the editor's secretary, where George Mitchell's grave was. Otto told her she didn't know the location of the grave, but could tell her when George Mitchell died. "That won't be necessary," Esther said. "I know when he died."

Soon after Esther had arrived on the coast it was reported in Corvallis's *Weekly Gazette-Times* that she was again in police custody.

> *She is now in the hands of the Provincial Police at Nanaimo* [British Columbia], *having been found horribly emaciated and heavy with opium in a Chinaman's shack at Departure Bay. She is held for vagrancy and will probably go to a rescue home.*
>
> *She escaped punishment on the ground of temporary insanity and has since fallen lower and lower, consort-*

*ing wholly with the Chinese of late, and living only to
satisfy her craving for the poppy.*

*Whether this report is true or not is not certain as it
is impossible to communicate at once with her relatives
over on the coast to find out if she is still there.*

"The lurid story," the *Gazette-Times* reported a week later,
"was evidently a deliberate fabrication." Esther was actually
living a quiet and uneventful life with the Hurts, whom she
stayed with for five years. In 1914, on the recommendation of a
physician, she was declared to be sane enough to have her
parole lifted, and in April of that year she married James Berry.
Within weeks of marrying, Esther complained of feeling ill and
friends noticed she was growing thin.

After supper on Saturday, August 2, James went to town to
help unload a boat while Cora Hartley and Esther did the dishes and dressed a couple of chickens for dinner the next day.
Cora said Esther "seemed in her ordinary spirits." At 9:30
Esther went to her bedroom, and about 11 o'clock Cora heard a
noise as though of someone in distress. She went upstairs and
found Esther on her bed in a spasm. Cora asked what she could
do for her. Esther said, "Nothing." Cora then tried to turn her
on her side. "You hurt me," Esther cried. "Let me go." As Cora
let her go, Esther died.

On the nightstand Cora found a note:

> *Dear James:*
> *Please deed the two lots over to mother and father.*
> *Give the piano and ring I sent away today to Martha.*
> *The silver watch to Attie.*
> *Esther.*
> *P. S. Of course, this place is now free from mortgage
> and is yours—also the little money in the bank.*

Also on the nightstand was an empty bottle that had contained one dram (sixty grains) of strychnine and a glass of
water with some undissolved crystals still in it. Her death was
ruled a suicide, and it was now assumed that Esther's illness of
the past few months had been due to a previous suicide

attempt. She had taken enough poison to make herself ill but not enough to kill herself. Esther was buried next to Frank and Mollie Hurt. Her headstone says, not "Esther, Bride of Christ," but "Esther, wife of James Berry." She was twenty-six when she died.

After Maud had died, Esther said that Maud had told her things she couldn't bring herself to tell her parents. Asked what those things were, Esther said that she too would never tell anyone.

And she never did.

And no one ever asked.

***

The grace of our Lord Jesus Christ be with you all.
Amen.—Revelation 22:21

Epilogue

EYES OF WORLD FALL ON WALDPORT
Headline in Waldport's
South Lincoln County News, April 1, 1997

Waldport, Oregon, the setting for the final chapter of Creffield's story, was also the setting for the first chapter of another cult story. In September of 1975, when Marshall Herff Applewhite and Bonnie Lu Nettles invited people to a meeting at the Bayshore Inn where they said they were going to talk about their religious philosophies, more than 100 people showed up. Waldport's population at the time was about 700. Ron Sutton, chief criminal deputy for Lincoln County, wasn't one of the attendees. "What I heard it was going to be about was the dumbest thing I ever heard of, and I thought no one would show up," he said later. "I kick myself many times for not going to that meeting."

What Applewhite and Lu Nettles—a music professor and a nurse known as "Bo and Peep," "Do and Ti," and "The Two"—told the assembly was how they were from "a higher realm"—had a personal connection with God. They said that at some point they would be assassinated, lie in the streets for three days, and then "ascend to a higher evolutionary level via a

Author's collection

Waldport, Oregon

spaceship." Those who followed them, they said, would at the same time also ascend to a higher level via a spaceship. Those who wanted to find this salvation by spaceship were told to "forgo their worldly belongings"—all that is except for their automobiles—leave their families, and follow them to Colorado. About two dozen people did leave town with them—leaving everything behind, some even leaving their children behind. The story made national headlines and the group was dubbed by the media as "The UFO Cult."

And as in Creffield's story, worse was yet to come.

The assembly at the Bayshore Inn was the first successful recruitment meeting held for the group that eventually became known as Heaven's Gate. Over the next twenty-two years the group grew, until in 1997 Applewhite and thirty-eight of his flock "abandoned their containers" in a mansion in California at Rancho Santa Fe. Believing the spaceship from "the Level Above Human" that was going to take them to "their world" in the Heavens was trailing Comet Hale-Bopp, they committed mass suicide.

A hundred years from now, will people be familiar with the story of Heaven's Gate or will it be forgotten like Creffield's story? Fifty years from now will a student from Waldport High happen upon an article about the tragedy, and when she asks her parents for more information be told: "Why dredge up the dead? It'll only hurt the living. It was a one-time thing. Nothing like that could happen again. Or, anyhow, it couldn't ever happen again to *normal* people. Sane people. People like you and me."

<hr />

As was promised—the keys to Heaven's Gate are here again in Ti and Do (The UFO Two) as they were in Jesus and His Father 2000 yrs. ago.

Heading for Heaven's Gate's Internet site in 1997

BIBLIOGRAPHY

Trial Court Records
Circuit Court of the State of Oregon, County of Multnomah. State of Oregon vs. Edwin Creffield. Reg. No. A8559, Judgment No. 33605. Information. Filed 22 August 1904. Judgment. Filed 16 September 1904. Commitment. Filed 16 September 1904.

Superior Court of the State of Washington, King County, Department No 1, Hon. A. W. Frater, Judge, State of Washington Vs. Geo. Mitchell, No 3652. Information. 10 May 1906. Affidavit for Witnesses. 27 June 1906. Stipulation. 1906. Contempt of Court. 2 July 1906. Defendant's Request for Instructions. 9 July 1906. Order and Bill for Board or Lodging of Jurors. July 1906. Witness Cost. July 1906.

Insanity Commission Court Records
County Court of the State of Oregon for Linn County. The Matter of the Examination and Commitment of Atta [sic] Bray. Order of commitment. Filed 6 May 1903. Complaint. Filed 6 May 1903.

County Court of the State of Oregon for Linn County. The Matter of the Examination and Commitment of Frank Hurt. No. 1067. Complaint. Filed 30 April 1904. Order of commitment. Filed 30 April 1904.

County Court of the State of Oregon for Linn County. The Matter of the Examination and Commitment of Mollie Hurt. No. 1036. Complaint. Filed 30 April 1904. Order of commitment. Filed 30 April 1904.

County Court of the State of Oregon for Benton County. The Matter of the Examination and Commitment of Sarah M. Hurt. Complaint. Filed 27 June 1904. Order of Commitment. Filed 27 June 1904.

County Court of the State of Oregon for Linn County. The Matter of the Examination and Commitment of Rose Seely [sic]. Order of commitment. Filed 6 May 1904. Complaint. Filed 6 May 1904.

Insane Asylum Records
Admissions Book, Female, Oregon State Hospital, Vol. E
Admissions Book, Male, Oregon State Hospital, Vol. D
Discharge Book, Male and Female, Volume F, Oregon State Hospital
Index to Admissions Books, Male and Female, 1898-1919, Oregon State Hospital
Insane Complaint and Commitment Book, Linn County.
Personal History, Females, Volume 4B Oregon Insane Asylum, Oregon State Hospital
Personal History; Males, Volume 6A, Oregon Insane Asylum, Oregon State Hospital.

Calbreath, J. F. Superintendent of Oregon State Insane Asylum letter to the County Judge of Benton County, Oregon. 8 June 1904. 12 July 1904. 19 September 1904. 29 September 1904. 25 November 1904. 5 December 1904. 19 December 1904. 4 January 1905.

Calbreath, J. F. Superintendent of Oregon State Insane Asylum letter to the County Judge of Linn County, Oregon. 3 December 1904. 9 December 1904.

Newspapers and Periodicals
Albany Democrat. 25 December 1903. p2. "Holly Rollers in Linn County." 25 December 1903. p3. "Holly Rollers." 8 January 1904. p7. 15 January 1904. p1. "Saturday Night Thoughts" 15 January 1904. p4. "The Holy Rollers." 15 January 1904. p3. 29 January 1904. p4. "Holy Rollers." 5 February 1904. p5. 6 May 1904. p2. 6 May 1904. p4. "A Holy Roller Victim." 6 May 1904. p7.

"Frank Hurt Said." 6 May 1904. p7. "More Holy Rollerism." 6 May 1904. p5. "Taken To The Asylum." 6 May 1904. p7. 13 June 1904. p1. "More Holy Rollers." 13 May 1904. p5.

American Mercury. Stewart H. Holbrook. "Oregon's Secret Love Cult." February, 1937. pp. 167-174.

Benton County Republican. "Has Sad Christmas." 3 January 1907. p4. 7 February 1907. p2. 28 February 1907. p4. 4 April 1907. p4. 11 April 1907. p3. 8 April 1909. p3. 6 August 1914. p3.

Brownsville Times. "On A Charge Of Insanity." 6 November 1903. p1. 8 January 1904. p1. 15 January 1904. p1. 29 January 1904. p3. "Holy Rollers." 5 February 1904. p4. "Reward Is Offered." 1 April 1904. p1. "Holy Rollerism Again." 4 May 1906. p4. "Holy Rollers Insane." 6 May 1904. p1. "Young Girl Arrested." 6 May 1904. p1. "Holy Roller Creffield Killed." 11 May 1906. p1. "Another Holy Roller Victim. 17 June 1904. p4. "Holy Roller Captured." 5 August 1904. p1. "To The Grand Jury." 12 August 1904. p1. "Creffield Found Guilty." 23 September 1904. p4. 30 September 1904. p1. 7 October 1904. p1.

Capital Journal. "David P. Mitchell Dies in Waldport." 13 September 1963. p5.

Columbia Chronicle. "Father Says Hypnotism." 21 July 1906. p. 1.

Corvallis Gazette. 29 July 1887. 7 June 1889. 2 August 1889. p. 3. 19 April 1894. p. 2. 10 May 1894. p. 3. 28 May 1894. p. 5. 5 July 1894. p. 4. 16 April 1896. p. 3. 9 April 1897. p. 3. 10 December 1897. p. 3. 31 December 1897. p. 3. 8 April 1898. p. 3. 5 January 1900. p3. 19 January 1900. p3. 9 February 1900. p3. 7 December 1900. p3. "Fast Traveling." 1 November 1901. p3. "The Salvation Army." 6 March 1901. p3. 26 April 1901. p3. 3 May 1901. p3. 4 October 1901. p3. 1 November 1901. p3. 7 February 1902. p3. "Central Committee Meeting." 21 February 1902. p3. 25 February 1902. p3. 8 April 1902. p3. 15 April 1902. p3. 17 June 1902. p3. 20 June 1902. p3. 11 July 1902. p3. 4 November 1902. p3. "Functus Officio." 5 December 1902. p3. 9 December 1902. p3. 12 December 1902. p3. "Berry-King Nuptials." 5 January 1903. p3. 17 March 1903. p3. *Corvallis Gazette.* 31 March 1903. p3. 5 May 1903. p3. "Almost a Riot." 12 May 1903. p3. 24 July 1903. p3. 31 July 1903. p3. 4 September p3. 2 October 1903. p3. 30 October 1903. p3. 3 November 1903. p3. 6 November 1903. p2. "What our Neighbors Think of Us." 10 November 1903. p2. 24 November 1903. p2. 8 December 1903. p3. 11 December 1903. p2. "Linn County Holy Rollers." 22 December 1903. p3. 29 December 1903. p3. 1 January 1904. p2. 8 January 1904. p1. "A Mystery of the Night." 8 January 1904. p3. "Rollers are Rolled." 8 January 1904. p3. "Editorial Comment." 12 January 1904. p2. 15 January 1904. p3. 19 January 1904. p1. "Our Brainy Contemporaries." 19 January 1904. p2. 25 January 1904. p3. "Lebanon's Holy Rollers." 2 February 1904. p3. 19 February 1904. p1. 4 March 1904. p4. "Creffield A Fugitive." 22 March 1904. p3. 19 April 1904. p3. "Felton-Munkers Nuptials." 3 May 1904. p3. "Holy Rollers." 3 May 1904. p3. *Corvallis Gazette.* 6 May 1904. p5. "Committed To Asylum." 10 May 1904. p3. 1 June 1904. p1. "Seventh Day Adventists." 8 June 1904. p4. 11 June 1904. p3. "The Creffield Reward." 22 June 1904. p3. 29 June 1904. p3. 13 July 1904. p3, p4. 29 July 1904. p4. 2 August 1904. p1. "Creffield Captured." 8 August 1904. p1. 12 August 1904. p3. "The Creffield Reward." p19. August 1904. p1. 26 August 1904. p5. "Charge Against Apostle Creffield." 26 August 1904. p1. 30 August 1904. p1. 30 August 1904. p3. "Creffield Gets Two Years." 20 September 1904. p3. 4 October 1904. p3. 7 October 1904. p5. 14 October 1904. p3. 2 December 1904. p5. 13 December 1904. p3. 17 December 1904. "His Prison Life." 24 March 1905. p5. 26 April 1905. p4. 9 January 1906. p3. 20 February 1906. p3. "By The Rolling Sea. Holy Rollers" 1 May 1906. p1. 4 May 1906. p3. "Creffield Dead." 8 May 1906. p1. "The Creffield Tragedy." 11 May 1906. p1. "To Assist Mitchell." 11 May 1906. p1. 18 May 1906. p3, p4. "To Assist Mitchell." 22 May 1906. p4. "To Assist Mitchell." 25 May 1906. p4. "To Assist Mitchell." 29 May 1906. p4. "Local and Personal" 5 June 1906. p3. "Will You Help Him?" 15 June 1906. p1. "Additional Local." 19 June 1906. p2. "The Trial On." 26 June 1906. p1. "About The Trial." 29 June 1906. p1. "Against Her Brother." 6 July 1906. p1. "The Mitchell Trial." 10 July 1906. p2. "What Berry Told." 10 July 1906. p1. "Will be Acquitted." 10 July 1906. p3. *Corvallis Gazette.* "With Roar of Applause." 13 July 1906. p2. "Plotted to Kill." 16 July 1906. p1. "The Second Tragedy." 16 July 1906. p1. "Madness." 17 July 1906. p2. "Matron's Part." 17 July 1906. p2. 20 July 1906. p2. . "About the Trial." 20 July 1906. p1. "George Mitchell Buried." 20 July 1906. p2. "Murder the Charge." 20 July 1906. p1. "End to Troubles of Holy Roller Family." 24 July 1906. p3. "Fired at Random." 27 July 1906. p2. "Not Guilty." 27 July 1906. p3. 8 August 1906. p1. "Day 'Juice' Now." 14 August 1906. p1. "Ill in Seattle." 14 August 1906. p1. 24 August 1906. p3. 31 August 1906. p3. 11 September 1906. p3. "Local and Personal." 14 September 1906. p3. 18 September 1906. p3. "Secret Sessions in Mitchell Case." 18 September 1906. p1. "Insanity

Hearing May Close Monday." 18 September 1906. p1. "In Seattle." 21 September 1906. p1. 25 September 1906. p3. "May Go Free." 25 September 1906. p4. "Pronounced Insane." 25 September 1906. p2. Must Not Deport." 28 September 1906. p1. "Has Creffield Arisen?" 19 October 1906. p1. "Holy Rollers Again." 26 October 1906. p4. "'Tongues of Fire' Coming." 26 October 1906. p1. *Corvallis Gazette*. 6 November 1906. p3. 13 November 1906. p3. 16 November 1906. p3. "Death of Mrs. Creffield." 20 November 1906. p1. "Not Yet Obliterated." 20 November 1906. p1. "A Word for Her." 30 November 1906. p1. "Her Funeral." 23 November 1906. p1. "It Was Poison." 23 November 1906. p1. 23 November 1906. p3. 30 November 1906. p3. "Not For 'Common Herd.'" 1 January 1907. p4. "Esther Mitchell." 4 January 1907. p4. "Holy Howlers' the Latest." 4 January 1907. p2. "'Bride of the Lord' Talks." 8 January 1907. p2. "In Esther Mitchell Case." 11 January 1907. p3. 11 January 1907. p3. 25 January 1907. p3. 29 January 1907. p3. 5 February 1907. p3. 15 February 1907. p1. "Asylum at Last." 22 February 1907. p2. "'Tangled Tongues' Killing Her." 22 February 1907. p2. 1 March 1907. p3. " Feb. 22nd, 1857-Feb. 22nd, 1907." 1 March 1907. p1. 8 March 1907. p3. 23 March 1907. p3. 2 April 1907. p3. 9 April 1907. p4. 12 April 1907. p3. 15 April 1907. p3. "Not Dead." 26 April 1907. p1. "Believes in Creffield." 30 April 1907. p3. "Mrs. Elizabeth Starr." 26 July 1907. p1. *Corvallis Gazette Times*. Bergeman, Rich, "Play recreates bizarre Corvallis tale." 11 January 1986. p16. "Clarence M. Starr Dies at Waldport." 21 June 1939. p. 4. "Mrs. Baldwin Dies." 2 August 1941. p3. "James K. Berry Rites Held Here Today." 13 January 1943. p6. "Dies at Waldport." 14 June 1943. p4. "Oregon Pioneer Dies Thursday Night." 12 December 1947. p. 8. "Levine [*sic*] Passes." 2 November 1957. p. 10. "Levins Rites Slated At Waldport Chapel." 4 November 1957. p12. "Molly Adeline Berry." 20 May 1959. p. 12. "Corvallis scandal spawns a play. Review." 15 June 1978. p16.

Corvallis Magazine . Vol 3, #2. Tom Wilson. "Corvallis Holy Rollers." 1964. p20. Vol 2, 1963, #1, p. 15. Vol 2, #2. "From the Gilbert Beach Album." 1963. p. 6.

Corvallis Times. 28 December 1893. p3. 4 February 1895. p. 3. 14 December 1895. p. 3. "A Piece of Hoodlumism." 7 January 1897. p. 3. "Many are Prostrated." 8 December 1897. p. 3. "Salvation Army Affairs." 5 January 1898, p. 2. 3 November 1900. p3. 6 February 1901. p3. 24 April 1901. p1. 15 May 1901. p3. 18 May 1901. p3. 29 May 1901. p3. 12 June 1901. p3. 21 September 1901. p2. 28 September 1901. p3. 26 October 1901. p3. "Corvallis Men." 27 November 1901. p3. 25 January 1902. p3. 26 February 1902. p3. 1 March 1902. p3. 24 May 1902. p3. "Local Mining Men." 12 July 1902. p3. 19 July 1902. p3. 26 July 1902. p3. 2 August 1902. p3. 4 October 1902. p3. "Highest in Eleven Years." 28 January 1903. p2. "Fire! Fire Fire!" 7 January 1903. p2. 10 January 1903. p3. "The Salvation Army." 7 March 1903. p2. 14 March 1903. p3. 28 March 1903. p3. 6 May 1903. p3. "A Street Melee." 13 May 1903. p3. "Desertion From The Ranks." 10 June 1903. p3. 27 June 1903. p3. "J. K. Berry—Bicycles." 27 June 1903. p4. 22 July 1902. p3. 1 August 1903. p3. 5 August 1903. p3. 8 August 1903. p3. 12 August 1903. p3. 22 August 1903. p3. "Their Queer Acts." 31 October 1903. p2. "Flight of The Apostles." 4 November 1903. p3. "Holy Rolling." 4 November 1903. p2. "Is Creffield Back." 7 November 1903. p3. "Like Our Rollers." 7 November 1903. p4. "Mr. Hurt Talks." 18 November 1903. p3. "They Are Gone." 25 November 1903. p3. "Through Much Tribulation." 28 November 1903. p3. 9 December 1903. p3. "Now in Eugene." 16 December 1903. p4. "Is Crazy Now." 23 December 1903. p2. "Tarred and Feathered." 6 January 1904. p1. "Their Welcome Departure." 9 January 1904. p1. "White Caps Again." 9 January 1904. p1. "Where Brooks Went." 13 January 1904. p2. "Newspaper Holy Rollers." 20 January 1904. p2. 3 February 1904. p3. "Driven From Linn." 3 February 1904. p4. "Corvallis Abroad." 6 February 1904. p4. "Seventh Day Adventists." 27 February 1904. p2. 2 March 1904. p4. 2 March 1904. p3. "The Holy Gang." 5 March 1904. p1. "The Twin Rock Company." 5 March 1904. p2. 19 March 1904. p3. "Fugitive Creffield." 23 March 1904. p3. 23 March 1904. p4. *Corvallis Times*. 16 April 1904. p4. "After The Roller." 27 April 1904. p1. 4 May 1904. p4. 4 May 1904. p3. "Victims Of Creffield." 7 May 1904. p3. 21 May 1904. p4. "Attie Bray's Journey." 11 June 1904. p3. "They Want Creffield." 11 June 1904. p3. 2 July 1904. p4. "He May Own Up." 27 July 1904. p4. "Creffield In Jail." 30 July 1904. p3. "Says 'I Am Elijah.'" 3 August 1904. p1. "The Bogus Prophet." 3 August 1904. p3. "A Dangerous Man." 6 August 1904. p2. "Creffield To Answer." 6 August 1904. p3. "The Reward." 20 August 1904. p3. 24 August 1904. p3. "His Coming Trial." 3 September 1904. p2. 7 September 1904. p1. 9 September 1904. p4. 17 September 1904. p3. 21 September 1904. p3. "Creffield's Confession." 21 September 1904. p2. "Now In Penitentiary." 21 September 1904. p1. 1 October 1904. p3. 5 October 1904. p4. 12 October 1904. p3. 22 October 1904. p4. "For Cement Sidewalks." 19 November 1904. p2. 26 November 1904. p3. "An Ended Chapter." 10 December 1904. p2. 4 February 1905. p4. 8 April 1905. p4. 10 May 1905. p3. 24 May 1905. p4. 3 June 1905. p3. 12 July 1905. p3. 12 August 1905. p3. *Corvallis Times*. 23 August 1905. p3. 20

September 1905. p3. 4 October 1905. p4. 27 October 1905. p3. "Publisher's Notice." 14 November 1905. p2. "Of Peritonitis." 14 November 1905. p2. 24 November 1905. p5. 8 December 1905. p4. 12 December 1905. p4. "Gave His Own Bail." 22 December 1905. p3. 29 December 1905. p4. 9 January 1906. p4. 13 March 1906. p4. 23 March 1906. p4. 13 April 1906. p4. "In Benton Again." 24 April 1906. p2. "Camp Given Up." 1 May 1906. p2. "Is Not Dead." 11 May 1906. p1. "Justifiable Homicide?" 11 May 1906. p1. "Widow of Holy Roller Is Insane From Waiting to See the Dead Arise." 15 May 1906. p6. "Nearly Starved." 18 May 1906. p1. "Miss Esther." 22 May 1906. p1. "Begins Monday." 22 June 1906. p2. "The Trial." 26 June 1906. p1. "Trying Mitchell." 29 June 1906. p1. 3 July 1906. p1. "O. V. Hurt Testifies." 6 July 1906. p1. "A Great Battle." 10 July 1906. p3. "Another Tragedy." 10 July 1906. p1. "Levins' Letter." 10 July 1906. p4. "Mitchell's Trial." 10 July 1906. p1. "Editorial." 13 July 1906. p2. "Esther Declined to Be Reconciled." 13 July 1906. p4. "Is Not Guilty." 13 July 1906. p1. "Shot to Death." 13 July 1906. p3. "The Acquittal." 13 July 1906. p2. *Corvallis Times..* 17 July 1906. p1. "May Come to Oregon." 20 July 1906. p1. "Mitchell Buried in Oregon." 20 July 1906. p1. "Perry Mitchell." 20 July 1906. p3. "Pleads not Guilty." 3 August 1906. p1. "Esther Mitchell." 14 August 1906. p1. Esther Mitchell 14 August 1906. p1. 11 September 1906. p1. 14 September 1906. p1. 14 September 1906. p4. "She Swallowed Poison." 21 September 1906. p3. "May Go Scott Free." 25 September 1906. p1. 28 September 1906. p3. 19 October 1906. p3. 23 October 1906. p3. 23 October 1906. p4. 9 November 1906. p4. "Mrs. Creffield." 20 November 1906. p1. "Died From Poison." 23 November 1906. p1. "Fined For Fishing." 21 December 1906. 15 January 1907. p4. 2 April 1907. p3. "Still Hoping." 30 April 1907. p1. 23 July 1907. p4.

Daily Capital Journal. "Holy Rollers Have Her." 29 April 1904. p8. "Interviewed. Odd People Are Not Insane." 2 May 1904. p1. "Wife of Apostle Creffield and Another Sister Becomes Guests of State." 4 May 1904. p1. "Holy Roller Murderess Goes Free." 7 January 1907. p1.

Daily Gazette Times. "Esther Mitchell a Suicide." 3 August 1914. p4. "Frank Hurt Killed at Waldport." 12 January 1920. p1.

Daily Oregon Statesman. "Joe, The Turk, Here." 29 June 1902. p8. "On A Charge Of Insanity." 31 October 1903. p5. 4 May 1904. p2. 4 May 1904. p4. "Holy Rollers." 7 May 1904. p1. "Holy Roller Captured." 30 July 1904. p1. "Holy Roller." 31 July 1904. p4. "Join Lives For Glory Of Cause." 31 July 1904. p9. "Tongues of Fire—Gift of Languages and Holiness Union." 10 April 1906. p6. 10 May 1906. p2. "Holy Rollers Return Home." 17 May 1906. p7. "Mitchell on Trial." 26 June 1906. p3. "Attorneys Display Caution." 27 June 1906. p3. "Much Squabbling in Mitchell Trial." 28 June 1906. p1. "Starr Testifies in Mitchell Trial." 4 July 1906. "Hartley Testifies in Mitchell Trial." 6 July 1906. p1. "Fails to Shake Testimony." 8 July 1906. p6. "George Mitchell Acquitted by Jury." 11 July 1906. p1. "Esther Mitchell Kills Her Brother." 13 July 1906. "Mitchell a Model Prisoner" 13 July 1906. p1. "George Mitchell Was Not Insane." 14 July 1906. p1. "Fears For Her Life." 19 July 1906. p4. 20 July 1906. p2. "Churches, Where One May Go and Worship"Evening." 22 July 1906. p10. "He Insists on Trial." 25 July 1906. p1. 9 September 1906. p10. "May Go To Asylum." 11 September 1906. p6. "Holly [*sic*] Rollers Found Insane." 21 September 1906. p1. "Issued Order." 22 September 1906. p1. "Bits for Breakfast." 5 October 1906. p2. "Holiness Church." 6 October 1906. p5. 7 October 1906. p10. "Slow to Arrive." 10 October 1906. p2. "Are Not Holy Rollers." 10 October 1906. p2. "New Tongues." 20 November 1906. p6. "The Other Side." 20 November 1906. p6. "Case of Suicide." 21 November 1906. p1. "Editorial of the People." 25 November 1906. p2. "Jury Finds Martin Guilty." 20 December 1906. p5. "The Scoffing News Reporter." 20 December 1906. p1. "Pigs Squeak." 21 December 1906. p1. "Says No Restraint There." 21 December 1906. p4. "Editorials of The People." 23 December 1906. p10. "Insane Asylum." 1 January 1907. p12. "The State Penitentiary." 1 January 1907. p17. "Is It Mesmerism." 2 January 1907. p8. 2 January 1907. p4. "Tongues Will be Silent." 8 January 1907. p7. "Tales of the Town." 9 January 1907. p5. "Light Leaves Salem." 15 January 1907. p4. "Storm Gathers Over Tonguers." 19 May 1907. p4. "Island is New Home of the Holy Rollers." 17 March 1911. p1. "Divorce Granted." 18 March 1911. p. 5. "Tragedies of Yesterday." 28 August 1934. p8.

Eugene Morning Guard. "Holy Rollers Roll Into Eugene Church." 11 December 1903. p1.

Eugene Morning Register. "Holy Rollers Roll Out." 3 November 1903. p1. *Eugene Morning Register.* "Holy Rollers At Corvallis." 3 November 1903. p3.

Evening Telegram. Strandborg, W. P. "Frazer After Holy Howlers." 1 January 1907. p1. "Fanatics

In Court." 2 November 1903. p1. "Group of Holy Rollers, Religious Fanatics Having Their Headquarters at Corvallis, Oregon." 2 November 1903. p1. "Had Promise of Tar and Feathers." 3 November 1903. p5. "Creffield Reappears." 5 November 1903. p12. "Rollers Take On New Life." 6 November 1903. p1. "Excess of Holy Rollers May Yet Lead To Serious Clash If They Continue." 7 November 1903. p2. "'Apostle' Creffield Still Under Cover." 11 November 1903. p.6. "Can Roll No More." 23 November 1903. p1. "A Sensible Conclusion." 24 November 1903. p8. "O. V. Hurt Tells All He Knows." 24 November 1903. p3. "In Pursuit of Creffield." 25 November 1903. p5. "Holy Rollers are Crowded." 29 November 1903. p4. "Urges Girl to be Firm." 7 December 1903. p5. "Holy Roller Victim Worse." 21 December 1903. p16. "'Holy Roller' Victim Better." 23 December 1903. p3. "Creffield Again Out in the Cold." 30 December 1903. p4. "Creffield Disappears." 6 January 1904. p3. "Married at Corvallis." 6 January 1904. p3. "Has Power To Convert." 30 October 1903. p4. "Mines, Mining, And Miners." 5 March 1904. p10. "Like Oregon's Holy Rollers." 10 March 1904. p3. "Rocks Ahead For Joshua" 16 March 1904. p12. "Where Now Is The Apostle?" 17 March 1904. p1. "Called For His Wife." 21 March 1904. p1. "Reward For His Capture." 21 March 1904. p1. "No Trace Of Creffield." 24 March 1904. p4. "Reward Is Offered." 28 March 1904. p4. "Careful Search For Holy Roller." 31 March 1904. p10. "Holy Rollers To Put World Where Adam Entered It." 3 May 1904. p5. "Creffield Captured." 29 July 1904. p1. "Mob After Creffield." 30 July 1904. p1. "Holy Roller Chief Says God Will Be His Lawyer." 1 August 1904. p5. "Creffield Is Human Study." 2 August 1904. p14. "Did Intend To Lynch Creffield." 2 August 1904. p10. "Is Creffield A Hypnotist?" 3 August 1904. p14. On Trial Tomorrow." 3 August 1904. p8. "Wedding Will End In Folds Of Flag." 3 August 1904. p14. "Creffield To Answer." 4 August 1904. p1. "Roller Faith In Salem." 5 August 1904. p14. "Material Hell Says 'Apostle.'" 6 August 1904. p14. "No One Visits Edmund Creffield." 10 August 1904. p14. "All Victims Of Religion." 11 August 1904. p3. "The Holy Rollers And The Man Who Made Them." 13 August 1904. p15. "Elijah's Sway Is Not Lost." 20 August 1904. p5. "Needs No Lawyer To Defend Him." 23 August 1904. p14. 2 September 1904. p6. "Thinks Dowie Real Prophet." 15 September 1904. p4. "Goes To Salem For Two Years." 16 September 1904. p12. "Creffield's Punishment." 17 September 1904. p6. "Creffield To Go To Penitentiary." 17 September 1904. p10. "'Holy Jumper' Has His Wife." 14 October 1904. p12. "Prison Life Of Joshua Creffield." 22 March 1905. p4. "'Holy Rollers' Scatter From Secret Assembly." 2 May 1906. p4. "Corvallis Commend Deed." 7 May 1906. p1. "Creffield Seen in Linn County" 7 May 1906. p3. "Holy Roller Creffield Killed." 7 May 1906. p1. "Portland Man After Creffield." 7 May 1906. p1. "Arranging for Defense of Mitchell." 8 May 1906. p8. "Deed of Avenger Endorsed." 8 May 1906. p1. "Gold Medal For George Mitchell Who Killed Holy Roller Apostle." 8 May 1906. p1. "Buried Without Ceremony." 9 May 1906. p10. "Creffield Was Doomed Man." 9 May 1906. p10. "District Attorney John Manning Would Defend Apostle's Slayer." 9 May 1906. p1. "Fund For Slayer's Defense." 9 May 1906. p10. "Hurt Anxious to Clear Mitchell." 9 May 1906. p10. . "Has No Need of Manning's Help." 11 May 1906. p8. "Mitchell May Plead Temporary Insanity." 11 May 1906. p1. "Holy Rollerism Has Death Blow." 12 May 1906. p4. "Mitchell Denied Bail At Seattle." 12 May 1906. p8. "Gardner Would Help Mitchell." 15 May 1906. p14. "Abandon Hope For 'Messiah.'" 16 May 1906. p1. "Enticed to City." 17 May 1906. p8. "Exhausted Women Reach Corvallis." 17 May 1906. p8. "Mitchell's Plea 'Not Guilty.'" 19 May 1906. p8. "All Ready For Mitchell Trial." 23 June 1906. p5. "Mitchell Trial is Absorbing Topic." 23 June 1906. p4. "Much Caution in Mitchell Trial." 25 June 1906. p1. "Slayer of Holy Roller Creffield Begins Fight For Life in Seattle." 25 June 1906. p1. "No Headway Made in Mitchell Case." 28 June 1906. p3. "Dramatic Moment When Widow of Late Holy Roller Enters Court." 29 June 1906. p8. "Insanity Will be Mitchell's Plea." 2 July 1906. p1. "Converted at Revival, Woman. Pays Visit to Heaven in Trance." 3 July 1906. p16. "Called by God to Kill Prophet." 4 July 1906. p8. "Corvallis Man Wanted to Kill." 5 July 1906. p1. Women Battle For Mitchell." 6 July 1906. p1. "Mitchell and Manning Shake." 7 July 1906. p1. "Murder Kept from Mitchell Jurors." 9 July 1906. p11. "No Argument for Mitchell." 10 July 1906. p1. "Says Brother is Murderer." 11 July 1906. p1. "Sister Hiding From Mitchell." 11 July 1906. p3. "Members of Mitchell Family Reconciled." 12 July 1906. p8. "Deepening Tragedy." 13 July 1906. p6. "Esther Mitchell Draws Gun From Under Cape and Kills Geo. Mitchell." 13 July 1906. p2. "Esther Mitchell Says She is Not Insane." 13 July 1906. p1. "Mrs. Creffield Loaded Down With Weapons to Kill Geo. Mitchell." 13 July 1906. p8. "Mrs. Starr of Portland Declares Esther Mitchell, Her Sister, is Sane." 13 July 1906. p1. "Esther Hypnotized, He Says." 14 July 1906. p1. "Family Deserts the Murderess." 14 July 1906. p1. "Holy Rollers of Western New York." 14 July 1906. p26. "Brothers Bring Body to Oregon." 16 July 1906. p1. "Hurt's Letter Most Moving." 17 July 1906. p8. "Mitchell is Buried." 17 July 1906. p8. "Mrs. Starr Receives Threatening Letter." 18 July 1906. p3. "Roller Religion Dead Forever." 19 July 1906. p1. "Esther Mitchell Asks More Time." 23 July 1906. p1. "Greatly Hurt True Religion." 4 August 1906. p4. "Mitchell Boys in Drunken Row."

6 August 1906. p8. "Mitchell Denies Report of Fight." 7 August 1906. p9. "Roasts the 'Rollers.'" 8 August 1906. p9. "St. Louis Woman Coming to Convert 'Rollers.'" 8 August 1906. p9. "Esther Mitchell Shows Signs of Improvement." 13 August 1906. p4. "Sad Christmas For Holy Roller." 17 December 1906. p4. "Pile of Queer Lore Gets Fat." 22 December 1906. p4. "Interpreter for Tongues of Fire." 24 December 1906. p2. "Three Specimens of Writing in the 'Unknown Tongues.'" 25 December 1906. p4. "Tongues of Fire Get New Foothold." 31 December 1906. p4. "Padded-Cell Religion in Two Forms is Rampant in Portland." 31 December 1906. p1. "Fanatics Must Go Into Court." 2 January 1907. p7. "Says Esther Mitchell Seems Sane Enough." 2 January 1907. p5. "Judge Frazer Issues Ukase." 3 January 1907. p8. "'Bride of the Lord' Now Has a Severe Cold." 4 January 1907. p12. "Just as Soon Be in Asylum." 9 January 1907. p14. "Deaths." 18 February 1909. p. 16. "Esther Mitchell is Dead By Own Hand." 3 August 1914. p2.

Front Page Detective. Holbrook, Stewart H (under the pseudonym Chris K. Stanton). "The Enigma of the Sex Crazed Prophet." January 1938. pp. 4-9, 108-110.

God's Revivalist and Bible Advocate. Mrs. M. W. Knapp and Bessie, Publishers: Cincinnati, Ohio, Chicago, Illinois. Edmund Creffield. "He'll not Compromise." 21 August 1902. "God's Witnesses." Mrs. M. W. Knapp and Bessie, Publishers: Cincinnati, Ohio, Chicago, Illinois. 6 November 1902.

Heppner Gazette. "The Salvation Army." 25 July 1901. p5.

Hood River Glacier. "Nasty Story of Holy Rollers." 19 July 1906. p2.

Lincoln County Leader. 6 November 1903. p. 1. *y Leader.* 11 December 1903. p. 8. 20 April 1906. p. 8. 27 April 1906. supplement, p. 1. 4 May 1906. p. 1. 11 May 1906. p. 1. "More About Creffield." 18 May 1906. p. 1. "The Prevailing Opinion." 18 May 1906. p. 1. "Collector of Customs Hurt." 18 June 1909. p. 1. "Waldport Items." 9 April 1909. p. 8. "Married." 30 April 1909. p. 1. 7 May 1909. p. 5. "Waldport Items." 25 June 1909. p. 8. "County News." 10 April 1914. p. 1. 8 May 1914. p. 1. "Report of Coroner's Jury." 7 August 1914. p. 1. "Bert Starr Passed Friday, February 14, at Hospital." 20 February 1936.

Lincoln County Times. "Prominent Figure Laid to Rest." 17 June 1943. p1. "Card of Thanks!" 20 September 1945. p6. "Pioneer Lady Passes." 11 April 1946. p1. 11 April 1946. p1. "Molly Adeline Berry." 28 May 1959. p1.

Los Angeles Examiner. "Fanatic Killed by Brother of Victim." 8 May 1906. p3. "Tells How 'Holy Roller' Leader Ruined His Home." 4 July 1906. p13. "Slayer of Holy Roller Creffield Acquitted." 11 July 1906. p12. "Slayer of holy Roller Chief Killed by Sister." 13 July 1906. p1. "'I am Willing to Hang,' Says Holy Roller Avenger. 14 July 1906. p3. "Heartsick Father Seeks to Save Maud Creffield." 17 July 1906. p14. "'I am not Worrying' Says Slayer of Holy Roller." 18 July 1906. p3. "To Defend Woman Who Urged Death of His Client." 19 July 1906. p2.

Los Angeles Herald. "Kills Seattle Holy Roller." 8 May 1906. p1. "Record Quake at Washington." 2 June 1906. p1. "Murderer Pleads Insanity." 26. June 1906. p1. "To Try Creffield's Slayer." 27 June 1906. p1. "Murderer Pleads Insanity." 3 July 1906. p6. "Two Sworn to Kill Creffield." 6 July 1906. p1. "Seattle Jurors Acquit Mitchell." 11 July 1906. p1. "Protects Girl and Is Killed." 13 July 1906. p1. "Repays Brother With a Bullet." 13 July 1906. p2. "Sisters Discuss Murder Details." 14 July 1906. p1. "Will Try Women Jointly." 18 July 1906. p2. "Promises to Aid Mitchell's Slayer." 15 July 1906. p1. "Religious Fakers." 21 July 1906. p6.

Sunday Oregonian. Stewart Holbrook. "Joshua." 29 November 1936. sec. 2, p. 11. Stewart Holbrook. "Joshua Elijah Creffield." 22 November 1936. sec. 2, p. 1. Stewart Holbrook. "Murder Without Tears, Part One.." 8 February 1953. pp. 6-7. Stewart Holbrook. "Murder Without Tears, Part One.." 15 February 1953. pp. 14-15. Stewart Holbrook. "Murder Without Tears, Part One.." 22 February 1953. pp. 10-11. Stewart Holbrook. "Murder Without Tears, Part Four." 1 March 1953. pp. 14-15. Dick Pintarich. "The Strange Saga of Oregon's Other Guru." *Oregonian.* 7 January 1986. p. c1. David Shaw. "When Creffield's Cult Went to Corvallis.'" 24 February 1980. pp. 6NW-9NW.

Morning Oregonian. George White. "Holy Rollerism is Again Revived." 27 June 1906. p1. George White. "Jury is Secured to Try Mitchell." 28 June 1906. p1. George White. "Mitchell Trial on at Seattle." 26 June 1906. p1. George White. "New Tack Taken by the Defense." 28 June 1906. p1.

"To Conduct Salvation Army Meetings." 14 December 1902. p11. "Army Has a Lively Day." 15 December 1902. p14. "Had Troubles Of His Own." 18 January 1903. p24. "Would be Suicide Lives." 19 January 1903. p8. "Burn Up Goods." 31 October 1903. p1. "Anxiety For Infant." 1 November 1903. p7. "Holy Rollers' In Frenzy." 2 November 1903. p10. "Rollers Turned Out." 24 November 1903. p3. "Holy Rollers at Eugene." 12 December 1903. p3. "Put Tar on Rollers." 6 January 1904. p4. "Holy Rollers Run Out." 1 February 1904. p4. "Sharp Lookout For Creffield." 22 March 1904. p6. "Reward For Creffield." 24 April 1904. p10. "Months In Hiding." 20 July 1904. p5. "Apostle Downfall." 31 July 1904. p1. "Could Not Raise Mob." 31 July 1904. p10. "May Cure His Disciples." 31 July 1904. p10. "Prophet In Jail." 31 July 1904. p10. "Salvation Army Pioneer Coming." 31 July 1904. p 20. "Finds Paradise In Hawaii." 1 August 1904. p11. "Says 'I Am Elijah.'" 1 August 1904. p11. Wedding In The Army." 5 August 1904. p7. "Wife Second, Army First." 6 August 1904. p8. "He Goes To Prison." 17 September 1904. p8. "Coated With Tar." 13 March 1905. p1. "Creffield Stirs Up Holy Rollers." 24 April 1906. p7. "Lives With Negroes." 24 April 1906. p3. "Rollers Run Out." 2 May 1906. p6. 3 May 1906. p8. *Morning Oregonian*. "Funds for Mitchell's Defense." 8 May 1906. p6. "Held By A Spell." 8 May 1906. p6. "Holy Roller Shot Down Like A Dog." 8 May 1906. p1. "In Fear Of His Life." 3 May 1906. p6. "Slayers Sister Carried Messages." 8 May 1906. p6. "Edmund Creffield." 9 May 1906. p8. "Justifies The Shot." 9 May 1906. p6. "Manning Upholds Him." 10 May 1906. p6. "Not Dead, She Cries." 10 May 1906. p6. "Bail Is All Ready." 11 May 1906. p6. "Mitchell Will Ask Bail." 12 May 1906. p6. "Mitchell Is Denied Bail. 13 May 1906. p15. 14 May 1906. p6. "Looks For Spirit." 14 May 1906. p5. "Sister Is Against Avenger." 16 May 1906. p6. "Starving Near Heceta Head." 16 May 1906. p1. "Defender of his Honor Released." 17 May 1906. p3. "Public Sentiment Favors Mitchell." 17 May 1906. p3. "Women Rollers Denied Shelter." 17 May 1906. p1. "Creffield Says, 'Don't Worry.'" 27 May 1906. p4. "Witnesses From Corvallis." 23 June 1906. p6. "Trial is Monday." 24 June 1906. p5. "Witnesses for Mitchell." 24 June 1906. p3. "Story of Killing Told by Widow." 30 June 1906. p1. "Mrs. Maud Creffield, Who Testified in the Mitchell Trial at Seattle." 1 July 1906. p3. "Oregon Man Tells Revolting Story." 3 July 1906. p1. "Oregon Men Are Star Witnesses." 4 July 1906. p1. "Others Eager to Slay Creffield." 6 July 1906. p1. "Perry Mitchell Tells His Story." 7 July 1906. p1. "Manning Says Jury Will Acquit." 8 July 1906. p4. "Plan to Revive Holy Rollerism." 9 July 1906. p2. "Admit Jury Acquit Mitchell." 10 July 1906. p1. "Blesses the Newspapers." 11 July 1906. p4. "Calls Him a Creffield." 11 July 1906. p4. "Murder Cases Won by Attorneys." 11 July 1906. p4. "Slayer Mitchell Found Not Guilty." 11 July 1906. p1. "Criminal Legislation." 12 July 1906. p8. "Esther Declined to Be Reconciled." 12 July 1906. p5. 14 July 1906. p6. 16 July 1906. p4. 17 July 1906. p6. "Tongues of Fire Threaten." 31 December 1906. p4. "Color Line Obliterated." 31 December 1906. p4. "Girl Taken From Fanatical Cult." 26 January 1907. p10. "Her Body Quivers as She Worships." 27 January 1907. p4. "Attacked by Mob." 10 February 1907. p10. "Tonguers Refuse to Move." 18 August 1907. p1. "Old Steel Cell Removed." 18 March 1907. p10. "Esther Mitchell Leaves Asylum." 6 April 1909. p1. "Mitchell Girl Escaped." 7 April 1909. p6. "Girl's Career is Tragic." 3 August 1914. p4. "Holy Roller' Girl Slayer Is Suicide." 3 August 1914. p4. "Rocks, Eggs and Bloodshed Early Salvation Fare Here." 30 September 1934. p15. "NW Magazine." 24 February 1980. p. 9.

Newberg Graphic. 2 November 1891. p 3. 30 May 1906. p5. "A Second Mitchell Murder." 19 July 1906. p1. "Mitchell Boys Arrested." 9 August 1906. p8. "Obituary." 17 June 1926. p1.

Newport News. "V. P. Mitchell Services Held." 13 July 1961. page unknown. "David P. Mitchell Dies in Waldport." 13 September 1962. p20. "Obituaries. Attie Irene Levins." 22 June 1922. sec. 2, p2.

News Times (Newport, Oregon). Leslie O'Donnell. "Former follower of The Two looks back at experience." 2 April 1997. p. 1. Leslie O'Donnell. "Memories of The Two surface at news of mass suicide." 2 April 1997. p. A3.

New York Times. "Tapes Left By 39 in Cult Suicide Suggest Comet Was Sign to Die." 28 March 1997. p.1.

Oregon City Courier. "Check sent to Esther Mitchell." 20 July 1906. p2.

Oregon City Enterprise. "Meets A Tragic Death." 11 May 1906. p1. "Esther Mitchell Worked Here." 20 July 1906. p5. "Will Sacrifice His Home." 20 July 1906. p4.

Oregon Daily Journal. Fred Lockley. "Impressions and Observations of the Journal Man." 31 October 1932. p8. "'Holy Rollers' Are Quiet at Present." 2 November 1903. p4. "'Holy Rollers' Seem to Like Oregon." 4 November 1903. p10. "Holy Rollers Pursue Their Crazy Antics." 16 November 1903. p2. "O. V. Hurt Chases the Holy Rollers." 23 November 1903. p12. "Girl of Sixteen Almost Insane."24 November 1903. p12. "Will Make Burn Offering." 25 November 1903. p6. "The Lord May Starve Them."27 November 1903. p3. "'Holy Roller' Hurt Seen In Portland." 8 December 1903. p9. "'Holy Rollers' Not Liked at the Dalles." 29 December 1903. p9. "Brooks and His Feathers." 13 January 1904. p10. "Fred Mitchell Sought Death." 17 January 1903. p2. "Holy Rollers Are Still In Possession." 31 October 1903. p2. "'Holy Rollers' in Hobo Camp Life." 1 February 1904. p8. "Medium Mystify Corvallis People." 11 February 1904. p3. "The 'Holy Rollers' Offend Humanity." 1 March 1904. p1 8 March 1904. p6. "Warrant Out For Holy Roller." 16 March 1904. p4. "Old Mount Rainier May Become Active." 17 March 1904. p4. "'Roller' Prophet Is Still Missing." 17 March 1904. p4. "Apostle Creffield Gets Out Of Country." 18 March 1904. p4. "Chase For Holy Rollers Still On." 22 March 1904. p3. "After the Holy Roller." 30 March 1904. p10. "Holy Roller' Chief Very Badly Wanted." 1 April 1904. p9. "The Salvation Army Gets Mission Money." 3 April 1904. p10. "Not Religion But Murder." 4 April 1904. p6. "Holy Roller High Priest Is Seen." 18 April 1904. p3. "Officer Is On 'Apostle's' Trail." 24 April 1904. p5. "Officer To Seize Young Holy Roller." 29 April 1904. p11. "Frank Hurt Is Forced To Flee." 30 April 1904. p3. "'Holy Rollers' Lose A Convert. 30 April 1904. p3. "'Holy Rollers' Sent To Asylum" 1 May 1904. p3. "'Rollers' Would Restore Eden." 2 May 1904. p1. "Asylum Receives More Fanatics." 7 May 1904. p11. "Two Young Women Are Committed." 7 May 1904. p3. "Thinks Williams May Tell All." 22 July 1904. p1. "Prophet Creffield Is At Last In Jail." 29 July 1904. p1. "Creffield Takes A Bath." 30 July 1904. p3. "Holy Roller High Priest Is Coming." 30 July 1904. p3. "Creffield Says God Will Protect Him From People." 1 August 1904. p1. "No Mob At Corvallis." 2 August 1904. p4. "Apostle Does Not Dislike Prison." 2 August 1904. p2. "'I Know No Sin'—Apostle Creffield." 4 August 1904. p3. "Heavenly Talks In County Jail." 6 August 1904. p2. "Silks And Rags At Army Wedding." 6 August 1904. p3. "No Flowers For 'Apostle' Creffield." 9 August 1904. p2. "Creffield Reward Will Be Returned." 16 August 1904. p1. "Many Of Creffield's Victims May Recover." 19 August 1904. p3. "Creffield Refuses Aid Of An Attorney." 23 August 1904. p8. "Creffield Trial Will Come Soon." 24 August 1904. p3. "Would Sell Nerve Tonic To Creffield." 26 August 1904. p9. "Creffield Destroys His Revelations." 28 August 1904. p3. "Promotes Himself From Plain Elijah." 11 September 1904. p1. "Creffield Is Guilty." 16 September 1904. p1. "Creffield Goes To Penitentiary." 17 September 1904. p7. "Holy Roller Is Taken To Salem." 18 September 1904. p2. "Holy Rollers Gathering Near Waldport." 24 April 1906. p10. "Said To Have Tried To Kill Apostle Creffield." 29 April 1906. p13. "Leaves Home For Roller." 30 April 1906. p1. "Mrs. Starr Walks To Holy Roller Camp." 1 May 1906. p8. "Creffield Poses As Jeremiah." 2 May 1906. p4. "Holy Roller Leader Shot Dead." 7 May 1906. p1. "O. V. Hurt Leaves For Scene Of Shooting." 7 May 1906. p6. "Starr Happy to Get The News." 7 May 1906. p6. "Death of Roller Causes Joy." 8 May 1906. p8. "Creffield's Slayer To Escape, Disciples Disband." 8 May 1906. p1. "Creffield Won Victims of Telepathy." 8 May 1906. p1. "Widow Claims Holy Roller Will Arise From Grave." 9 May 1906. p1. "Mitchell Is Denied Release on Bail." 13 May 1906. p9. "Widow of Holy Roller Is Insane From Waiting to See the Dead Arise." 13 May 1906. p1. "Holy Rollers in Corvallis." 17 May 1906. p2. "Mitchell's Young Sister Esther to Testify Against Brother. 20 May 1906. p4. "Letters from the People." 21 May 1906. p4. "Still Believe In False Prophet." 22 May 1906. p2. "Mitchell's Attorney Goes To Corvallis." 26 May 1906. p8. "Mitchell is Placed on Trial." 25 June 1906. p1. "Sympathy With Mitchell." 26 June 1906. p3. Mitchell Trial Held up by Squabble." 27 June 1906. p8. "Gardner will Testify in the Mitchell Case." 29 June 1906. p8. "Mitchell Trial is Under Way." 29 June 1906. p8. "Mrs. Creffield Testifies." 30 June 1906. p5. "Esther Mitchell on Stand." 2 July 1906. p2. "Creffield Ruined Entire Family." 3 July 1906. p8. "Mitchell and Thaw." 5 July 1906. p8. "Baldwin Tells of His Man Hunt." 5 July 1906. p10. "Old Lady Grills Prosecutor." 6 July 1906. p7. "Mitchell Jury is Kept in Dark." 9 July 1906. p7. "Mitchell's Fate Now With Jury." 10 July 1906. p1. "George Mitchell is Acquitted." 11 July 1906. p3. "Holy Rollers to go to Canada." 11 July 1906. p8. "Manning Says Mitchell Did Just Right." 11 July 1906. p8. "Are They Insane." 13 July 1906. p6. "Esther Mitchell Should Pay Penalty, He Says." 13 July 1906. p2. "Fear Esther Mitchell Will Commit Suicide." 13 July 1906. p1. "Had Three Guns." 13 July 1906. p2. "Hurt Prostrated." 13 July 1906. p6. "Mrs. Starr Not Sorry for Crime." 13 July 1906. p1. "Story of Crime." 13 July 1906. p2. "Upton Drunk." 13 July 1906. p2. "Will Plead Guilty." 13 July 1906. p2. "Wires Congratulations." 13 July 1906. p2. "Women Went Armed." 13 July 1906. p2. "Worked at Oregon City." 13 July 1906. p2. "Both Killed in Same Way." 14 July 1906. p8. "Esther Mitchell, Maud Creffield are Both Charged With Murder." 14 July 1906. p1. "Gallows Shadow Over Two Women." 14 July 1906. p8. "Body is Shipped to Oregon." 16 July 1906. p6. "Manning Scored by Frater." 16

July 1906. p6. "Says Frank Hurt is Innocent." 16 July 1906. p2. "Lies Beside His Mother." 17 July 1906. p6. "In First Degree." 18 July 1906. p1. "Mitchell is Buried." 18 July 1906. p3. "Holy Roller Family is Leaving Corvallis." 19 July 1906. p2. "Holy Rollerism is Dead Forever." 19 July 1906. p2. "Will Defend Women." 19 July 1906. p2. "Attorney Morris Offers Aid." 20 July 1906. p12. "To Sacrifice Oldest Child." 20 July 1906. p1. 21 July 1906. p2. "Mysterious Note to O. V. Hurt." 21 July 1906. p8. "End to Troubles of Holy Roller Family." 22 July 1906. p13. "Esther Mitchell Sheds Tears." 22 July 1906. p20. "Holy Rollerism is Discussed." 23 July 1906. p3. "Laws Are Needed, Says Pastor." 23 July 1906. p3. "Women Arraigned for Murder." 23 July 1906. p8. "Withdraws Complaint." 27 July 1906. p3. "Not Guilty, Plea of Murderess." 31 July 1906. p8. "Holy Roller Makes Human Torch as Sacrifice." 25 August 1906. p12. "White Women Join Negroes in Frenzy of Religious Orgy." 4 September 1906. p1. "Woman Robs Husband to Join Holy Rollers." 8 September 1906. p12. "Esther Mitchell Close to Death from Typhoid." 12 August 1906. p1. "Development of Bohemia." 12 September 1906. p13. "To Examine Minds of Slayers." 10 September 1906. p7. "Mrs. Creffield's Trial Set for Next Month." 16 September 1906. p14. "Glad Mitchell is Murdered." 18 September 1906. p10. "Ship Murderess to Oregon." 19 September 1906. p8. "Both Women May Go Free." 21 September 1906. p8. "Corvallis Woman Takes Dose of Poison." 21 September 1906. p8. "Frater Must Not Deport Women." 24 September 1906. p7. "Holy Roller Woman Dies While in Trance." 1 October 1906. p2. "California Holy Rollers Will Invade Capital City." 4 October 1906. p14. "Epilepsy Ends Mad Revel of Holy Rollerism." 10 October 1906. p2. "Holy Roller Mania Has Seized Women." 22 October 1906. p6. "Says Alliance Is Not Holy Roller Church." 23 October 1906. p6. "Ask Police Aid." 15 November 1906. p3. "Maud Creffield Dies in Jail." 17 November 1906. p12. "Poison May Have Caused Death." 18 November 1906. p26. "Only What He Expected." 18 November 1906. p26. "Creffield's Widow Died From Poison." 20 November 1906. p1. "Deaths." 18 February 1909. p. 12. "Esther Mitchell Did Not Break Parole." 8 April 1909. p11. "Holy Roller Principal Suicide." 3 August 1914. p14. 9 January 1937. p4.

Oregon Sunday Journal. "Murderess Cursed by Brothers." 15 July 1906. p1.

Oregon Magazine. March, 1983, p. 44.

Oregon Union. 4 February 1898. p. 3.

Pacific Christian Advocate (Portland). "Religious Fakirs." No. 22. 16 May 1906. p. 4.

Polk County Observer. "The Holy Rollers. 6 November 1903. p1.

San Francisco Chronicle. "May Offer Up Human Sacrifice." 1 November 1903. p19. "Holy Rollers Leave in Fear. 3 November 1903. p1. "Leader of Holy Rollers Returns to his Flock. 6 November 1903. p3.

Seattle Daily Times. Walter Deffenbaugh. "Creffield's Ghost Controls His Flock." 1 July 1906. p. 3. Walter Deffenbaugh. "Esther Mitchell at Brother's Trial." 30 June 1906. p. 1. Walter Deffenbaugh. "Mitchell is at Last on Trial." 29 June 1906. p. 1. Walter Deffenbaugh."Mitchell Meets His Aged Father." 28 June 1906. p. 1. Walter Deffenbaugh. "Still Working on Mitchell Jury." 26 June 1906. p. 1. E. O. Kelsey. "O. V. Hurt, Star Witness for Mitchell Defense, Gives His Testimony." 3 July 1906. p1. E. O. Kelsey. "Mitchell Weeps While Starr Testifies." 4 July 1906. p1. E. O. Kelsey "Attorneys Argue Many Wary Hours." 5 July 1906. p1. E. O. Kelsey. "Audience Shouts Approval of Verdict." 11 July 1906. p1. E. O. Kelsey. "Killing of Emory May Effect Mitchell." 9 July 1906. p3. E. O. Kelsey. "Mitchell Case Goes to Jury." 10 July 1906. p1. E. O. Kelsey. "Mitchell Jury to be Given Case Wednesday." 8 July 1906. p17. E. O.Kelsey. " Signal Victory for Mitchell Defense." 7 July 1906. p1. E. O. Kelsey. "Visits Wrath on Head of State's Attorney." 6 July 1906. p1. "New Officers Take Up Religious Work." 25 April 1906. p5. "Creffield's Followers In An Insane Asylum." 7 May 1906. p2. "Creffield Shot To Death." 7 May 1906. p1. "Justifiable Homicide?" 8 May 1906. p1. "Mitchell to Get Medal For Murder." 8 May 1906. p1. "Doings of Holy Rollers at Corvallis." 10 May 1906. p1. "Bullet Only Way to Save His Sisters." 10 May 1906. p1. "Mitchell To Be Arraigned At Once." 11 May 1906. p1. "Statue Prevents Granting Bail To Mitchell." 12 May 1906. p1. "Creffield is Due To Rise Today." 13 May 1906. p1. "Creffield Victim Tells Sad Story." 15 May 1906. p1. "Let The Law Take Its Course." 15 May 1906. p6. "Oregon Citizens Plan Aid for Mitchell." 15 May 1906. p1. "Creffield Said To Stay." 16 May 1906. p4. "Creffield Made No Denial Of His Acts." 17 May 1906. p4. "Five Refugees Return." 17 May

1906. p5. "Holy Roller Wife Would Be Forgiven." 17 May 1906. p5. "Religious Fanatic Terrifies Sailors." 17 May 1906. p5. "Creffield Driven From Vermont." 18 May 1906. p4. "Mitchell Enters His Formal Plea." 19 May 1906. p1. "New Head of the Police Department of Seattle. 20 May 1906. p1. "Joshua Says Not to Worry." 27 May 1906. p10. "Claims Mitchell Rid World of a Fiend." 1 June 1906. p1. "Talesman to Try Mitchell." 16 June 1906. p5. "Many Witnesses For Mitchell." 19 June 1906. p5. "Mitchell Trial Tomorrow." 24 June 1906. p12. "Mitchell Trial Begins." 25 June 1906. p1. "Says She Talked With God." 25 June 1906. p2. "Still Endeavoring to Secure a Jury to Try Mitchell." 27 June 1906. p1.Witnesses at the Mitchell Trial. 30 June 1906. p1. "Esther Mitchell on Witness Stand." 2 July 1906. p1. "Comes to Testify in Behalf of Mitchell." 4 July 1906. p1. "Claims Mitchell was Insane." 6 July 1906. p14. "Mitchell Seeks Aid." 8 July 1906. p21. "Thompson is Charged with First Degree Murder." 10 July 1906. p1.11 July 1906. p6. "Mitchell Seeks His Sister." 11 July 1906. p9. "Much Credit Due Prosecuting Attorney." 11 July 1906. p1. "General Rejoicing at Mitchell's Acquittal." 12 July 1906. p2. "Avenge Death of Creffield" 4th Extra. 12 July 1906. p1. "Is Reconciled to Her Father." 5 o'clock edition,12 July 1906. p9. "Brothers Will Testify Against Esther Mitchell." 13 July 1906. p13. "Creffield's Followers in Camp at Kiger's Island." 13 July 1906. p13. "Creffield's Widow Had Three Revolvers." 13 July 1906. p1. "Declares Esther is Surely Insane." 13 July 1906. p1. "Esther Mitchell is Willing to Hang." 13 July 1906. p2. "Murder Causes a Sensation in Portland." 13 July 1906. p13. "Murder Mania is Denounced by Lawyers." 13 July 1906. p3. "Pay Last Tribute to Memory of Jurist." 13 July 1906. p2. "Spangenberg Sold Woman Revolver." 13 July 1906. p13. "Suicide Rumor Causes Sheriff Much Trouble." 13 July 1906. p3. "The Times Scoops." 13 July 1906. p1. "Walla Walla Man Glad Mitchell Died." 13 July 1906. p2. "Wagner Would Aid Women in Fight." 13 July 1906. p2. "Wanton Murder!" 13 July 1906. p1. "Was One of Most Fanatical of Sect." 13 July 1906. p13. "Woman's Great Crime Causes Loss of Friend." 14 July 1906. p4. "Brothers Refuse to Aid Esther Mitchell." 14 July 1906. p1. "Four Holy Rollers Living at Everett." 14 July 1906. p4. "Seek to Raise Money to Bury Their Brother." 14 July 1906. p4. "The Insanity Farce." 14 July 1906. p6. "Follows in Steps of Creffield." 16 July 1906. p11. "Body is Shipped to Oregon." 16 July 1906. p4. "Mitchell's Murderers Talk to a Lawyer." 16 July 1906. p10. "Will Look After His Daughter's Defense." 16 July 1906. p5. "Mitchell Buried in Oregon." 17 July 1906. p8. "Murderers Are Examined Daily." 17 July 1906. p8. "Cheap 'Economy' Talk." 19 July 1906. p6. "Esther Mitchell Receives $1." 22 July 1906. p8. "Holy Rollers in California." 22 July 1906. p11. "Hurt Thinks Both Women Are Insane." 22 July 1906. p44. "Frater Favors a Commission of Alienists." 23 July 1906. p10. "Mackintosh Will Oppose Calling Commission." 24 July 1906. p5. "Army Has Moved to Seattle." 26 July 1906. p11. "Esther Mitchell Pleads Not Guilty." 31 July 1906. p9. "Esther Mitchell Very Ill." 13 August 1906. p5. "Criminal Court to be Busy." 1 September 1906. p1. "Esther Mitchell May Escape Trial." 10 September 1906. p1. "Sets Creffield Case for Trial in October." 15 September 1906. p14. "Insanity Inquest Unfinished." 17 September 1906. p4. "Maud Creffield Anxious to Hang." 18 September 1906. p1. "Declares Slayers of Mitchell Insane." 20 September 1906. p1. "Insanity Excuse Arouses Much Indignation." 21 September 1906. p1. "Where is This Thing to End!" 22 September 1906. p6. "Murders Must Be Tried." 23 September 1906. p1. "Judge Frater is in Very Small Business." 25 September 1906. p1. "Supreme Court Acts." 24 September 1906. p1.Insanity Board Not Paid." 28 September 1906. p13. "Murder Epidemic as Result of 'Insanity' Folly Predicted by Times." 2 October 1906. p1. "Neighbors Object to Religious Sect." 17 October 1906. p1. "Religious Excitement Raging in Salem, Ore." 27 October 1906. p4. "Maud Creffield Dies in County Jail." 17 November 1906. p2. "Death May End a Hypnotic Spell." 18 November 1906. p1. "Mrs. Creffield's Father Coming." 18 November 1906. p4. "Esther Mitchell Breaks Down at Funeral." 19 November 1906. p7. "Mrs. Creffield Killed Herself with Poison!" 20 November 1906. p1. "Daily Statistics." Deaths." 21 November 1906. p16. "Religious Frenzy in Ballard." 30 November 1906. p10. "Recent Insanity Hearings Provoke Startling Charges." 4 December 1906. p1. "Bar Association Will Investigate Charges Against Frater!" 5 December 1906. p1. "Strikes Blow at Insanity Plea Dodge." 5 December 1906. p2.

Seattle Mail and Herald. Myron Haynes. "The Creffield Murder—Shall it be Condoned" 16 May 1906. p4. "Salmagundi." 12 May 1906. p3. "Reaping the Whirlwind." 21 July 1906. p3.

Seattle Post-Intelligencer. Sam Angeloff. "He Raised His Voice in Holy Anger." 15 May 1906. page unknown. "Marriage Licenses." 4 April 1906. p11. "History of the 'Holy Rollers.'" 8 May 1906. p11. "Leader Of 'Holy Rollers' Killer." 8 May 1906. p1. "Crefeld [*sic*] is to be Buried Today." 9 May 1906. p1. "Oregon Prosecutor Would Aid Mitchell." 10 May 1906. p1. "Shows No Emotion At Husband's Grave." 10 May 1906. p1. "Insanity May Be Mitchell's Plea." 11 May 1906. p5. "Mitchell May Ask Court for Bail." 12 May 1906. p5. "Court Denies Bail to Geo. Mitchell." 13 May

1906. p5. "Crefeld [sic] Fails to Rise From Dead." 14 May 1906. p12. "Mitchell to Enter Plea Tomorrow." 18 May 1906. p5. "Mitchell to Enter Plea of Not Guilty." 19 May 1906. p5. "F. M. Dow Denies Knowing Crefeld [sic]." 20 May 1906. p5. "Attorneys Ready For Mitchell Trial." 23 June 1906. p9. "Mitchell Declares He Is Not Guilty." 30 May 1906. p5. "Select Jurors in Mitchell Trial." 26 June 1906. p1. "Mitchell Trial Advances Slowly." 27 June 1906. p1. "Special Venire in Mitchell's Trial." 28 June 1906. p1. "Thirty More Named as Special Jurors." 28 June 1906. p5. "Evidence against Mitchell Today." 29 June 1906. p1. "Maud Crefeld [sic] on Witness Stand." 30 June 1906. p1. "Crefeld [sic]'s Doings Plea of Defense." 1 July 1906. sec. 2, p7. "Insane Delusion Mitchell's Plea." 3 July 1906. p1. "Tell How Homes Were Broken Up." 4 July 1906. p1. "Oregon Attorney Here for Mitchell." 5 July 1906. p5. "Witnesses from Portland Called." 5 July 1906. p5. "Say They Wished to Kill Crefeld [sic]" 6 July 1906. p1. "Mitchell's Defense Soon Will Close." 7 July 1906. p16. "Mitchell Insane Expert Testifies." 8 July 1906. p12. "Mitchell Trial About Concluded." 10 July 1906. p4. "Mitchell Freed by Jury's Verdict." 11 July 1906. p1. "Mitchell's Father Leaves for East." 12 July 1906. p5. "Attorney Miller Goes to Morgue." 13 July 1906. p5. "Both Sleep Soundly at the County Jail." 13 July 1906. p5. "Chester Thompson is Not Informed." 13 July 1906. p5. "Crowds Try to Get Look at Murderess." 13 July 1906. p4. "George Mitchell Killed by Sister." 13 July 1906. p6. "Holy Rollerism' Cause of Tragedy." 13 July 1906. p5. "Hurt Hopes Esther Will Be Punished." 13 July 1906. p1. "Judge W. H. Upton Offers Assistance." 13 July 1906. p1. "Maud Crefeld Was Given Revolver." 13 July 1906. p4. "Mitchell Bade Jailers Good-Bye." 13 July 1906. p4. "Mrs. Starr Smiles at Brother's Death." 13 July 1906. p1. "Obituaries." 13 July 1906. p11. "Perry Mitchell Tells of Killing." 13 July 1906. p4. "Planned to Kill Mitchell Herself." 13 July 1906. p4. "Says She Does Not Regret Shooting." 13 July 1906. p4. "Sisters Conversed Daily Over Phone." 13 July 1906. p4. "Sister Said She Would Have Killed." 13 July 1906. p4. "State's Attorney Makes Statement." 13 July 1906. p5. "Too Easy to Get Pistols." 13 July 1906. p6. "Widow Blamed for the Tragedy." 13 July 1906. p4. "Attorney Manning Discusses Murder." 14 July 1906. p1. "Wanted to Assist Distressed Women." 14 July 1906. p1. "Declares Murder Was for Revenge." 14 July 1906. p10. "Deny Religion Led to Killing." 14 July 1906. p10. "Prosecutor Will File Information." 14 July 1906. p10. "Shows Mitchell had Normal Brain." 14 July 1906. p1. "Surprised by the Action of Manning." 15 July 1906. p5. "O. V. Hurt Sends Aid to Daughter." 15 July 1906. p7. "Both Women Will Ask for Attorney." 16 July 1906. p14. "Says She Has Kept Religion Out of It." 16 July 1906. p14. "Still Loves His Daughter Maud." 17 July 1906. p16. "May Take Esther Mitchell South." 18 July 1906. p1. "Threaten Sister of George Mitchell." 18 July 1906. p10. "Information Filed in Mitchell Case." 19 July 1906. p10. "Says Roller Creed is Dead Forever." 19 July 1906. p5. "The Insane of Criminal Impulse." 19 July 1906. p6. "To Arraign Esther Mitchell Monday." 20 July 1906. p5. "Mitchell Boys to Stand by Esther." 21 July 1906. p1. "Says Crefeld [sic] Was 'Good Godly Man.'" 22 July 1906. p14. "Esther Mitchell Sent Dollar Back." 23 July 1906. p14. "Esther Mitchell Appears in Court." 24 July 1906. p9. "Headquarters of Province Here." 27 July 1906. p7. "Write Letters to Esther Mitchell." 28 July 1906. p5. "Relatives to Help Esther Mitchell." 1 August 1906. p16. "W. A. Holzheimer Will Defend Mrs. Crefeld [sic]." 6 August 1906. p11. "Esther Mitchell Not Seriously Ill." 13 August 1906. p4. "Charges Mitchell Girl is Insane." 11 September 1906. p4. "Esther Mitchell Objects to Help." 13 September 1906. p1. "State to Oppose Insanity Charge."14 September 1906. p1. "Secret Sessions in Mitchell Case." 15 September 1906. p5. "Crefeld [sic] Murder Trial on Oct. 22." 16 September 1906. p7. "Insanity Hearing May Close Monday." 16 September 1906. p7. "New Evidence in Sanity Hearing." 18 September 1906. p16. "Mitchell Crefeld [sic] Hearing is Ended." 19 September 1906. p5. "Insanity Board May Report Today." 20 September 1906. p7. "Esther Mitchell and Mrs. Crefeld [sic] Insane." 21 September 1906. p1. "Miller Objects to Board's Report." 22 September 1906. p1. "Supreme Court to Determine Sanity." 23 September 1906. p1. "Injunction Issued in Mitchell Case." 25 September 1906. p1. "Restraint Might Only Delay Case." 27 September 1906. p7. "Monday Was Time For Crefeld [sic]." 21 October 1906. p5. "Crefeld [sic]-Mitchell Case is Submitted." 27 October 1906. p8. "Mrs. Hurt Visits Daughter in Jail." 11 November 1906. p5. "Believes Death Came Naturally." 17 November 1906. p1. "Maud Crefeld [sic] Dies in the County Jail." 17 November 1906. p1. "Tragic Record of the Holy Rollers." 17 November 1906. p1. "Cause of Death Not Determined." 18 November 1906. p4. "Esther Mitchell Refuses Visitors." 18 November 1906. p4. "Girl May Attend Funeral Services." 18 November 1906. p4. 18 November 1906. Classified Albany Democrat Section, p1. "Gives Opinion on Crefeld [sic] Autopsy." 19 November 1906. p5. "O. V. Hurt Arrives From Corvallis." 19 November 1906. p16. "Says Friend Did Not Kill Herself." 22 November 1906. p4. "Holy Roller Leader Buried Beside Wife." 22 November 1906. p4. "Decided Change in Esther Mitchell." 20 November 1906. p10. "Funeral Held to Late Mrs. Crefeld [sic]." 20 November 1906. p10. "Special Notices—Deaths and Funerals." 20 November 1906. p14. "Poison is Found in the Stomach of Mrs. Crefeld [sic]."

21 November 1906. p1. "Esther Mitchell Goes to Asylum." 21 February 1907. p4.

Seattle Star. "I Got My Man." 7 May 1906. p1. "Revolting Creed Of Holy Rollers." 7 May 1906. p3. "Justifiable Homicide Is the Defense." 8 May 1906. p1. "'He Is Not Dead But Will Arise.'—Mrs. Edmund Creffield." 9 May 1906. p1. "Why? The Case of George Beede." 9 May 1906. p1. "Will Try His Best To Hang. Geo. Mitchell." 9 May 1906. p1. "Offers of Aid for Mitchell Are Pouring In." 10 May 1906. p1. "Writes Plea for Mitchell." 10 May 1906. p3. "Holy Roller Ruled by Hypnotic Power." 11 May 1906. p1. "Mitchell Must Remain in Jail." 12 May 1906. p1. "What an Honorable Man Thinks of Geo. Mitchell." 12 May 1906. p1. "Creffield's Widow Watches at Grave." 14 May 1906. p1. "Sister Turns on Mitchell." 14 May 1906. p6. "Holy Roller Hurt Back From Oregon." 15 May 1906. "Miss Mitchell to Be Chief Witness." 15 May 1906. p3. "Attack on Mitchell Fails to Carry." 16 May 1906. p7. "Were Half Starved But Still Faithful." 17 May 1906. p7. "Creffield (obliterated text) Rail In Vermont." 18 May 1906. p1. "Expert Writes on Creffield Case." 18 May 1906. p1. "Esther Mitchell." 19 May 1906. p1. "'Not Guilty' Is His Plea." 19 May 1906. p1. "Gets Message From Messiah." 28 May 1906. p7. "Creffield's Influences." 1 June 1906. p1. "Witnesses Called in Mitchell Case." 19 June 1906. p1. "Mitchell's Brother Here for the Trial." 22 June 1906. p1. "Will Testify For Mitchell." 23 June 1906. p1. "George Mitchell on Trial For His Life." 25 June 1906. p1. "Mitchell's Brother Here For the Trial." 25 June 1906. p1. "Mitchell Jury is Selected with Care." 26 June 1906. p1. "Slow Work to Pick the Mitchell Jury." 27 June 1906. p1. "State and Defense Weed Out Jurors." 28 June 1906. p1. "Mitchell Trial is Now on in Earnest." 29 June 1906. p1. "State Will Close its Case Monday." 30 June 1906. p1. "'God Bless You, George; We're Praying For You.'" 2 July 1906. p1. "Hurt Tells the Horrible Story of Holy Rollerism." 3 July 1906. p1. "Wanted a Chance to Kill Creffield." 5 July 1906. p1. "Are Sure Mitchell Was Out of His Mind." 6 July 1906. p1. "Insanity Expert on the Witness Stand." 7 July 1906. p1. "Mitchell Jury is Kept in Ignorance." 9 July 1906. p1. "Esther Mitchell Makes Her Escape." 10 July 1906. p1. "Mitchell May Know Fate before Night." 10 July 1906. p1. "George Mitchell is Now a Free Man." 11 July 1906. p1. "Mitchells Go to Portland." 12 July 1906. p7. "Climax of Crime in History of Seattle." 13 July 1906. p1. "Crowds Flock to View Body." 13 July 1906. p1. "Demands Arrest of Frank Hurt." 13 July 1906. p6. "Do Not Believe Hurt Implicated." 13 July 1906. p7. "Esther Tried to Hide Name." 13 July 1906. p1. "'Flower Girl' Visits Morgue." 13 July 1906. p7. "Girl's Heart Will Break." 13 July 1906. p1. "Intimate Study of the Face of Esther Mitchell." 13 July 1906. p1. "Her Good-Bye Was a Missile of Death." 13 July 1906. p1. "Hurt Cleared of Suspicion." 13 July 1906. p1. "Mrs. Creffield Bought Gun." 13 July 1906. p7. "Mrs. Creffield Did Planning." 13 July 1906. p6. "Murder in First Degree." 13 July 1906. p1. "Sister Smiles Over Murder." 13 July 1906. p7. "Sleeps the Sleep of a Care-Free Girl." 13 July 1906. p1. "Will Hold a Post-Mortem." 13 July 1906. p1. "Brain Shows no Insanity." 14 July 1906. p1. "Doesn't Blame His Daughter." 14 July 1906. p3. "Dr. Haynes Roasts Seattle Reporter." 14 July 1906. p1. "Father's Love is Still Alive." 14 July 1906. p1. "File Charge Next Week." 14 July 1906. p1. "Flowers Deck Body of Boy." 14 July 1906. p1. "Holy Rollers at Everett." 14 July 1906. p7. "Insanity Plea is Loophole in Law." July 1906. p1. "Mitchell Boys Are Done With Esther." 14 July 1906. p1. "Need Money for Mitchell Funeral." 14 July 1906. p1. "Women Have no Defense Plans." 14 July 1906. p1. "Money is Raised to Bury Mitchell." 16 July 1906. p8. "Pastors Talk of Tragedies." 16 July 1906. p8. "Will Mortgage His Home for Daughter." 16 July 1906. p1. "Early Trial for Women Slayers." 17 July 1906. p1. "Let's Think When We Talk." 17 July 1906. p4. "Will Provide for Daughter." 17 July 1906. p1. "Esther Mitchell to Have Defense." 18 July 1906. p1. "Threatens His Sister's Life." 18 July 1906. p1. "Mrs. Creffield Weeps in Jail." 19 July 1906. p1. "Mitchell's Slayers are Arraigned." 23 July 1906. p1. "Holy Rollers Seek Home in Wyoming." 27 July 1906. p1. "Esther Mitchell Pleads Tomorrow." 30 July 1906. p1. "Esther Mitchell Says Not Guilty." 31 July 1906. p1. "Will Defend Mrs. Creffield." 4 August 1906. p5. "Are Like the Holy Rollers." 11 August 1906. p1. "Esther Mitchell is Far From Death." 13 August 1906. p1. "Terrible Tale of Illness of Esther Mitchell." 14 August 1906. p1. "Will be Tried Next Month." 8 September 1906. p1. "Hurt Thinks His Daughter Insane." 12 September 1906. p7. "Women Not Agitated." 14 September 1906. p1. "Trial Set for Mrs. Creffield." 15 September 1906. p1. "Mrs. Creffield on Stand." 17 September 1906. p1. "Did Only What the Spirits Commanded." 18 September 1906. p7. "Are They Sane or Insane?" 19 September 1906. p6. "Says Examination Was Only a Farce." 21 September 1906. p1. "Writ for Frater." 25 September 1906. p6. "Where Women are 'Inspired.'" 12 November 1906. p1. "'God's Children' Rejoice Joyfully." 16 November 1906. p8. "Third Fatality in Holy Roller Drama." 17 November 1906. p1. "Mrs. Creffield Laid to Rest." 19 November 1906. p3. "Maud Creffield Died by Her Own Hand." 20 November 1906. p1. "They Still Scout Theory of Suicide." 21 November 1906. p1. "Washing Dirty Linen." 4 December 1906. p1. "Say It Is Up to Judge Frater." 5 December 1906. p1. "Judge Frater Hits Back at Mackintosh." 6 December 1906. p1. "Baptized in

Icy Waters." 19 December 1906. p1.

Seattle Sunday Times. "An Epidemic of Murder." 15 July 1906. p1. 15 July 1906. p6. "Says Daughter is Not Insane." 15 July 1906. p1. "Hurt Will Come to Aid of His Daughter." 15 July 1906. p1.

South Lincoln County News (Waldport, Oregon). Colleen Nickerson. "Waldport Heritage Museum." 24 August 1999. p. 2. "Eyes of World fall on Waldport." 1 April 1997. p. 1. "Obituary." 20 April 1999. p. 2.

Tacoma Daily News. "Holy Roller is Shot Down in Street." 5 May 1906. p. 1. "Are to Defend Holy Roller Slayer" 8 May 1906. p. 1.

The Dalles Daily Chronicle. "Salvation Army." 22 September 1900. p3. 18 October 1900. p3. 1 November 1900. p4. "Grand Farewell Meeting." 3 November 1900. p4.

The Dalles Semi-Weekly Chronicle. 24 June 1903. p3. 22 July 1903. p3. "False Doctrine." 25 July 1903. p4. 22 August 1903. p3. 2 September 1903. p3. "Local Items." 5 September 1903. p3. "Fanatics Antics Excite Corvallis." 4 November 1903. p1. "Crefield [sic] Reappears." 7 November 1903. p1. "Had Promise of Tar and Feathers." 7 November 1903. p1. "Alice, Arise, I command Thee." 11 November 1903. p1. 21 November 1903. p1. "Holy Roller Insane." 28 November 1903. p1. "Rollers Rolled in Feathers." 9 January 1904. p3. "Officers to Seize Young Holy Roller." 4 May 1904. p1. "The Doomed Murderer." 16 July 1904. p3. "Creffield is Captured." 3 August 1904. p1. "Not Creffieldites." 3 August 1904. p4. 17 September 1904. p3. "Two Years in Pen." 21 September 1904. p3. 24 September 1904. p2. "Tar and Feather Case." 18 March 1905. p3. "Shadow of Scaffold." 22 July 1905. p2.

The Dalles Weekly Chronicle. 19 April 1902. p3. 23 April 1902. p3. 1 October 1902. p3. 3 December 1902. p3. 10 December 1902. p3. "Holy Rollers Gathering." 27 April 1906. p1. "Won Following by Telepathy." 11 May 1906. p1. "Slaying the 'Prophets.'" 11 May 1906. p4. "For Defense of Mitchell." 18 May 1906. p4. "Ready to Try Mitchell." 22 June 1906. p3. "Creffield's Slayer on Trial." 29 June 1906. p9. "Joshua's Ghost in County Jail." 29 June 1906. p1.

The War Cry. Crefeld [sic] Edmund. 21 September 1901. "Holiness." p3. 4 November 1899. p13. 25 November 1899. p11 ."Promotions." 25 November 1899. p16. "War Cry Booming in Reality. Report Seattle Corps No. 1." 18 August 1900. p. 10. 12 January 1901. p6. 23 February 1901. p11. "Promotions." 16 March 1901. p8. "A visit from the P. O." 6 July 1901. p10. "Pacific Coast Notes" 20 July 1901. p2. 27 July 1901. p. 8. 1 November 1902. p11. 13 December 1902. p7. 14 January 1903. p10. "Pacific Coast Provincial Notes." 24 January 1903. p10. 21 February 1903. p10. "Revival Marks Our Field Reports This Week." 28 February 1903. p14.

The West. Tompkins, Peter. "Oregon's Bearded Prophet." March 1972. pp. 28-29, 50-55.

Weekly Gazette-Times. "Esther Mitchell Found in a Hut." 20 August 1909. p7. "Mitchell Girl at Waldport." 27 August 1909. p6. 28 April 1911. p8.

Weekly Herald Disseminator. "Holy Rollers Again Scattered." 1 January 1904. p2. "Creffield Has at Last Been Caught." 4 August 1904. p1. "Holy Roller." 8 August 1904. p7. "Holy Roller Mania." 26 April 1906. p5. "Holy Rollers in Albany." 3 May 1904. p5. "Burned His Shoes in County Jail." 5 May 1904. p1. "Holy Rollers in the Public Eye." 5 May 1904. p7. "A Reminder of Creffield." 17 May 1906. p7. "Took Strychnine." 22 November 1906. p1. "Weeps Like a Child." 22 November 1906. p. 12.

West Side Enterprise. "Passed Through." 4 August 1904. p2. "Passed Through." 24 August 1904. p3.

Yamhill County Reporter. "Corvallis and Eastern Railroad." 19 April 1906. p4. "Holy Roller Craze Again." 26 April 1906. p2. 3 May 1906. p3. "Married." 9 April 1914. p1. 6 August 1914. p1. 13 August 1914. p3. 3 April 1919. "Vernon LaMar Hartley Called." 7 August 1919. "Frank Hurt Meets Death by Gun Accident." 15 January 1920. p1. "Mrs. Warren Hartley Dies Following Long Illness." 2 November 1933. 14 December 1894. p3. 6 November 1903. p8. 13 November 1903. p4. 20 November 1903. p4. 12 February 1904. p5.

Yaquina Bay News. "Holy Roller Craze Again." 26 April 1906. p2. "Mrs. J. K. Berry Commits Suicide." 6 August 1914. p1. "Frank Hurt Meets Death by Gun Accident." 15 January 1920. p1.

Miscellaneous Sources

Apostolic Faith Mission. The Apostolic Faith Publishers. Portland, Oregon. 1965.

Bahn, Elizabeth. Interview with Robert Blodgett. July 13, 1996.

Beach, Robert Homer and Pauline. Interview with Robert Blodgett. October 5, 1996.

Beam, Maurice. *Cults of America.* MacFadden Books, New York. 1964.

Bowen, Ezra, ed. *This Fabulous Century, 1900-1910.* "Scandal of the Decade." New York: Time-Life Books. 1969.

Buchanan, John. Letter to Stewart Holbrook. 1 March 1953.

Burgess, Stanley M. and Gary B. McGee, eds. *Dictionary of Pentecostal and Charismatic Movements.* Grand Rapids, MI: Regency Reference Library. 1988.

Castle, Darlene. *Yaquina Bay 1778-1978.* Lincoln County Historical Society. Newport, OR. 1978.

Chamberlin, Ellen. Letter to Stewart Holbrook. 1 December 1936.

Crimes and Punishment, Volume 1. "The Socialite and the Playboy." BPC Publishing Limited: United Kingdom. 1973. pp. 43-47.

Fagan, David D. *History of Benton County, Oregon.* 1885.

Halperin, David A. *Psychodynamic Perspectives on Religion, Sect and Cult.* John Wright•PSG Inc. Boston, Bristol, London. 1983.

Hayes, Marjorie H. *The Land That Kept Its Promise, (A History of South Lincoln County).* Lincoln County Historical Society, Newport, OR. Copyright 1976, Third Printing, January 1991.

Hexham, Irving and Karla Poewe. *Understanding Cults and New Religions.* William B. Eerdmans Publishing Company. Grand Rapids, MI. 1986.

Holbrook, Stewart H. *Murder out Yonder.* "Death and Times of a Prophet." MacMillan Company, New York. 1941. pp. 1-22.

Holbrook, Stewart, *Wildmen, Wobblies & Whistle Punks.* "Death and Times of a Prophet." Oregon State University Press, Corvallis. 1992. pp. 41-60.

Knapp, Martin Wells (ed). *Bible Songs of Salvation and Victory.* Cincinnati: M. W. Knapp. 1901.

Langford, Gerald. *The Murder of Stanford White.* Bobbs-Merrill Company, Inc. Indianapolis, New York. 1962.

Hayes, Marjorie H. *The Land That Kept Its Promise, (A History of South Lincoln County).* Lincoln County Historical Society, Newport, OR. 1991.

http://omhs.mhd.hr.state.or.us/ORHIST.htm

http://www.ci.corvallis.or.us/historic/indextxt.html

http://www.findagrave.com/pictures/10789.html

http://www.halcyon.com/jennyrt/WABios/kmackintosh.txt.

http://www.halcyon.com/jennyrt/WABios/wmorris.txt.

http://www.historylink.org/output.cfm?file_id=2800

http://www.wolfe.net/~dhillis/history9.htm

Johnson, Joan. *The Cult Movement.* Franklin Watts. New York, London, Toronto, Sydney. 1984.

Kent, Eugene. *The Siletz Indian Reservation 1855-1900.* Portland State University. Portland, OR. 1973.

Lane County Historian. Lane County Historical Society. Summer, 1981

Lincoln County Extension Office. *Lincoln County Histories.* Newport, Oregon. 1976.

McCormack, Win and Dick Pintarich. *Great Moments in Oregon History.* New Oregon Publisher, Inc. Portland, OR. 1987.

Porterfield, Kay Marie. *Straight Talk About Cults.* Facts on File, An Infobase Holdings Company. New York, NY. 1995.

Price, Richard L. *Newport, Oregon.* 1866-1936. Lincoln County Historical Society, Newport. 1975.

Reynolds, Minerva Kiger. *Corvallis In 1900.*

Shaw, David. "Wanted, Edmund Creffield, alias 'Joshua.'" (photo-copied article with no source or date written on it.)

Shirley (like Cher, she has no last name). Interview with Robert Blodgett. 1996.

Special Reports. Religious Bodies: 1906. Department of Commerce and Labor, Bureau of the Census. Government Printing Office, Washington, D. C. 1910.

Stevens, Virginia. Interview with Robert Blodgett. July 13, 1996.

Shumway, G W. Study of "The Gift of Tongues." AB thesis, University of Southern California, 1914.

Vanzandt, J. C. *Speaking in Tongues.* J.C. Vanzandt, Portland, Oregon, 1926.

Van de Velde, Paul and Henriette R. *South Lincoln County and its Early Settlers, I. Charles L. Litchfield.* Lincoln County Historical Society, Publication No. 4-A.

Washington State Archives. An undated biography of Judge Archibald Wanless Frater, handwritten by an unknown author.

Yunker, Susanna Beck. *Proved Up on Ten Mile Creek, The Story of the Early Settlers of Ten Mile Creek Lane County, Oregon.* 1991.

Marriage Certificates

Hurt, Frank E and Mollie Sandell. Benton County, Oregon. 20 July 1903.

Crefeld [*sic*], F. E. and Maud Hurt. Linn County, Oregon. 5 January 1904.

Crefeld[*sic*], Franz E. and Ida M. Hurt. King County, Washington. 3 April 1906.

Johnson, Frank Oscar and Eva Mae Hurt. Lincoln County, Oregon. 29 April 1909.

Berry, James K. and Tensie Johnson. Lincoln County, Oregon. 9 March 1910.

Mitchell, Velley. P and Sophie Hartley. Lincoln County, Oregon. 25 November 1913.

Berry, James K. and Esther Mitchell. Lincoln County, Oregon. 7 April 1914.

Berry, J. K. and Donna Starr. Lincoln County, Oregon. 4 April 1916.

Benton County Marriages, Index to Marriage Recorder, Vol. 1.

Divorce Court Records

Circuit Court State of Oregon for Benton County. Lewis Hartley (Plaintiff) vs. Cora A. Hartley (Defendant). No. 4377.
Complaint. Filed 11 May 1906.
Summons. 11 May 1906.

Circuit Court State of Oregon for Benton County. Lewis Hartley (Plaintiff) vs. Cora A. Hartley (Defendant). No. 4466.
Decree. Filed 23 November 1908.
Order for Publication of Summons. 8 October 1908.
Demurrer. 12 November, 1908.

Circuit Court of the State of Oregon for the County of Multnomah. Coral D. Worrell (Plaintiff) vs. John F. Worrell. (Defendant). Reg. No. B-5338. Judgment No. 40866A.
Complaint. 27 May 1909.
Summons. Filed 27 June 1909.
Judgment. Filed 15 June 1932.

Circuit Court of the State of Oregon for Benton County. Maud Creffield (Plaintiff) vs. Edwin Creffield (Defendant). No. 4334.
Complaint. Filed 6 July 1905.
Summons. 27 May 1905.

Circuit Court State of Oregon, For Benton County. Alice Berry (Plaintiff) vs. James K. Berry (Defendant).
Complaint.
Amended Complaint.
Affidavit. 6 October 1927.
Reply.

Circuit Court of the State of Oregon for Lincoln County. James K. Berry (Plaintiff) vs. Clara May Berry (Defendant). Complaint. Filed 23 July 1908.

Circuit Court of the State of Oregon for the County of Multnomah. Donna Berry (Plaintiff) vs. James K. Berry (Defendant). Reg. No. G8063.
Complaint in Equity. Filed 20 June 1919.
Summons. Filed 1 July 1919.
Affidavit. Filed 5 August 1919.
Order for Entering Default of Defendant. Filed 15 July 1919.
Findings and Conclusions. Filed 15 July 1919.
Decree. Filed 22 July 1919.
Judgment. Filed 12 September 1919.

Death Certificates

Berry, James Kemmer. Benton County, Oregon. State File No: 9 Local Registered No: 10. 16 January 1943.

Berry, Kenneth. Death Certificate. Benton County, Oregon. State Registered No: 82 Local Registered No: 78. 14 September 1931.

Berry, Virginia Esther. Death Certificate. Lincoln County, Oregon. State Registered No:7 Local Registered No: 1. 24 January 1912.

Crefield, Franz E. Death Certificate. King County, Washington. Volume No:1906, Register No: 16307. 7 May 1906.

Crefield, Ida M. Death Certificate. King County, Washington. Volume No: 1906, Register No: 17252. 16 November 1906.

Hartley, Cora Alice . Death Certificate. Lincoln County, Oregon. State File No: 5853 Local Registered No: 23. 10 September 1945.

Hartley, James Lewis. Death Certificate. Lincoln County, Oregon. State Registered No: 2 Local Registered No: 15. 1 January 1937.

Hurt, Frank. Death Certificate. Lincoln County, Oregon. State Registered No:1 Local Registered No: ?. 10 January 1920.

Hurt, Orlando Victor. Death Certificate. Lincoln County, Oregon. State Registered No:67 Local Registered No: 6. 14 June 1943.

Mitchell, Charles. Death Certificate. Lincoln County, Oregon. State Registered No: 37 Local Registered No: 4. 11 June 1926.

Mitchell, George. Death Certificate. King County, Washington. Volume No:1905, Register No: 1697. 12 July 1906. 16 November 1906.

Starr, Burgess Ebb. Death Certificate. Lincoln County, Oregon. State Registered No: 18 Local Registered No: 9. 14 February 1936.

Vander Kelen, Peter Johananas. Death Certificate. Multnomah County, Oregon. State Registered No: 442 Local Registered No: 2. 1 March 1918.

Miscellaneous Records

Federal Census of Oregon for 1870, 1880, 1890, 1900 and 1910.
Federal Census of Washington for 1900.

Mitchell, Esther, Case No. 2251, 1903 record from the archives of The Boys' and Girls' Aid Society of Oregon.

Creffield, Edmund. Oregon State Penitentiary. Convict Record, Great Register, 1894-1910. page 183.

Brooks, Charles E. Brooks. Salvation Army Record. 1903.
Creffield, Edmund. Salvation Army Record. 1901.
Sandell, Mollie. Salvation Army Record. 190

THE AUTHORS

T. McCracken lives in Waldport, Oregon, where many descendants of the people in this story are her friends and neighbors. She teaches natural history for Lane Community College and works as a naturalist on the Discovery, a ship that does sea life cruises out of Newport. She is also a cartoonist. Her work has appeared in hundreds of publications ranging from the *Oregonian* to the *Saturday Evening Post*. She first wrote about Edmund Creffield while working for the U. S. Forest Service compiling anecdotes about Northwest history. That research was part of the reason she was named 1994 Pacific Northwest Region Forest Interpreter of the Year.

Robert Blodgett lives in Corvallis, Oregon, and has long been interested in the Creffield story. He originally became aware of it through conversations with several long-time denizens of the city, while he was a graduate student at Oregon State University in the 1980s. Subsequent research into the story has led to thousands of hours spent staring at old newspapers on microfilm readers and many visits and much correspondence with numerous archives in the Pacific Northwest.

By profession, Blodgett is a paleontologist/stratigrapher unraveling the fossil and rock record of ancient western North America.

OTHER BOOKS FROM CAXTON PRESS

Massacre Along the Medicine Road

ISBN 0-87004-387-0 (paper) $22.95

ISBN 0-87004-389-7 (cloth) $32.95

6x9, 500 pages, maps, photos, bibliography, index

The Oregon Trail
Yesterday and Today

ISBN 0-87004-319-6 (paper) $12.95

6x9, 200 pages, illustrated, maps, index

On Sidesaddles to Heaven
The Women of the Rocky Mountain Mission

ISBN 0-87004-384-6 (paper) $19.95

6x9, 268 pages, illustrations, index

Dreamers: On the Trail of the Nez Perce

ISBN 0-87004-393-5 (cloth) $24.95

6x9, 450 pages, photographs, maps, index

Yellow Wolf: His Own Story

ISBN 0-87004-315-3 (paper) $16.95

6x9, 328 pages, illustrations, maps, index

Outlaws of the Pacific Northwest

ISBN 0-87004-396-x (paper) $18.95

6x9, photographs, map, 216 pages, index

For a free Caxton catalog write to:

CAXTON PRESS
312 Main Street
Caldwell, ID 83605-3299

or

Visit our Internet Website:

www.caxtonpress.com

Caxton Press is a division of The CAXTON PRINTERS, Ltd.